p 3 - Franciscans + P...
p. 9 - typology
p. 10 - Three strands o...

D1323222

Olivi and the Interpretation of Matthew
in the High Middle Ages

Received 11 July 2007.
I went in for a meeting with
David, Philip + Hugh.

Olivi

and the
Interpretation of
Matthew in the
High Middle Ages

KEVIN MADIGAN

UNIVERSITY OF NOTRE DAME PRESS

Notre Dame, Indiana

Copyright © 2003 by University of Notre Dame
Notre Dame, Indiana 46556
www.undpress.nd.edu
All Rights Reserved

Manufactured in the United States of America

Library of Congress Cataloging-in-Publication Data
Madigan, Kevin, 1960–
Olivi and the interpretation of Matthew in the high Middle
Ages / Kevin Madigan.
    p. cm.
Includes bibliographical references and index.
ISBN 0-268-03715-9 (alk. paper)
ISBN 0-268-03716-7 (pbk.: alk. paper)
1. Bible. N.T. Matthew—Criticism, interpretation, etc.—
History—Middle Ages, 600–1500.   2. Olivi, Pierre Jean,
1248 or 9-1298.   I. Title.
BS2575.52.M25   2003
226'.06'0902—dc21
2003009074

∞ *This book is printed on acid-free paper.*

To Stephanie & Amanda

Contents

Acknowledgments

This book began as a dissertation completed at the University of Chicago in 1992. I would like to thank my advisor, Bernard McGinn, for his sound guidance and encouragement over the three years it took to complete the project. I also want to thank Bernie for his kind friendship and encouragement in the years since I graduated. To his example of scholarship and integrity, I owe more than I can easily say. It gives me great pleasure to offer him acknowledgments and thanks here.

I would also like to thank Robert Lerner for initially responding to a bewildered graduate student casting about for a dissertation topic in the general area of medieval exegesis and apocalyptic thought. It was Professor Lerner who first suggested that I take on Olivi's Matthew commentary as my topic, and for that I was and remain very grateful.

Once I settled on the topic, I immediately contacted David Burr. Since then, we have had many conversations, in person, by letter, and by email about our mutual friend Petrus Iohannis. On every occasion, David's fathomless generosity expressed itself, whether it was in suggesting avenues of research or thought, writing me letters of introduction, lending me microfilms, reading my dissertation (for which he deserves, minimally, a plenary indulgence), putting me in contact with other scholars of Olivi, and keeping me up-to-date on Olivi scholarship. David is the greatest scholar of Olivi of this generation. He is also an exemplary human being, and I have learned from him much about how to treat fellow scholars. Readers of this book will recognize how deeply I am indebted to his scholarship. But let me thank him deeply for his friendship and all of the other ways in which he has put me in his debt and for which he has asked no repayment.

I would like to thank David Flood, O.F.M., for invaluable bibliographical help, given generously just as I was beginning this project. Thanks, too, for encouragement and helpful reading to E. Ann Matter and E. R. Daniel.

In the years since I completed my dissertation, my thinking about Olivi's Matthew commentary has changed considerably. My conscience is clear when I say that this is not a "warmed-over" dissertation. Indeed, the existence of my dissertation in the University of Chicago Library and on microfilm is something of an embarrassment to me. This is because I am, in particular, less sure that Olivi's Matthew commentary was *directly* influenced (as I argued with rather glib confidence in my thesis) by Joachim of Fiore's *Tractatus super Quatuor Evangelia*. It *may* have been, but it's hard to say with surety. I do remain fully convinced, however, that Olivi's Matthew commentary was deeply influenced by the broader Joachite corpus, and, having read much more widely in the Matthew commentaries of the twelfth, thirteenth, and fourteenth centuries over the past years, I am more persuaded than ever that Olivi's commentary on that gospel is one of the most original—and daring—in the High Middle Ages.

For their friendship and support, I am forever grateful to my graduate school peers Brent Sockness, Barbara Pitkin, Richard Rosengarten, Margaret Mitchell, and Amy Hollywood. I am very honored to have been part of this remarkable group of students, from whom I have learned much and whom I have been delighted but not the least surprised to watch flower into leaders in their respective fields.

For financial support, without which this project could not easily have been completed, I wish to thank the Institute for the Advanced Study of Religion of the University of Chicago. I would especially like to thank the Institute for International Education for a Fulbright Fellowship to Italy (1991–92). There I was able to use the manuscripts of the Vatican Library, the Franciscan Library in Assisi, the University of Perugia Library, and the Laurenzia Library in Florence. To the administrators and librarians at these four libraries, who smoothed my way and made scholarly materials available to me, I extend profound thanks.

I wish to thank two anonymous readers from the University of Notre Dame Press for careful reading and invaluable suggestions. Let me also extend special thanks to Carole Roos of the University of Notre Dame Press for an exemplary job of copyediting. Naturally, any mistakes that remain are mine.

Finally, let me extend my deepest thanks to my wife, Stephanie Paulsell. With her, I shared much joy as a fellow graduate student at the University of Chicago (implausible a venue for joy as that might seem), including (more plausibly) a memorable year in Italy. In the years since, she has been a saint of patience and support as this project slowly found its way to completion. In those years, she has also become the mother to our beloved daughter, Amanda, who has given us both inexpressible happiness. It is to these two, Stephanie and Amanda, that I dedicate this book with great affection.

Abbreviations

Petrus Iohannis Olivi. *Lectura super Matthaeum*. Oxford New College MS 49.

Rabanus Maurus. *Commentariorum in Matthaeum libri octo. PL* 107, cols. 727–1156.

Remigius of Auxerre. *Homiliae in Matthaeum. PL* 131, cols. 865–932.

Thomas Aquinas. *Lectura super Matthaeum*. Turin and Rome, 1951.

Lk.—Commentary on the Gospel of Luke, given with commentator's name.

Ambrose of Milan. *Expositio Evangelii Secundum Lucam*. Edited by M. Adriaen. *CC* 14. Turnhout, 1957.

Bede. *In Lucae evangeliam expositio*. Edited by D. Hurst. *CC* 120. Turnhout, 1960.

Bonaventure. *Commentarius in Evangelium S. Lucae*. In *Opera Omnia*. Edita studio et cura PP. Collegii a Bonaventure. 11 vols. Quaracchi, 1882–1902. Vol. 7: 3–604.

Petrus Iohannis Olivi. *Lectura super Lucam*. MS Vat. Ottab. lat. 3302.

Jn.—Commentary on the Gospel of John, given with commentator's name.

Petrus Iohannis Olivi. *Lectura super Johannem*. MS Vat Ottab. lat. 3302.

PERIODICALS, BOOKS, AND SOURCE COLLECTIONS

AF	*Analecta Franciscana.*
AFH	*Archivum Franciscanum Historicum.*
Archiv	*Archiv für Literatur- und Kirchengeschichte des Mittelalters.* Berlin, 1885–90.
BF	*Bullarium Franciscanum.*
CC	*Corpus Christianorum, Series Latina.*
CF	*Collectanea Franciscana.*
CSEL	*Corpus Scriptorum Ecclesiasticorum Latinorum.*
EF	*Études Franciscaines.*
FS	*Franciscan Studies.*
OFP	David Burr. *Olivi and Franciscan Poverty*. Philadelphia, 1989.
OPK	David Burr. *Olivi's Peaceable Kingdom*. Philadelphia, 1993.

PL	*Patrologiae Cursus Completus.* Series Latina. Paris: Migne, 1844–66.
RTAM	*Recherches de théologie ancienne et médiévale.*
SC	*Sources chrétiennes.* Éditions du Cerf, 1949–.
SF	*Studi Francescani.*

Introduction

On February 8, 1326, Pope John XXII issued a condemnation of an Apocalypse commentary written some three decades earlier by the Franciscan *lector* Petrus Iohannis Olivi.[1] That Olivi's Apocalypse commentary was condemned by the pope is well known. Less widely known is that, as part of the process of examination leading to the censure, John's investigators examined other works written by Olivi, including his *Commentary on Matthew*. In fact, there is evidence that proves at least one of them liked this commentary no more than the one on the Apocalypse. Other evidence suggests that it was so little appreciated that it, too, was condemned at the same time as the Apocalypse commentary. Had his examiners inspected his other gospel commentaries, they would surely have found much to deplore in them as well.

Curiously enough, much of Olivi's Matthew commentary is derivative and, by any measure, innocuous. (The same might be asserted of his other gospel commentaries.) The work is, in many ways, a standard, wholly unremarkable product of mendicant academic culture. Produced by a Franciscan *lector* for use in his order's classrooms, it exhibits to a large degree the kind of exegesis Olivi learned as a student at Paris—and from masters not appointed for being habitually subversive of the "institutional" church. Indeed, much of it is indistinguishable from gospel commentaries produced by his more respectable peers. So inoffensive and even prosaic are vast stretches of it that one manuscript could travel under the name of the irreproachable Franciscan regent master Nicholas of Lyra.[2] Few works of medieval exegesis are likely to generate as little intellectual *frisson* as Thomas Aquinas's *Catena Aurea*. Yet (when he does not plagiarize it verbatim), Olivi borrows ideas from no other contemporary exegetical writing in his Matthew commentary as liberally as he does from that innocuous work, a papally commissioned mosaic of unthreatening opinions collated from the writings of the orthodox fathers.[3] Given Olivi's altogether solid Parisian education and his unimpeachable choice of major exegetical sources, how was it that his Matthew commentary came, apparently, to be condemned? What could an early fourteenth-century scholar have found objectionable about it? How, at least, would he have found it different from others produced by mendicant *lectores* and *magistri* educated at Paris? And what would have persuaded him that parts of it had strayed so far from the truth, that its opinions posed so grave a threat to the church, that it was worthy of papal censure? Indeed, what would have aroused him to examine it in the first place?

To begin with, there is the fact of Olivian authorship. Olivi was a man who, in David Burr's apt description, was "apparently born to polarize opinion."[4] He was a man who, already in 1283, had been condemned for a battery of philosophical and theological errors. By 1285, he was being described, rightly or wrongly, as the leader of a sect.[5] Though rehabilitated after a few (though personally painful) years, it was not the last time Olivi's orthodoxy would be questioned.

In fact, his death coincided with a new and vigorous debate on this issue, one in which his ever more zealous supporters, or *sectatores* (as his critical examiners preferred to call them), did precious little to help their hero's cause. Some announced that Olivi's views had been formed under the inspiration of the Holy Spirit; his readers, therefore, should naturally be prepared to accept them as gospel truth. Others identified him with one of the angels of the Apocalypse—thus investing him with the sort of apocalyptic significance with which he had endowed Francis. Others went dangerously further, arguing that the papacy had, because of certain errors and sins, been divested of its pontifical authority. This had now been transferred to the elect, the true priests who observed gospel poverty.[6]

Once such opinions were ventilated, it could not be long before the papacy would launch an investigation into their sources and propagators. With the election in 1316 of Pope John XXII, a major offensive against the "Spirituals"[7] in the Franciscan Order was launched with the new pope's blessing. The results were disastrous for the Spirituals—not least for the four who, for defying papal authority, were consumed in an *auto-da-fé* in the marketplace of Marseilles in May 1318. Before long, Olivi's supporters were viewing events through the prism his writings supplied. As David Burr has put it, "As they watched the events unroll, they saw Olivi's apocalyptic scenario incarnated before their eyes. The church of Rome was turning into the whore of Babylon."[8] Soon enough a vernacular digest of Olivi's commentary on the Apocalypse, and at least fragments of his Matthew commentary, were circulating among supporters. These had the effect of strengthening his followers' will to resist. They also likely confirmed them in their belief that Olivi's prophecies concerning the carnal church, and particularly the pope, were, horrifyingly, being realized before their very eyes. Whatever Olivi meant by his words, his followers were applying them in ways that can only be described as subversive; and so it was inevitable that they, and Olivi, would come under scrutiny. Thus a second reason Olivi's Matthew commentary came under investigation is the context in which it was being read and used.

It is not surprising, then, that John XXII, as part of his campaign against the now-distinct Spiritual wing of the Franciscan Order, had commanded an examination of Olivi's commentary on the Apocalypse. A committee was entrusted to inspect this commentary, while other masters were charged with examining some of Olivi's other works. Also not surprisingly, they found the Apocalypse commentary, and the Matthew commentary, rife with error. The former was denounced for its opinions on the "carnal church" (which the investigating commission simplistically identified with the "Roman church"), for its celebration of the piety and distinctive mission of Francis and his order, and for other errors. Shortly after this process got underway, the General Chapter of the Franciscan Order met in 1319, not without significance, in Marseilles. It denounced Olivi's writings as erroneous. Seven years later, the pope finally condemned the Apocalypse commentary. This condemnation was accompanied, according to some sources, by a condemnation of Olivi's Matthew commentary, which, in the eyes of those who examined it, deplorably contained "many similar errors."

Olivi's examiners almost certainly recognized the conventional quality of much of his Matthew commentary. However, parts of the commentary lay far outside the conventional lines of thinking in thirteenth-century exegesis of the gospels, as was demonstrated by the late Beryl

Smalley. In the preface to the third edition of her pathbreaking study, *The Study of the Bible in the Middle Ages,* Beryl Smalley remarked of medieval commentators: "The reader of a text . . . was expected to be more active and less passive than his modern counterpart . . . he put his own meaning into it."[9] As a general rule, that may be true, though it would, of course, require much elucidation. But one of the major conclusions of Smalley's own important study of medieval gospel commentaries[10] is that, with few if any exceptions, scholastic commentators in the twelfth and early thirteenth centuries did *not* "put their own meaning into it."[11] They put their predecessors', especially patristic predecessors', meaning into it. In studying the *postillae* of the first generation of friar doctors, Smalley established the curious fact that Dominican and Franciscan presuppositions and values tended *not* to influence mendicant exegesis of the gospels very deeply. Nor did the particulars of the ecclesial and social context in which they wrote. The gospel commentaries of the Dominican Hugh of St. Cher (written 1234–35) or of the Franciscans Alexander of Hales (probably written post–1235) and John of LaRochelle (written 1236–45) were all highly traditional and conservative efforts.[12] Smalley describes Hugh of St. Cher's gospel commentaries, not wrongly, as "a mosaic of quotations."[13] Alexander, she observes, shows "no particular interest in poverty" and never mentions the friars.[14] Nothing in his commentaries "gives an inkling that he was a potential or actual recruit to the Order of Friars Minor."[15] John of LaRochelle identifies himself as a Franciscan, "but not in the sense that he strongly defended poverty or begging."[16] "The first friar doctors at Paris," Smalley quite accurately concludes, "were by no means anxious to stress their novelty as postillators. . . . One has to probe deeply to find Mendicant traits in any of them." Rather than innovate, they "quietly slip[ped] into the tracks of their predecessors."[17] Anyone who has ploughed laboriously through these commentaries in search of qualities unique to the mendicants can only confirm the accuracy of these remarks.

The event which decisively transformed this sort of exegetical conservatism was the secular-mendicant controversy. Once the secular clergy launched its attack on the mendicant life and apostolate, mendicant gospel commentaries (especially Franciscan ones) began to reflect their authors' own distinctive concerns and values. The trend is first evident in the gospel commentaries of Bonaventure. What differentiates Bonaventure from his mendicant predecessors, Smalley asserts, "is his reading of Franciscan values into his lecture courses. . . . Poverty is stressed wherever the text gives occasion for it."[18] Some ten years before the publication of Smalley's book, Dominic Monti had made the same point about Bonaventure's Luke commentary:

> in its own way, it too is a 'Defense of the Mendicants,' although not so much directed against their outside assailants as to confirm the friars in their belief that they were indeed living out the way of life specifically proposed by Christ himself.[19]

Mysteriously enough, the change described by Smalley and Monti is especially (perhaps even only) evident in Franciscan gospel commentaries. For reasons which have still not been explored, the attack by the seculars on the mendicants did not affect Dominican gospel commentaries in analogous fashion. Though he was every bit as involved in the literary side of the conflict as was Bonaventure, Thomas Aquinas shows almost no consciousness in his gospel commentaries of writing as a mendicant friar, nor do typically Dominican presuppositions seem to govern his exegesis of the gospels in any significant way.[20] The same could be said of Albertus Magnus. Be that as it may, the point is that the secular-mendicant controversy decisively transformed the genre of Franciscan gospel commentary.

As the controversy wore on, the genre seemed to undergo change again in a more subtle fashion and again in response to pressures from the secular clergy. The John commentaries of Franciscan friars such as John of Wales and John Pecham, written as much as two decades after the original composition of Bonaventure's Luke commentary, are marked in many places by distinctively Franciscan concerns. However, they tend to be significantly more polemical and defensive than the commentaries written by Bonaventure. Bonaventure's Luke commentary was not, in Monti's words, "directed against outside assailants." According to Smalley, the John commentaries of John of Wales and Pecham begin increasingly to focus upon those "items of gospel history which figured into polemic."[21] John of Wales, she says, "went further than Bonaventure in his more polemical defense of gospel poverty," while "Pecham's teaching on poverty reflects a time when polemic had descended to niggling over certain texts."[22] The purpose of the gospel commentary in this next generation of friar postillators was not only to "confirm the friars in their belief that they were living out the way of life specifically proposed by Christ himself"; a corollary purpose was now to discredit those obnoxious readings of the gospel advanced by the friars' detractors that argued that the mendicants were living a way of life contrary to the example and teachings of Christ and the apostles. Bonaventure's response to the seculars in his gospel commentaries was irenic, implicit, and offensive. The response of Pecham and Wales was polemical, explicit, and defensive.

Olivi's gospel commentaries continue and heighten the Franciscanizing exegesis of the gospels begun in Bonaventure. Unlike those *postillae* written by the first generation of friar doctors at Paris, Olivi's gospel commentaries are easily identifiable as the work of a Franciscan. Like Bonaventure's Luke commentary, they stress poverty (I use Smalley's words here) "wherever the text gives occasion for it." Along with the John commentaries of Pecham and Wales, they represent a defensive and polemical form of exegesis which attempts to invalidate potentially damaging readings of the gospel. Unlike these two commentaries, however, Olivi's *postillae* also reflect his involvement in two subsequent disputes over the issue of poverty.

Even before the conclusion of the secular-mendicant controversy, some members of the two mendicant orders had exchanged fire over the relative perfection of each order, a polemic which focused upon the importance of poverty. Then, with a logic peculiar to the first century of Franciscan existence, once the fire of this controversy began to die out, the flames of an intramural dispute on the issue of *usus pauper* were fanned by Olivi and his detractors within the order. As we will see, the particulars of each of these three polemics influenced, though in varying degrees, the way in which Olivi interpreted the gospels. That is, it is impossible fully to understand Olivi's gospel commentaries unless one sees them as, in part, a response to the secular clergy, to Dominican detractors (like Thomas Aquinas, against whom Olivi launches a long and—even for him—extraordinarily angry and sarcastic diatribe in his Matthew commentary),[23] and to the author's Franciscan opponents in the *usus pauper* controversy.

What made Olivi's commentary even more daring is that, unlike virtually any other Franciscan commentator on the gospels, Olivi gave Francis, his order, and its fundamental values (as interpreted, of course, by Olivi himself) apocalyptic, absolute, and uncompromising significance and found continuous and ample warrant in the text of Matthew for doing so. Indeed, Olivi found both positive and negative apocalyptic meaning in Matthew. In the text of Matthew, Olivi perceived countless prophecies of the appearance of Francis and his band of spiritual, evangelical men and the re-emergence, after many centuries of decline, of evangelical values.

He also perceived in the gospel text countless prophecies of the persecution of these spiritual men and their values by those whom he designates members of the "carnal" church (which Olivi surely did not intend to identify with the Roman church *simpliciter*) that has opposed the true and the good throughout the history of the church.

If these features put Olivi outside the mainstream of mendicant exegesis of the gospels, then another feature of the commentary put him even further outside the pale. One early modern reader of MS Oxford New College 49, a manuscript which contains a copy of the Matthew commentary, perceptively indicated just how far in a cursive warning he left on the last folio of manuscript.

> There was a certain heretic named Peter of John, a confederate of the heresiarch Abbot Joachim. Since it is not clear which Peter of John wrote this work, I have thought it my duty to warn the unwary reader.[24]

That reader knew his exegetical tradition and his history, and he had read the Matthew commentary with care. In fact, the commentary is saturated—and that is the word—with ideas that clearly had their origin in the exegetical corpus of Joachim of Fiore (ca. 1135–1202). As Decima Douie observed in 1975, "The most interesting and original feature of the *Postilla* is that it shows that Olivi was already an exponent of the theories associated with the name of the famous abbot Joachim."[25] My research into more than ten lengthy mendicant commentaries on Matthew, and many others on the other three gospels, indicates that Olivi was the only author in the thirteenth and fourteenth centuries whose gospel commentaries were deeply influenced by Joachite thought, as well as what we might call the basic exegetical approach or (to use the modern category) hermeneutic applied in Joachim's simultaneous commentary on all four gospels, the *Tractatus super Quatuor Evangelia*.[26]

One field of inquiry left open after the publication of Professor Smalley's book is the influence of Joachim's thought and hermeneutic on subsequent generations of interpreters of the gospels. Smalley had little sympathy with Joachim or with works influenced by him, though her book on the gospel commentaries certainly seems to be leading up to Olivi's Joachite commentary. She once dismissed the Calabrian abbot and Joachism as "an attack of senile dementia" in the "spiritual reading of the gospels," a position she later retracted, though indicating still a certain lingering antipathy to Joachite thought.[27] It seems possible that Smalley chose to end her study of the gospels in 1280 at least in part because that was the year in which Olivi wrote his first gospel commentary, the one on Matthew, which was profoundly shaped by Joachite thought.[28]

Smalley's antipathy has not been shared by all. Over the course of the twentieth century, there has been a staggering volume of work completed on the life, thought, and influence of Joachim, and this flood of work has shown few signs of subsiding.[29] In recent years, a number of editions of his authentic works have been finished, and more are planned.[30] Joachim's *figurae* have been analyzed carefully.[31] Some of the pseudepigraphal Joachite works have been edited and studied.[32] The early spread of Joachite thought and especially its influence on the Franciscan Order and other orders, has been intensively analyzed.[33] Much attention in recent years has been given to Joachim's influence on the second and third generations of Franciscans, like Bonaventure and the Spiritual Franciscans.[34] But Joachite specialists have ignored the influence of Joachim's thought on commentaries on the gospels. This neglect contrasts markedly with the enormous attention lavished upon the question of the possible influence of Joachim's *Expositio in Apocalypsim* on Franciscan Apocalypse commentaries, especially Peter Olivi's.[35] Of course, there are good reasons for this. The *Tractatus* almost certainly circulated much less widely than Joachim's other major works. Consequently, it could not have exercised the same sort of influence.

Nonetheless, we know from a passage in Salimbene that Joachim's *Tractatus* was known by the early Spirituals. Moreover, Olivi's gospel commentaries are profoundly influenced by the assumptions and exegetical methods enshrined in Joachim's exegetical corpus, including his gospel commentary. So pervasively do Olivi's gospel commentaries appropriate the methods found in Joachim's *Tractatus* that one is almost tempted to say that Olivi's gospel commentaries are like those Joachim might have written had he lived a century later and been a Franciscan. At the very least, one can regard Olivi's Matthew commentary as an example of how earlier traditions of prophecy could be reworked and modernized in light of new ecclesiastical realities.

The argument I wish to make can be expressed with more precision if we reflect upon the fact that the *Tractatus* was an unfinished work. Joachim never got around to commenting on roughly the last three-quarters of each of the gospels. Consequently, there can be no question of the *Tractatus* directly influencing Olivi's interpretation of the greater part of each of the gospels. Generally, the influence I am describing is more oblique. The influence of the *Tractatus* on Olivi's gospel commentaries is, generally speaking, the influence of a certain *kind* of exegesis or way of interpreting the gospels.

Like virtually all of his patristic and medieval contemporaries, Joachim was convinced that the Hebrew Scriptures could and should be read typologically. Figures, events, images in the Hebrew Scriptures—all of these could be and indeed should be interpreted by the Christian exegete as "types" or representations of New Testament figures, events, and images. Indeed, it was only this sort of typological exegesis that revealed the deeper and true meaning of the Old Testament. Joachim shared and put into practice this conviction. But Joachim was convinced that the *New* Testament could be read typologically as well. Some of his patristic predecessors and some of his contemporaries undoubtedly have shared this conviction in theory, but very, very few were prepared to put it into practice in systematic fashion. Joachim was. Indeed, Joachim was prepared to read each of the narratives of the gospel in a typological sense (*sensus typicus*). In fact, the *Tractatus* consists of virtually nothing but typological interpretation.

What this meant concretely for his exegesis of the gospels is that the figures, events, and images of New Testament history could be taken as types of the future history of the church. That is to say, the gospels could be taken as historical books not only in the sense that they pointed backward to the past history of Christ and the apostles but in the sense that they pointed forward to the future of salvation history. The gospels were, in a word, prophetic and apocalyptic books. Joachim's exegetical principle here, even if he did not live to see it entirely realized, is that the nativity, baptism, temptation, teaching, miracles, passion, death, and resurrection of Christ all were historical occurrences which should be interpreted typologically to reveal the future of salvation history. Thus there was nothing at all preposterous in assiduously studying the details of the Temptation account, for example, for particular knowledge of how the church would be tempted in the days of the Antichrist, nor in meditating on the details of Christ's passion for signs of how the mystical body of Christ might be persecuted in its imminent eschatological tribulation. It was in the conviction, expressed in the *Tractatus* as elsewhere in Joachim's writings, that the gospels could and should be interpreted typologically, that Joachim most profoundly influenced Olivi's gospel commentaries. That is to say, even where Olivi was not and could not have been directly depending on Joachim's *Tractatus,* it is still possible to detect Joachite influence. The influence, however, is of the indirect variety; it is the influence of a certain kind of exegesis, of certain exegetical assumptions, and of certain key ideas present in all of Joachim's works.

It is, finally, the conviction that the gospels should be read typologically that distinguishes Olivi's gospel commentaries from those written by his mendicant peers. However much they are marked by Franciscan concerns, contemporary gospel commentaries are almost totally untouched by Joachite influence. That this should be so is quite curious in the case of Franciscan confreres, like Bonaventure, who were not otherwise immune to Joachite influence. As is well known, some of Bonaventure's non-exegetical works are highly indebted to the eschatology of Joachim. Nonetheless, his gospel commentaries are utterly innocent of Joachite influence. Bonaventure was not at all anxious to read the gospels of Luke and John typologically. The same can be said, with few if any exceptions, of the rest of Olivi's mendicant confreres. For Olivi's contemporaries, the gospels were simply not about the future, at least not in the sense that they were predictive of it.

Thus, by the time Olivi began his Matthew commentary ca. 1280, there were essentially three distinct exegetical strands in commentaries on the gospel: the scholastic, the Franciscan, and the Joachite. The first tradition is represented by early friars such as Hugh of St. Cher and Alexander of Hales, as well as the French masters and texts from the twelfth century on whom Smalley has proven they depended: the *Glossa Ordinaria,* a Matthew commentary of unknown origin sometimes attributed to Master Geoffrey Babion, and commentaries by Peter Cantor and Peter Comestor, as well as Peter Lombard.

The second tradition, one which begins to be influenced by elements of Franciscan mythology developed in the 1240s and 1250s, is represented, to some extent, by John of LaRochelle and, more obviously, by John Pecham and others. The appearance of Franciscan mythology in commentaries on the gospels not only coincides with, but seems to have been caused by, the emergence of the Franciscan Order in the mid-thirteenth century into an atmosphere of bitter ecclesiastical polemics, especially in its battle with secular clergy and masters over sacred and academic privileges and prerogatives.

The third tradition, the Joachite, is represented by Joachim alone and his *Tractatus.*

In the following chapters, especially in the first part of the book (chapters 1–3), I describe and analyze each of these three traditions. In the second part (chapters 4–7), I take a close look at Olivi's Matthew commentary. In some ways, Olivi's commentary represents the culmination of each of these trends in the high medieval exegesis of Matthew. From one perspective, it appears to be the commentary to which trends in the late twelfth and thirteenth centuries were leading. It is, so it seems, the only commentary of the century in which these three traditions merge. It is obviously scholastic in form and influenced by the sort of scholastic exegesis Olivi heard while a student in Paris. Second, it is (to borrow a term from Gordon Leff) a "complete Francisanizing" of the Gospel of Matthew. Third, it is highly, and uniquely influenced by content and especially methods found in the exegetical corpus of Joachim of Fiore. Finally, it was forged in a polemical matrix of personal vicissitude and attack on the Franciscan Order as a whole, and its exegetical opinions both reflect and vigorously respond to these. Three separate exegetical roads led, finally in 1280, to Olivi.

In the third part of the book (chapter 8 and conclusion), I argue that forty years later these roads had separated, never to merge again in medieval exegesis of the gospels. In the fourteenth century—in the exegesis of Nicholas of Lyra, for example—Franciscan exegesis of the gospel returns to the model established by the French masters of Paris and Laon and the earliest friar commentators on the gospels. None of these commentaries is so much as touched by Joachite influence, nor do they show any interest in prophecy or apocalyptic thought. None celebrates the Franciscan Order or its mission and values as unambiguously or absolutely as did Olivi, if at all. Indeed, reading gospel commentaries written in the early fourteenth century is very much like reading ones written in the early thirteenth. It would be impossible to tell, if one did not know, that the commentator was writing as a friar.

It is just possible that this was no accident. In the first quarter of the thirteenth century, Pope John XXII would bring to heel not just the dissident Spirituals but would, finally, undermine the self-understanding of all Franciscans, even the heretofore innocuous "conventuals." Some might want to argue that one of the consequences of this papal disciplining of the order was the disappearance in commentaries on the gospels of virtually any element that was distinctively Franciscan or Joachite in character. From 1250 to roughly 1315, Franciscan gospel commentaries became increasingly "Franciscan," polemical, and, finally, with Olivi, apocalyptic. With the ascent of John XXII to Peter's throne, that exegetical trend was quite suddenly reversed. Is it possible to view John's condemnation as having a chilling effect on Franciscan exegesis?

In the end, it is impossible to say. With the present state of evidence, my own inclination is to regard the connection between the condemnation and this exegetical sea-change as coincidental rather than causal. What is not in doubt is that, after the condemnation, exegesis of Matthew ceases to be distinctively Franciscan or apocalyptic. Instead, exegesis in the fourteenth century becomes increasingly like it was in the beginning of the twelfth. The story I will tell, then, has the form of a circle. It is a story of a kind of exegesis that strays further and further from its point of origin, incorporating new elements along the way, only to shed those new elements and to return, intellectually speaking, to its Parisian birthplace.

CHAPTER ONE

The Scholastic Gospel

Matthew Commentaries in Laon and Paris, ca. 1140–1240

What did it mean for a commentary on Matthew to be "scholastic" in the High Middle Ages? In order to begin to address that question, we will be examining three important, characteristic, and influential Matthew commentaries written in the period ca. 1140–1240: the Matthew commentary "written" (perhaps "compiled" would be the better word) by Ralph of Laon (d. 1136) for the immensely influential *Glossa Ordinaria;* a less well-known but very influential commentary of unknown authorship, also composed, though some years after the *Gloss,* in Laon, entitled *Enarrationes in Evangelium Sancti Matthaei;* and the *Postilla super Matthaeum* written by the indefatigable exegete

Hugh of St. Cher and his Dominican colleagues in the new university setting of Paris in the mid-1230s.

As it turns out, the answer to our question shifts over the period in response to changing curricular and institutional needs and settings and the emergence of new forms of religious life. Still, it is possible to suggest a number of elements that define a "scholastic" commentary on Matthew in the late twelfth and early thirteenth centuries. First, *all* commentaries in the period under consideration, no matter how brilliant and creative their authors, rely heavily—very heavily—on carefully selected and ordered extracts from patristic commentary on Matthew. Sometimes the reliance on such authorities is so nearly total that the scholastic *glossator* (a term which signifies neither a *compilator* pure and simple nor a "writer") remains buried under their weight; he can hardly shine through at all. In such cases, it is difficult, if not impossible, to say much about the author; anything we venture to say about him must be on the basis of the extracts he selects and manages. His commentary is not inscribed at all with signs of ecclesial conflict, debate, or tension. His exegesis tends, in this sense, to be "generic," that is, standard, universally applicable, ordered to preaching and moral application. Whatever the differences among our three authors, this is the sort of exegesis we see in all three commentaries under consideration here.

A second feature of scholastic commentaries on Matthew is that the expository style so characteristic of late eleventh-century exegesis yields in the twelfth and thirteenth centuries to something more dialectical and theological, something more obviously required by the scholastic classroom setting for which these lecture-commentaries were often written. This shift is marked organizationally and structurally by the introduction of the theological *quaestio* and *responsio*. These begin to occupy more and more intellectual space in the twelfth-century classroom lecture and, hence, the biblical commentary.

Third, scholastic authors by the thirteenth century at the latest begin in each chapter of the commentaries to divide the biblical text into ever smaller and smaller fragments and to concentrate their exegetical attention on almost atomistic pieces of the biblical text.

Finally, beginning with mendicant exegetes in Paris, we begin to see small flashes of personality shine through and to have glimpses into the social and ecclesial realities of the day. The hurly-burly of university life, of intramural and extramural dispute, of debates on the nature of the most perfect form of religious life—these all begin to be perceivable in commentaries on the gospel and to shape—subtly at first, then, by the late thirteenth century, less and less so—how commentaries on the gospels were conceived and executed.

The Patristic Heritage on Matthew and the "Synoptic Problem"

These three commentators, and, for that matter, virtually all high medieval and early modern commentators, were in essential agreement on issues regarding the date, place of composition, and purpose of the Gospel of Matthew (which all recognized as having a subtly but definably different intention than the other gospels). Nearly all medieval commentators, regardless of their libraries or exegetical orientation, came heavily under the influence of leading patristic thinkers, especially Jerome and Augustine, on these questions. These "synoptic questions" they conventionally treated at the outset of their commentaries in one, two, or even (as, in the fourteenth century, with Nicholas of Lyra) three prologues.

By the late twelfth century, it had become standard practice to open one's first (and in many cases only) prologue with reflection upon a scriptural text, usually from the Hebrew Bible. One of the most popular texts was Ezekiel's vision of four living creatures: "Each had four faces, and each four wings" (Ez. 1:4 ff.). The same cast of creatures reappears in Apocalypse 4:7–8; some Latin exegetes refer to this vision and not to Ezekiel's. If there was a second prologue, it was usually a reflection on Jerome's prologue to his own commentary on Matthew. The third prologue, if such there was, was a commentary on the *Glossa Ordinaria's* prologue to its commentary on Matthew.

In prologues to commentaries on Matthew, most thirteenth- and fourteenth-century exegetes would reflect on the text from Ezekiel not just as a way to begin interpretation of the first gospel but also as a way to consider questions organized today under the rubric of "the synoptic problem." Why were four gospels written rather than just one? What was the order in which the gospels were written, and where were they composed? What were the distinct qualities of each of the gospels, and what were the evangelists' specific aims? Why did the evangelists not all write uniformly but with different narrative order and often with apparent contradiction?

No patristic figure reflected more influentially on these issues, and especially on the question of the order in which the gospels were written and the interrelations among them, than Augustine (354–430). In modern biblical scholarship, the hypothesis of Marcan priority has been accorded a high degree of probability by scholars.[1] However, this hypothesis, proposed only at the end of the eighteenth century and widely accepted only in the middle of the nineteenth, overturned more than fourteen centuries of adherence to the Augustinian theory. In his *De Consensu Evangelistarum,* Augustine made a strong and enduring case for the priority of the Gospel of Matthew. In fact, he argued that the temporal order of composition of the gospels was identical to the canonical order: Matthew-Mark-Luke-John.[2] Although modern scholars think it highly probable that Matthew used Mark, Augustine suggested the opposite possibility, namely that Mark borrowed heavily and almost exclusively from Matthew. In fact, he calls Mark the "epitomator" (*breviator*) of Matthew because he has so much material in common with Matthew, while he appears to record almost nothing not included in the first gospel.[3] Augustine was not the first to suggest this order of composition. Nevertheless, by lending the authority of his name to it, it became the favored explanation throughout the pre-modern period.

To these theories about the order in which the gospels were written, Jerome (ca. 342–420) added some important remarks in the *praefatio* to his commentary on Matthew on the date and place of composition of the gospels. These remarks are, in turn, dependent upon traditions deriving ultimately from Papias of Hierapolis (ca. 125) and proximately from Eusebius (ca. 260–ca. 340). In the *Historia Ecclesiastica,* Eusebius quotes Papias as saying: "Matthew compiled the *Sayings* in the Aramaic language, and everyone translated them as well as he could."[4] Curiously, scores of patristic and medieval commentators echo this comment without ever speculating on who put these sayings into their present narrative framework or suggesting how exactly they got translated into their final Greek form. In any event, Eusebius also quotes Papias on the origin of the Gospel of Mark. Papias designated Mark the "interpreter" of Peter[5] and, for that reason, Rome was very early credited as the place of origin of that gospel. Modern scholars have given good reasons for doubting that Peter was Mark's major source, though, interestingly, some have found the suggestion of Roman origin more plausible.[6] In the preface to his commentary on Matthew, Jerome canonized these traditions, as well as the other patristic traditions that held that Luke was the third gospel written in Achaia and John the fourth.[7] In the High Middle Ages, no Latin exegete proposed an order of composition or suggested places of origin different from those proposed by Jerome and Augustine.

Patristic and medieval interpreters also appreciated that each of the evangelists had significantly different intentions and that each had highlighted one major aspect of Christ's person or work. Both Augustine and Jerome, as well as Gregory the Great, attempted to distinguish the different christological tendencies of the evangelists and to highlight the different emphases and qualities of their gospels. The most popular way to get at these questions in the patristic period, as well as in the thirteenth and fourteenth centuries, was to ask which of the four faces (man, eagle, ox, lion) of the creature in Ezekiel's vision (or, much more rarely, of John's in Apocalypse 4:7–11) corresponded to which of the four evangelists, and why? All Latin commentators from Jerome and Augustine to Nicholas of Lyra agreed that John was represented by the eagle, for he had soared to ponder the mysteries of Christ's divinity and the secrets of heaven. Too, there was substantial agreement that Luke should be represented by the ox, either because Luke wished to show Jesus' priestly character or to represent him as the victim of a priest.[8] There was less agreement on how the other two faces corresponded to the gospels of Matthew and Mark. Augustine proposed that Matthew be represented by the lion, because he wished to emphasize the regal character of Christ, and Mark by the face of the man, since he wished to show his human nature.[9] Gregory argued that Matthew should be represented by the man, since he begins with the human genealogy of Christ, while Mark should be represented by the lion, since he begins with a voice crying in the desert.[10] Finally, there was widespread and almost unanimous agreement among Latin patristic exegetes that, whatever their differences, the first three gospels were concerned with demonstrating the humanity of Christ and the fourth with exhibiting his divinity.

Many of these opinions were to be incorporated by Ralph of Laon in the preface to the *Glossa Ordinaria,* to which we are about to turn. Since later commentators would treat the *Gloss's* preface in their own preliminary remarks, these opinions carried tremendous weight for centuries.

The *Glossa Ordinaria*

If the origins and authorship of the *Glossa Ordinaria*[11] have until fairly recently been shrouded in obscurity, the depth and range of its influence are not in doubt. The *Gloss* was, from ca. 1150 to the middle of the fourteenth century, *the* standard medieval commentary on the Bible. As such, it was reproduced in hundreds of manuscripts and printed editions. By the thirteenth century, it had become so central in the activity of biblical interpretation that exegesis inevitably entailed direct or indirect exegesis of the *Gloss* as well as of the biblical text. Only three or four medieval theological textbooks had the sort of profound, widespread, and lasting impact of the *Gloss;* in the years 1150–1350, none was more important in the realm of biblical study.

The early twelfth century was an age not only of theological, exegetical, and canonical creativity and invention in the schools, it was also an age of scholarly compilation, of the production of textbooks for classroom and library use. These textbooks typically took the form of carefully selected extracts from ancient authors stitched together to form a continuous exposition or "gloss" on an authoritative text. Once produced, they formed the basis for lectures, commentaries, and sermons.

The result, for biblical scholarship, was the production of the *Standard Gloss* or *Glossa Ordinaria.* The *Gloss* appeared inevitably with the text of the Latin Bible, which appeared on the manuscript page in a central block. This text was commented upon, or "glossed," both between the lines of the biblical text (thus the "interlinear" gloss) and, usually more fully, in the margins (thus the "marginal" gloss) surrounding the text. In every manuscript and printed edition of the *Gloss* to have survived, the interlinear and marginal glosses appear together. In the "final edition" of the *Gloss,* each book of the Bible was annotated in this fashion. The *Gloss* was far too large to appear in a single pandect. Instead, glossed texts were usually grouped together, often under the influence of Cassiodorus's famous definition of the nine codices which made up the Bible.[12] Accordingly, the four books of glossed gospels were often found together in manuscript and incunabulum.

The edition of the *Gloss* published in Migne perpetuates a hoary fifteenth-century legend, according to which Walafrid Strabo (d. 849), a student of Rabanus Maurus and later abbot of Reichenau, wrote the marginal glosses.[13] According to the same legend, Anselm of Laon wrote the interlinear glosses. This legend had remarkable longevity; respectable scholars were keeping it alive through the mid-twentieth century.[14] At about the same time, other scholars began to demonstrate its implausibility.[15] Actually, it was proven that Strabo contributed to the *Gloss* only fragments on Genesis and Exodus. He had nothing to do with its over-all conception or content.

The origins of the *Gloss* are in fact tied up with the much later history of the cathedral school of Laon, the center of Christian theological work in the early twelfth century.[16] The two leading figures of the school in that generation were the brothers Anselm (d. 1117) and Ralph (d. 1136). Virtually all the important theologians and exegetes of the succeeding generation, including Gilbert de la Porée and Peter Abelard, learned scholastic method and matter from these two men (though the latter famously, and typically, had less than full respect for Anselm).[17]

Their work on the *Gloss* was largely editorial. Anselm and Ralph were gifted compilers with massive learning and a sure sense for what from the exegetical tradition should be preserved and highlighted. Consequently, glossators like them were spoken of, as Smalley points out, "as having 'ordered' (*ordinare*) [a] *Gloss*."[18] In truth, they were not "authors" of the *Gloss* in any modern sense of the term. "Ultimately," as Margaret Gibson has usefully reminded us,

> the principal contributor to the *Gloss*—the giant who bears it on his shoulders—is Jerome. He was responsible for the text of the Bible, for many of the explanatory prefaces to individual books [including the one on Matthew], and for the learned and comprehensive exegesis of most of the Old Testament and part of the New [again, of Matthew].[19]

Relying heavily on extracts lifted from Jerome (perhaps pre-arranged in already existing glosses), Ralph assembled the gloss on Matthew in Laon. From there, it, along with the rest of the *Gloss*, spread to Paris. It is not impossible that the monks or canons of a particular scriptorium there, maybe St. Victor, established a "definitive edition."[20] In any case, following some sort of process of revision and standardization, such an "edition" spread outward from Paris to all of Latin Christendom, and within its boundaries, it was everywhere accepted as a standard work. By the 1160s and 1170s it was being used by Peter Comestor, Peter Cantor, and Stephen Langton in their lectures and commentaries on the gospels.[21] Indeed, their lectures are, among other things, glosses on the *Gloss*. The tradition of gospel exegesis that had begun in Laon in the first decade of the twelfth century had arrived thus in Paris early in the second half of the century.

From Paris, the *Gloss* would exercise enormous influence on interpretation of the gospels for the next two centuries and beyond.

THE *ENARRATIONES IN EVANGELIUM SANCTI MATTHAEI*

One of the most important, influential, and representative early scholastic commentaries on the Gospel of Matthew, one demonstrably influenced by the *Gloss,* is now printed under the name of Anselm of Laon in the *Patrologia Latina* with the title *Enarrationes in Evangelium Sancti Matthaei.*[22] For a variety of reasons—chronological, formal, and material—Anselmian authorship is impossible to sustain. For one thing, the author of the *Enarrationes* borrowed from sources which in turn used the *Glossa Ordinaria.*[23] Aside from the fact that the existing external evidence makes it likely that Ralph wrote the *Gloss* on Matthew, there are strong internal and material grounds for ruling Anselm, or any early twelfth-century writer, out of the picture. Among other things, the *Enarrationes* used the term *vicarius Christi* when referring to the pope. That term replaced *vicarius Petri* only after the mid-twelfth century, or some twenty to thirty years after Anselm's death in 1117.[24]

Positive attribution is a much more perplexing affair. J. P. Bonnes has proposed that the author be identified as one Geoffrey of Loroux, otherwise known as Geoffrey Babion.[25] This proposal, however, is not without its difficulties, most of which have been identified by D. Van den Eynde.[26] This tradition of attribution to Geoffrey began with Peter Comestor, who referred to Babion's "solemn and authentic" glosses.[27] That tradition of attribution lasted until the mid-twentieth century, when Stegmüller linked the forty or so manuscripts of the *Enarrationes* he knew under the name of Geoffrey with Master Geoffrey Babion.[28]

However, analysis of matters of style and content makes it virtually impossible to conclude that Babion was the author of the *Enarrationes.* There seem to be no other plausible candidates for authorship. Accordingly, "it seems wiser" in the end (as Smalley has concluded), to leave the author anonymous.[29] (Following Smalley, we will hereafter refer to the author simply as *B.*) More certain than his name and precise identity is that *B* wrote in the mid-twelfth century in some school in northern France, perhaps Laon, then took a religious habit and wrote the *Enarrationes.* In so doing—whether or not he ever actually studied in Laon—

he drew on the scholastic tradition of gospel exegesis in Laon that reaches back to the first decade of the twelfth century.[30]

If the matter of authorship must finally be viewed with caution, the importance and influence of the *Enarrationes* is not in doubt at all. This is a commentary which formed a vital link between the early twelfth-century Laon tradition and the later twelfth- and thirteenth-century Parisian tradition of Matthew exegesis. Indeed, it used at least one early Laon commentary on Matthew and was used in turn by both Peter Comestor and Peter Cantor, who were in turn used by Hugh of St. Cher. For his part, Hugh was used by and influenced Alexander of Hales and later mendicants including John of LaRochelle, John of Wales, John Pecham, and Thomas Aquinas.[31] Thus *B* exercised an important direct and indirect influence on early mendicant exegesis of the gospels. More than that, he helped put exegesis of Matthew "on the map," to use Smalley's image[32]—that is, on the agenda of the schools. Up until the mid-twelfth century, there were relatively few commentaries written on Matthew or, for that matter, on any of the gospels; commentaries on the psalter and on Paul, on the other hand, abound in the late eleventh and early twelfth centuries.[33] From 1150 or so on, probably partly in response to the new enthusiasm for literal imitation of the *vita evangelica et apostolica*, commentaries on the gospels proliferate.

Aside from putting the academic exegesis of the gospels on the curricular and scholarly agenda of the schools, *B* also took compilations which had their origins in Laon (including the *Gloss*) and supplied them with (the words are again Smalley's) "a more scholastic form and equipped them with theological *quaestiones*."[34] In other words, this is one of the earliest commentaries on Matthew to include almost all the technical terms, exegetical material, and structural elements that would qualify it to be described as fully "scholastic."[35] This commentary thus satisfied a need in the schools; as Smalley puts it, it "fulfilled a desideratum,"[36] namely for a commentary which put the old wine of established exegetical traditions into the new skins of emerging scholastic terminology and structure. Most important for our purposes, the *Enarrationes* began and made quite popular a mode of non-particularistic and generic, largely moral exegesis of Matthew which was to have deep influence in the mendicant schools and in the university milieu of Paris in the thirteenth century. It popularized a form of exegesis that was to become enshrined in, among other works, the gospel commentaries of Hugh of St. Cher.

HUGH OF ST. CHER'S *POSTILLA SUPER MATTHAEUM*

Between the commentaries produced by secular masters at Laon and the ones produced in Paris in the 1230s lay, among other things, the founding of the two mendicant orders, growing interest in the implications of living the *vita evangelica vel apostolica*, the rise of the universities, and the gradual entrance into their theological faculties of Dominican and Franciscan masters of theology. Among the leading theologians of the first generation of friar-masters and without doubt the leading practitioner of biblical exegesis was the Dominican master Hugh of St. Cher (ca. 1195–1263).[37] By the time Hugh completed his *Postilla super Matthaeum*,[38] probably ca. 1235,[39] he was regent master at St. Jacques. Hugh commented on all four of the gospels, and did so in canonical order. The Matthew commentary forms only part of a massive *Postilla super Totam Bibliam*. Dondaine, Smalley, and Lerner all have concluded that these *postillae* were given first as lectures and then edited for "publication."[40] Given the scope of the project, and of Hugh's other duties, all agree also that the commentary on the whole Bible was a product not of Hugh himself but of a fairly large "team" of Dominican research assistants, captains, and amanuenses under Hugh's supervision. "Hugh," as Robert Lerner has concluded, "was never really one author but always a consortium."[41] In Smalley's words, this sprawling commentary was a *travail d'équipe* of Hugh and his assistants.[42]

Hugh's intention, for himself and for his team, was not to produce a work of great invention but something rather like a *Catena Aurea,* with brief comments made for modernizing contemporary (especially moral) application. Smalley has concluded that all parts of the commentary on the Bible, and not just the *postillae* on the gospels, form a mosaic of quotations. Hugh's purpose was to provide masters and students of the sacred page with "a vast *instrument de travail,* incorporating traditional and more nearly contemporary sources into its framework. . . . Hugh wanted . . . to equip his colleagues with the best means to continue and enlarge the work of his secular predecessors." At the same time, as Smalley also observed, this should not discourage the reader for looking for "flashes of personal opinions." If Hugh's intention did not "permit that fresh approach to the Gospels which we might expect from a Friar Preacher,"[43] he was attempting to "modernize" the patristic and secular tradition. Accordingly, his management of the tradition is not purely slavish. In fact, he shapes the exegetical tradition in accordance with new realities and aims his personal comments especially to an audience of future prelates and preachers.

To see just what is meant by "non-particularistic," "generic," and "largely moral" exegesis, we turn below to an analysis of how *B* treated materials he had inherited from the exegetical tradition, particularly from the *Gloss*, when interpreting two pericopes from Matthew and, then, to how the Laon tradition was received and reworked by Hugh.

Persecution of Herod (Mt. 2:13–23)

The *Gloss* inaugurated an important medieval line of interpretation of the Persecution of Herod. Aside from regarding the account as a historical episode in Jesus' infancy, the *Gloss* historicizes the story—that is to say, reads it as a type of historical development to come in the life of the earliest church. According to this reading, Joseph's flight to Egypt represents the bringing of the gospel to the gentiles after its rejection by the Jews.[44] The persecution of Jesus in his infancy represents the persecution of the church in its infancy. As soon as Christ appears in the world, the persecution against him begins; so, analogously, does the persecution of the saints. Indeed, the death of the male infants signifies the coming death of the martyrs.[45]

B follows the *Gloss* quite closely, if anonymously, though he underlines more emphatically the "blindness of the Jews." Joseph takes Mary and Jesus to Egypt in the middle of the night in order to emphasize, *B* says, that the Jews remained "in the night of ignorance" (*in nocte ignorantiae*).[46] Again, the flight of Christ represents the apostles—Christ in his members—fleeing to the gentiles, and Rachel's cries the church bewailing its murdered martyrs.[47] In terms of the content of his exposition, then, *B* cleaves to the path laid out by Ralph of Laon.

There is, however, a notable structural difference. If the *Gloss* was a more or less continuous exposition of text, with very few theological *quaestiones* inserted, we see in *B* a proliferation of such questions.[48] This signals a change of some moment, for such questions will become a conventional and significant component of exegesis of the gospels in the thirteenth-century Parisian tradition. Here, in *B*, we observe a new genre of gloss, where the continuity of exposition is frequently stalled by the introduction of theological *quaestiones* posed by the biblical text. Eventually, such *quaestiones* will be separated from their exegetical context altogether and become, once rearranged under the appropriate theological rubrics, systematic theological commentaries—namely, *Quaestiones in Sacra Pagina*, *Sentence* commentaries, and *summae*. In *B*, there is yet no real distinction between the study of the sacred page and the study of doctrine. Still, *B* represents an important move away from the simple expository glossing he found in Ralph's *Gloss*, a move away from the style of learning found in the cathedrals and toward that found in the universities. Hugh of St. Cher follows these two secular texts very closely, and, in fact, explicitly cites the *Gloss*.[49] And the influence of the "biblical-moral" tradition is never absent. For Hugh, Herod signifies the Devil, "who is disturbed when Jesus, that is, salvation, is born in the heart of a man."[50]

Nevertheless, "flashes of personality" do shine through. When talking about the alacrity with which Joseph obeys the angel's command to take the child and his mother to the land of Israel (Mt. 2:20), for example, Hugh comments that, just so, one who has been elected to the prelature or to preaching should go to their posts with zeal.[51] In short, Hugh is taking here the secular and early scholastic tradition and modernizing it for use in the mendicant and university setting in Paris in the thirteenth century.

The Temptation (Mt. 4:1–11)

Most medieval commentaries on Matthew interpret the Temptation as an actual historical encounter between Jesus and the Devil. In fact, many commentators felt confident enough to identify its location: the desert between Jerusalem and Jericho, indeed the desert of which Luke speaks in the parable of the Good Samaritan (Lk. 10:30–37).[52] Nonetheless, the *Gloss* and, then, most medieval commentaries interpret the Temptation account as a sort of historically based moral parable carefully orchestrated and enacted by Christ for the education of the baptized. The *Gloss* argues that Jesus proceeded immediately and intentionally to the solitude of the desert after his baptism to confront and withstand the onslaughts of the Enemy. He did so in order to instruct the baptized to leave the world, serve God in quiet, and gird themselves for battle with the Devil.[53]

The author of the *Enarrationes* also interprets the Temptation not only as a historical account of an actual encounter of Christ with the Devil after his baptism. He also reads it as an allegory of the inevitability of temptation in the life of the newly baptized Christian and an example of how the freshly baptized ought to resist temptation when it comes. Christ intentionally permitted himself to be tempted after baptism, not before, precisely so that he might teach the baptized how to meet temptation. And, following the *Gloss, B* argues that Christ goes into the desert immediately after having been baptized in order to show every faithful person that after baptism one should regard the world as of secondary importance, seek the desert of the mind (or a physical desert), and prepare for war against the Devil.[54]

In fact, Christ's behavior throughout the narrative is quite consciously and carefully calculated to demonstrate how to frustrate the Devil. For example, Christ deliberately allows himself to grow hungry after his forty-day fast precisely in order to invite the Devil to tempt him with bread. The Devil takes the bait, but Christ admonishes him with words from Deuteronomy: *Non in solo pane* (Dt. 8:3). Why? So that Christ might teach us to resist temptation with "the shield of the Scriptures" (*clypeum Scripturarum*).[55] Similarly, Christ admonishes the Devil not to tempt the Lord God. And he does so in order to demonstrate that when we petition God we should do so confidently, but not to tempt God.[56] In short, Christ is understood here to be functioning purposefully as a moral exemplar whom Christians are to imitate in trial and temptation.

These lines of interpretation are not new. Indeed, this interpretation of the account can be found in any number of ancient and early medieval sources, including, as we have seen, the *Gloss*.[57] What is novel, however, and what will exercise considerable influence in the following centuries is that the text of the commentary is periodically punctuated by new scholastic forms of inquiry and analysis: the *quaestio* and the *responsio*. At one point in his analysis, the author of the *Enarrationes* pauses to wonder, "how were these temptations effected?" Perhaps, some say, they occurred in the soul, so that they were not visibly achieved. Others say—and more truly (*verius*)—that the Devil visibly appeared as a man (*ut homo*) to Christ and spoke with him.[58] But then how did the Devil lead Christ to the pinnacle of the temple? Some say that, with Christ's permission, he transported and placed him there; others, that he led Jesus on the road to Jerusalem and that they ascended the temple together, "as other men do."[59] These *quaestiones*—often quaint and seemingly digressive—and the discussion and resolution of competing responses which follow are something new in mid-twelfth–century exegesis of the gospels. In the following century, they will become utterly conventional.

Hugh's commentary on the Temptation follows the general interpretive lines set down by the *Gloss* and B. He accepts the traditional consensus that the Temptation was a historical encounter between Christ and the Devil and that it occurred in a precisely identifiable spot.[60] Hugh, too, puts great emphasis on the moral meaning of Christ's decision to proceed directly to the desert after his baptism. Just so, we too, having accepted the grace of the Holy Spirit, ought to come to the desert and inclaustrate ourselves from the world. There, we will find a real paradise and garden of delights.[61]

Thus far, Hugh follows his predecessors from Laon, especially *B,* quite closely. While he continues to do so for the remainder of the chapter, a distinctively Dominican note is inserted when Hugh begins to explain the meaning of the Devil's first temptation. Why does Christ answer the Devil's first temptation with a *riposte* lifted from Deuteronomy? In order to defend the harmony (*convenientiam*) of the Law, Prophets, and the Gospels. Indeed, Christ's specific target here was the Manichees, who argued that the Old Law was diabolical in origin.[62]

One of the features of medieval exegesis that receives special emphasis among the Dominicans is that Christ was understood to be constantly (and that is the word) being, acting, and speaking so as to neutralize the arguments of heretics who, he knows, will plague the church after his death, resurrection, and ascension. This emphasis, while present in Hugh, will become especially pronounced in the Matthew commentary of that ever-vigilant Dominican hammer of heretics, Thomas Aquinas. As Beryl Smalley observed, "Thomas wins the prize as a heresiologue . . . in his search throughout the Gospels for anti-heretical arguments"; his commentary is "a relentless pursuit of heretics."[63] But this is merely the culmination of a Dominican tradition that had its origin in the commentaries of Hugh.

A second Dominican note that Hugh subtly introduces throughout the commentary and here in this chapter consists of moral application to the lives and work of religious, prelates, and, above all—and not surprisingly—preachers. Beryl Smalley has correctly observed that Hugh was "working in the tradition of the 'biblical moral' school."[64] However, he modernizes that tradition by making his *moralitates* applicable always to his Dominican confreres. For example, the invitation by the Devil to Christ, "If you are the Son of God, command these stones to become loaves of bread" (Mt. 4:3), Hugh interprets as a moral allegory. Applied to contemporary mendicant experience, it represents the devil's attempt to soften the preacher's harsh admonitions for the sake of temporal emolument.[65] Or, again, the stones represent the austerity of penance. The Devil's words, translated, mean: "You have been in the convent long enough . . . go to the infirmary. Relax."[66] At the level of contemporary moral interpretation, they are a specific sort of temptation for the Dominican preacher.

The number of examples like this could be multiplied. But the important point to grasp is that the Friar Preacher does occasionally declare himself, if usually *sotto voce*. Smalley is again correct to note both that, "A new vision of poverty and the apostolate does come through"[67] and that this element of the commentary is "less obvious, indeed elusive."[68] In the end, Hugh stands with one foot in the Laon tradition from which he borrows so freely. Hugh *is* a compiler, and his commentary "a mosaic of quotations."[69] His intention was, in the end, to provide masters and students with a reference work of extracts carefully selected from the patristic and secular tradition.

At the same time, he "tweaks," improvises, and modernizes the biblical-moral tradition he inherits. If Smalley is correct to have observed that "Hugh never mentions either his Order or its founder,"[70] it is important to underline that this is a commentary which is meant for mendicant consumption. If we do not see in Hugh "that fresh approach to the Gospels which we might expect from a Friar Preacher,"[71] signs of religious identity do flicker through on occasion. The Temptation account in Hugh's hands, for example, remains a moral parable carefully manipulated and enacted by Christ for the education of the baptized—but above all for the baptized who have an apostolic preaching mission, who dedicate their lives to study, pastoral care, and contemplation. Consequently it is rather less—but just a little less—generic and more particularistic than the secular sources from Laon on which it so thoroughly depends.

CONCLUSION

By the time we get to Hugh of St. Cher, then, we begin to see a fully formed, mature new genre of commentary that contains all of the elements usually associated with the word "scholastic." Hugh's Matthew commentary is a compilation of patristic extracts and citations from the "modern" scholastic tradition of Laon, particularly the *Gloss* and B. It contains many theological *quaestiones* and lengthy responses. If the exegesis is largely "generic" and intended for moral application, matters of convent and church do begin to shape the way in which the commentary is conceived and written. Hugh borrows freely from the school of Laon and from the "biblical-moral" tradition. But the new worlds of which he is a part—thirteenth century, university, mendicant—make his commentary subtly different from the twelfth-century secular works on which he so heavily depends. His is essentially an updating of that twelfth-century secular tradition for the new world in which he and his audience find themselves. In this sense, he is a bridge figure who helped to link the traditions of Laon and Paris.

It is also worth noting, by way of brief anticipation, how Hugh's commentary differs from the later thirteenth-century tradition of which Olivi is the culmination. In Hugh's *postilla*, long stretches of commentary can pass before we perceive a distinctively mendicant or thirteenth-century note. There is little hint of intramural or extramural tension or debate. There is almost nothing that attempts to reinforce or reflect the values of a particular religious order; the moral exegesis ladled out by Hugh and his team is food for all Christians. Above all, such debates as Hugh ever so delicately alludes to are never framed in the language of prophecy or eschatology, nor elevated to the level of apocalyptic struggle or reformation. "Certain it is that Joachimite types of speculation had no appeal for [Hugh]."[72] All too true. To see what Smalley meant by this, and all that her comment implied, we turn now to the gospel commentary of Joachim of Fiore. For Joachim and, then, for Olivi, the gospels were full of prophecy, of war and rumors of war. And much else besides.

CHAPTER TWO

The Joachite Gospel

The *Tractatus super Quatuor Evangelia*

By the time Joachim began writing in the mid-twelfth century, scores of Greek and Latin thinkers had produced hundreds of commentaries on the gospels and the Apocalypse. Among those who had written on these biblical texts were the most illustrious figures in patristic exegesis—thinkers like Origen, Chrysostom, Bede, Jerome, Ambrose, Gregory, and Augustine. No exegete writing in the twelfth century, no matter how isolated, could have been unaware of some, at least, of the exegetical writings of these patristic giants, and none, however inventive, could have remained immune to their influence.

Joachim is no exception. It has been well established that Joachim's interpretation of the Apocalypse is partially indebted to the dominant "Tyconian-Augustinian" exegetical tradition, which emphasized the moral and ecclesiological content of the book and minimized its prophetic and historical dimensions.[1] Joachim's interpretation of many of the other biblical writings is also dependent on traditional patristic assumptions.

Significant though his debt to tradition might be, Joachim was acclaimed by contemporaries and is studied by modern scholars for very different qualities. Joachim himself was persuaded that he had achieved a deeper insight into the meaning of the scriptures than the fathers, and those medieval readers who embraced him with such enthusiasm did so because they shared that conviction. Nowhere was the novelty and, to contemporaries, prophetic power and truth of his exegesis more evident than in his reading of the Apocalypse. In that last book of the Bible, Joachim had discovered not just a timeless moral message about the soul and the church, but a detailed revelation about God's plan for history. That was the idea that exhilarated contemporaries and motivated many to action.

That Joachim discovered, or thought he discovered, a detailed message about God's plan for history in the Apocalypse is well known. Less widely known and discussed is that he saw that message inscribed also, if differently, in the four gospels. Indeed, for Joachim, that was *the* message of the Bible, and it was announced, though here literally and there spiritually, in all its parts. The importance of the *Tractatus* is, as Henri Mottu has put it, "the importance of an exegesis of an apocalyptic type applied to the Gospels."[2]

For his part, Olivi shared both of Joachim's convictions, namely that God's plan for history was revealed in a special way in the Apocalypse but given in all books of the Bible as well. Unlike any contemporary mendicant commentator, Olivi also depended in his own gospel commentaries on many of the central assumptions and methods of Joachim's gospel commentary, even if he did not know the text directly. For that reason it seems appropriate to begin this chapter with an examination of the kind of exegesis enshrined in the abbot's *Tractatus super Quatuor Evangelia*. We will discover a much more *heilsgeschichtlich* mode of exegesis than we have seen in the scholastic Matthew commentaries examined in the last chapter. It is the combination of scholastic structure and Joachite method and content that (along with elements of Franciscan experience and thought, to be considered next chapter) make Olivi's commentaries so unique.

THE *TRACTATUS*: METHODS AND ASSUMPTIONS

The way in which Joachim's *Tractatus* influenced Olivi's gospel commentaries has to be distinguished from the way in which other medieval exegetical works influenced them. Olivi did not depend upon the *Tractatus* in the same systematic and continuous way that he did, for example, on the *Catena Aurea*. That he even read it may be doubted.³ In fact, an analysis of the contents of the *Tractatus* and the context in which it was written points to an oblique influence of exegetical approach and assumptions, rather than of direct borrowing.

Though quite long, the *Tractatus* is an unfinished and probably late work of Joachim.⁴ It is a simultaneous commentary on all four canonical gospels, though Joachim concentrated his attention on Luke and John.⁵ The commentary is divided into three tractates. The first is devoted primarily to the infancy accounts, the second to the synoptic accounts of the earliest stages of Jesus' ministry, and the third primarily to John 2–5. Thus, Joachim did *not* say much, or anything, about most of each of the four gospels. He says virtually nothing, for example, about the last twenty-three chapters of Matthew; he died before he got around to commenting on them. Nonetheless, Joachim took his own unique assumptions about the nature of the revelation contained in the Bible and applied them to his exegesis of the gospels. The result was a highly original mode of interpretation that Olivi, though often with different results connected to his own Franciscan presuppositions, appropriated in his own gospel commentaries.

Perhaps the most important assumption Joachim brought to his gospel commentary is that the entire Bible, not just those books traditionally taken to be "historical" or "prophetic," reveals what he called "the fullness of history" (*plenitudo historiae*).⁶ As has been pointed out by Bernard McGinn, what is truly distinctive of Joachim's approach to exegesis is that none of his predecessors had made so central in their biblical commentaries the notion that the scriptures reveal the history of the past, present, *and* future.⁷ Joachim took this basic idea and applied it to his interpretation of the Apocalypse. However, he was also prepared to apply this notion systematically to the four canonical gospels. Consequently, Joachim interpreted the events of the four gospels above all as "types" or "concords" of the future. It was through Olivi's appropriation of this fundamental assumption that Joachim's *Tractatus* exercised its profound, if indirect, influence on his gospel commentaries.

Certain methods of exegesis go hand-in-glove with the assumption that all of the Bible reveals the fullness of history, including the future. Most of these methods are not original to Joachim. However, Joachim applied them so much more systematically than his predecessors that they may be regarded as distinctive of his approach to the Bible.

The most important of these has already been implied, namely, that the events and teachings of the New Testament may be interpreted as "types" or "figures" of future events. Typology is a mode of exegesis produced by the Christian community in the context of second-century struggles with the Jewish community over the ownership and meaning of the Hebrew Scriptures. Typology is, therefore, a term used most often to denote a mode of early Christian interpretation of the *Old* Testament. It is normally understood as that system of exegesis which demands that events in Israelite history be read in the light of subsequent Christian history and as prophetic of key events (especially the crucifixion) in that history. Practitioners of typology read the Old Testament in light of the New. Indeed, the method assumes that the meaning of the Old Testament is incomplete and even false without reference to the contents of the New. Consequently, the deepest meaning of the sacrifice of Isaac (Gn. 22:1–19) or of the role of the "suffering servant" in Isaiah 52–53 can only be fathomed by reference to the passion and crucifixion of Christ. By the mid-second century, Christian exegetes such as Justin Martyr (d. 165) were reading the Hebrew Scriptures in precisely this way.[8]

No later than the mid-third century, however, exegetes such as Origen were interpreting the *New* Testament typologically as well.[9] That is, Origen was willing to regard certain episodes of the New Testament as prophecies or "types" of the future of the church.[10] Nonetheless, there is a crucial difference between Origen's brand of typologizing and that found in Joachim and Olivi. Origen was prepared to regard some events of the New Testament as prophesying *in general* about the future history of the church. But both Joachim and Olivi were willing to go one critical step further. Both assumed that the New Testament, and the gospels in particular, contained episodes which could be *specifically* correlated with concrete events which had occurred, were occurring, or would occur at specifiable moments in the history of the church. It is one thing to say that the temptation account is a general type of the temptations to be endured by the church in the future. It is quite another to say that it is a type of temptations that will occur, in predictable forms, after 1,200 years of church history. This kind of typologizing is particularly dangerous if one is willing to state or imply who the tempters in question are, and to specify the nature of their temptations. Both Joachim and Olivi sometimes were. Few other interpreters of the New Testament in the first thirteen centuries of Christian history would be willing to concede, in theory, that the gospels embodied this kind of prophecy and fewer still, in practice, to hazard their own typological reading of the gospels.

One of the corollaries of the typological reading of the Bible, or at least of the New Testament, is implied in Joachim and Olivi's interpretation of the Temptation account. Again, it is not original with Joachim. The principle of "head and members" was classically articulated by the fourth-century Donatist exegete Tyconius in his *Liber Regularum*, a set of seven exegetical principles that would shortly achieve canonical status by their inclusion in Augustine's *De Doctrina Christiana*.[11] According to this principle, those things predicated of Christ may also be referred to his mystical body, the church. What is said about the "head" may be applied to the "members."[12]

At one point in the *Liber Concordie*, Joachim makes a crucial hermeneutical statement: "There are many things written about the Lord Jesus Christ, which by no means can reasonably be understood, except as referring to his body."[13] This is a hermeneutic which Joachim uses to great effect in the *Tractatus*. Again, though not original to Joachim, he applied it in a more historicizing fashion than virtually any of his predecessors. In Joachim (and, for that matter, Olivi) we see a *heilsgeschichtlich* way of employing the application of this ancient biblical hermeneutic. Both Joachim and Olivi, for example, interpret the temptation of Christ "the head" as a type of the temptation of his "members" by the devil in the age of eschatological tribulation. Olivi would frequently exploit this principle in a similar fashion throughout his gospel commentaries.

More distinctive of Joachim is his own particular definition of "allegory." This term has a longer history than typology, going back at least as far as the Pythagorean interpreters of Homer. It was subsequently popularized in Alexandria by Philo and by Origen. Augustine would discuss it at great length in *De doctrina christiana*.[14] In Christian theories of biblical hermeneutics, it usually refers to that level of exegesis, usually but not always taken to be dependent upon some prior determination of the fundamental literal or historical meaning of a text, which reveals articles of belief or the doctrinal contents of the faith. In actual exegetical practice, however, it usually refers more generally to levels of meaning acknowledged to be non-literal or non-historical.

Joachim's definition of *allegoria* is rather different: "Allegoria is the similarity of any small thing to an extremely large one, for example of a day to a year, or a week to an age, of a person to an order, or a city, or a nation, or a people, and a thousand similar instances."[15] Again, the example of the Temptation account provides a good illustration of how both Joachim and Olivi exploit this principle. As we shall see, both agree that the forty days of Christ's fasting in the desert before his temptation symbolize the forty generations of the church which would elapse before the eschatological temptation of the devil. In his gospel commentaries, Olivi shows no signs of approving, or even knowing, Joachim's theoretical definition of *allegoria*. However, this is a principle he applies *in practice* throughout his interpretation of the first gospel.

Olivi applies this notion of allegory most often when he encounters numbers which appear in the texts of the gospels. Numerological exegesis is a highly characteristic feature of medieval exegesis. It is used particularly often, but not only, in connection with the interpretation of prophetic and eschatological books (such as Daniel or the Apocalypse) or in apocalyptic parts of books not otherwise usually taken to contain information about the future (such as the "Apocalyptic Discourse," found in slightly different forms in Matthew 24, Mark 13, and Luke 21). Many pre-modern exegetes (as well as less illustrious twentieth-century successors) have assumed that an understanding of the numbers contained in these books was essential to an appreciation of their meaning, especially to a comprehension of the secrets of the future they contained.

There can be no doubt about the importance that Olivi attached to an understanding of numbers in the gospels. On several occasions, he pauses to make explicit his understanding of what certain numbers ordinarily signify.[16] In his gospel commentaries, the most important numbers are those connected with theologies of history developed by predecessors of both Joachim and Olivi, especially the sevenfold pattern of church history found in Bede and others.[17] How Joachim actually used these numerological and exegetical principles in his apocalyptic exegesis is a topic to which we turn now.

Joachim's Apocalyptic Thought

The originality of Joachim's apocalyptic thought can perhaps be appreciated only against the background of the previous Latin exegetical tradition. With few exceptions, exegetes of the Apocalypse in Latin Christianity from the fifth century to the late twelfth interpreted the book in a "spiritual" rather than historical sense. That is, most Latin exegetes from ca. 400 to ca. 1180 interpreted the book *primarily* as a timeless message about the life of the church and the individual in the present, rather than as a detailed prophecy about the course of future history. Most read the book in terms of the struggle of virtue and sin in the individual soul and the church in all ages rather than in terms of the crisis and persecution to be endured by the faithful in an imminent age of eschatological tribulation.

Almost all lingering traces of classical apocalypticism[18] in the West, as well as any remaining tendencies toward chiliasm[19] or of the historicizing reading of the Apocalypse, were doomed by Augustine's refusal to read the signs of the times as evidence of the divine plan for humanity or to read the Apocalypse in any but a spiritual sense.[20] Only in the twelfth century, in exegetes such as Rupert of Deutz, do we begin to see a movement away from a thoroughgoing spiritual reading of the Apocalypse.[21] However, Rupert marks only the first tentative steps to the historicizing readings found in Joachim. In the last analysis, the German Benedictine is still very faithful to the spiritualizing and moralizing reading that almost completely eclipsed all rivals in the long centuries between the African bishop and the Calabrian abbot.

The extensive historicizing of the Apocalypse found in Joachim's *Expositio super Apocalypsim*[22] should not lead us to conclude that he utterly neglected the traditional spiritual reading of the book. He did not. However, Joachim did see the Apocalypse of John primarily as a detailed, continuous prophecy of the entire course of church history in seven ages and of the enjoyment of beatitude by the saints in the eighth "age" of eternity.[23] Indeed, the very structure of the *Expositio* reflects Joachim's conviction that the Apocalypse was intended principally as a prophecy of the future of the church in seven ages (*tempora*).[24] The commentary is divided into eight parts, one for each of the seven periods of church history and one for the "age" of eternal beatitude.[25] We can therefore represent Joachim's outline of the Apocalypse and of church history in the following schematic form.

JOACHIM'S SYNOPSIS OF THE APOCALYPSE

Tempus	*Apocalypse*	*Major Symbols*
First	1:1–3:22	Letters to Seven Churches
Second	4:1–8:1	The Seven Seals
Third	8:2–11:18	The Seven Trumpets
Fourth	11:19–14:20	Dragon and Beasts from Sea and Earth
Fifth	15:1–16:17	Seven Bowls of Wrath
Sixth	16:18–19:21	Whore of Babylon
Seventh	20:1–10	Reign of Christ and Saints; Gog/Magog
Eighth	20:11–22:21	New Heaven and New Earth

Joachim's originality consists in correlating these symbols and events in the Apocalypse, not with a general moral and ecclesiological message, but with concrete events in salvation history (especially church history) which had occurred, were occurring, or would occur. Thus, to cite just one example, Joachim interprets the onslaughts of the unnamed beast of the fourth part of the Apocalypse as a symbol of Moslem attacks on the church in the seventh century.[26]

Joachim did not limit the scope of the Apocalypse's revelation to New Testament history alone. As has already been implied, Joachim regarded the Apocalypse as an epitome of the entire course of salvation history, including what we might call Old Testament history. Throughout his writings, Joachim was anxious to find in the scriptures as a whole, and in the Apocalypse in particular, precise parallels in the histories of the Israelite and Christian peoples of God. As is well known, Joachim was convinced that the "similarities" (*concordiae* or *concordantiae*) between or "harmony" (*concordia*) of Old and New Testament history were given in the literal sense of the scriptural text.[27]

These parallels were particularly evident to Joachim in the seven seals of the Apocalypse (4:1–8:1). There Joachim found a literal representation of successive persecutions to be endured by the church, trials which precisely paralleled those undergone by the Israelites in Old Testament history. Joachim returned again and again to this theme in his writings, so these concords vary somewhat throughout his works. For our purposes, however, the basic structure is stable enough to be represented in the following schematic form.[28]

JOACHIM'S CONCORD OF PERSECUTIONS

Tempus	*Old Testament*	*New Testament*
First	Egyptian	Jewish
Second	Canaanite	Roman Empire
Third	Syrian/Philistine	Arian/Barbarian
Fourth	Assyrian	Persian/Saracen
Fifth	Babylonian	German Empire
Sixth	Assyrian/Persian	Saladin/Antichrist
Seventh	Age of Peace	Age of Peace

As will later become evident, Olivi departed from all of his exegetical predecessors and contemporaries, except Joachim, in finding in the gospels (and especially in the parables) similar concords of salvation history and persecution. Olivi, of course, would see the parallel persecutions in terms of his own Franciscan presuppositions. He would also stipulate that they were given in the spiritual rather than the literal sense of the gospel text.

Olivi would also follow Joachim closely in the Calabrian abbot's decision to place himself at a moment of decisive transformation in the history of the church. At the beginning of the *Expositio*, Joachim states that his own historical moment is that of the transition between the fifth and sixth *tempora*, or the moment of the opening of the Sixth Seal.[29] He also speaks of this transition in all of his major works in terms of his more famous Trinitarian scheme, according to which history unfolds in terms of three successive, overlapping *status*, each primarily under the aegis of one of the persons of the Trinity. Each *status* is also characterized by a particular way of life, or *ordo*. The *status* of the Father, which is coterminous with the seven ages of Old Testament history, began with Adam and ended with the coming of Christ. Its characteristic way of life was that of the married (*ordo coniugatorum*). Since the three *status* are overlapping, those of the Son and of the Holy Spirit have their beginnings (*germinationes*) in the previous *status*. The *status* of the Son, which corresponds roughly but not perfectly with the first five *tempora* of New Testament history, began with King Josiah, achieved fruition in Christ, and would end "in these times," that is, at the end of the twelfth century. Its characteristic way of life was that of clerics (*ordo clericorum*). The *status* of the Holy Spirit, which corresponds roughly to the sixth and seventh *tempora* of church history, had its beginning in St. Benedict, would reach fruition in the relatively near future, and would last until the end of the world. Its characteristic way of life was that of monks (*ordo monachorum*).[30] Joachim usually places himself explicitly at the beginning of the third *status*.[31] The beginning of this *status* or the sixth *tempus* was to be marked both by an extraordinary advance in the understanding of the Bible and by a frightening increase in the persecution of the spiritual church by the forces of evil.

It is no exaggeration to say that, for Joachim, the goal or end of the entire historical process was the clear "spiritual" understanding of the Bible. As McGinn has put it, "the meaning of world history is the history of exegesis."[32] To be sure, Joachim affirms that the spiritual understanding of scripture had been given to the people of God in past ages. However, it had always been a partial and unfinished endowment. Joachim concedes that some members of the people of God in Old Testament history had been given glimpses into the spiritual meaning of the scriptures. However, the first great insight into the spiritual meaning of the scriptures took place only in the resurrection. It was only at that moment, when the "tomb of the letter" was opened, that the spiritual understanding (*intellectus spiritalis* or *intelligentia spiritalis*) of the Bible emerged in a truly decisive way.[33] Nonetheless, the revelation given at the resurrection, though decisive, was not conclusive.

Much as Joachim insists that Christ imparted to believers the first spiritual understanding of the scriptures, he is equally insistent that he did not entrust to them that understanding of the scriptures in its fullness. Joachim maintains that the revelation of the spiritual meaning of scriptures would be given by the Holy Spirit only gradually over the course of church history. In the *Tractatus,* he states quite explicitly that the spiritual understanding of the scriptures was given "more fully and openly" (*plenius et apertius*) to Ambrose, Jerome, and Augustine than to their apostolic predecessors.[34] But the logic of Joachim's progressivist position drives him to declare in the *Liber Concordie* that the fullness of understanding had not been granted even to this illustrious group of fathers. That would be conferred by the Holy Spirit upon *viri spirituales* only in the final *status* of salvation history.[35] For Joachim, the coming perfection of the monastic life could be described in terms of the increasing spiritual understanding of scripture and the emphasis on the contemplative life which this understanding alone makes possible. Following Bonaventure, Olivi would see the future of the Franciscan Order in similar terms but also insist far more than Joachim on the importance of poverty as a condition for the observance of the perfect contemplative life.

Despite these optimistic and positive apocalyptic signs, Joachim reminds us that persecution of the faithful is a perennial feature of ecclesiastical life. Indeed, Joachim characterizes each ecclesiastical *tempus* primarily in terms of its own peculiar travail and conflict. Thus, the first ecclesiastical *tempus* is generally depicted in the abbot's works and illustrated in his *figurae* in terms of the clash between the apostles and the Judaizers. The second is characterized by the attack of the pagan Roman emperors on the martyrs and the third in terms of the battle of the ancient heretics and doctors. The fourth *tempus* is often represented chiefly in terms of the assault of the Persians and Moslems on the church, while the fifth is exemplified by the onslaught of the Great Whore Babylon (sometimes understood as the German Emperor). Quite clearly, the clash of two new inimical forces, one good and one evil, gives each age its own special character. Still, there is a strong element of continuity in the first five *tempora* of church history for Joachim. In each of its first five ages, the church is plagued by a hostile force intent on its dissolution and championed by a class of Christian heroes intent on its vigor and well-being.

When Joachim turns to describe the persecution of the dawning sixth *tempus,* he does not emphasize similarity or identity with previous ages. He stresses difference. For Joachim, the sixth *tempus* is exceptional in Christian history in the depth of the perception by its *viri spirituales* of the spiritual meaning of the scriptures and in the excellence of their practice of the monastic life. In parallel fashion, it is unprecedented in the severity of the persecution suffered by the faithful. Indeed, a survey of late twelfth-century events and developments convinced Joachim that he was living in times of unparalleled evil and chaos. Joachim found a number of developments worthy of concern, but he himself emphasizes the resurgence of Islamic power under Saladin, the growth of heresy, the continuing conflict of papacy and empire, and the deepening corruption within the church. In short, Joachim embodies the classical apocalypticist's conviction that he was living in a time of dire crisis, of unusually cruel persecution of the righteous, and of the mounting power of the wicked.

Perhaps not surprisingly, Joachim found prophetic representations of the evil forces of his own age in the *dramatis personae* of the Apocalypse. In the beasts from Land and Sea of Apocalypse 13, Joachim perceived a prophecy of the union of Islam and the Western heretics (whom he often calls "Patarini"). Under the leadership of the Antichrist, these two forces would, as predicted in Apocalypse 13:5, be permitted to persecute the church for forty-two months or three and a half years.[36] At one point in the *Expositio,* Joachim implies that this persecution has been well underway by the time he writes. The Antichrist, he says, is now present in the world but has not been revealed; his persecution has three years left to run.[37] Joachim also interprets the seven heads of the dragon of Apocalypse 12 as a series of seven persecuting kings throughout church history. The last two are identified as Saladin and the Antichrist and the fifth as the Emperor Henry IV.[38] Finally, in the Great Whore Babylon, Joachim saw an image not only of the German Empire but of the corrupt members of the church.[39]

According to Joachim, two powerful forces would arise to confront the Antichrist and his minions in the dark days ahead. One was a holy pope who would preach to the pagans at a time of persecution immediately preceding that of the Antichrist.[40] The second was a pair of new groups of "spiritual men" (*viri spirituales*) who would resist the onslaught of the Antichrist. One of the groups of spiritual men would be preachers in the spirit of Elijah. Its mission would be to clarify the mysteries of faith while the Antichrist attempted to pervert them by twisting the meaning of the scriptures.[41] The second group would be a band of contemplative hermits in the spirit of Moses. Its mission would be to intercede for the world in prayer.[42] The work of both groups would help to prepare the way for the contemplative order of the third *status*. It was, of course, this notion that was the source of the apocalyptic hopes and self-understanding of many religious orders in the thirteenth through the sixteenth centuries and beyond. Within decades of Joachim's death, a variety of religious orders, including the Franciscan, began to identify themselves as one of the groups of *viri spirituales* prophesied by the abbot Joachim.[43]

In his gospel commentaries, Olivi would be deeply influenced by three of Joachim's principal themes. First, that the New Testament had prophesied the dawn of a new age of the spiritual understanding of the scriptures and the practice of a new, more perfect observance of the religious life. Second, that the church in that new age would be subject to unusually fierce persecution by the Antichrist and his forces, a persecution which was to be resisted by two new groups of "spiritual men" (*viri spirituales*). Third, that the defeat of the Antichrist would usher in a final, brief period of this-worldly sabbatical peace and contemplation. Joachim expressed these themes not only in his *Expositio* but in his gospel commentary as well, as the following examples will demonstrate.

Joachim's Apocalyptic Thought and the *Tractatus*

The Synoptic Problem

Like his patristic and scholastic predecessors, Joachim begins reflections on the gospels with some reflections on the interrelations of the four gospels. To some extent, he depends on Augustine's *De Consensu Evangelistarum*. Mottu is not entirely wrong in arguing that the debt of Joachim to this Augustinian work is "undeniable."[44] On the other hand, Joachim, as always, has some interesting and innovative things to say about "the synoptic problem." For these he owes precious little to the patristic tradition in general or to Augustine in particular.

To start with, though he accepts the argument that Matthew, Mark, and Luke preceded John,[45] he is less comfortable with the traditional patristic view that the canonical order and the chronological order are identical. In fact, he argues quite explicitly than a proper interpretation of the vision of Ezekiel would suggest not that Mark wrote before Luke, but afterward, and that there were good pedagogical reasons for the Holy Spirit to have inspired the evangelists to write in this sequence (Matthew, Luke, Mark, John). If we move through the gospels in this order, Joachim argues, we ascend from the more humble to the sublime.[46] Thus, each evangelist concentrates attention on one phase of Christ's life: Matthew, on the nativity; Luke, on the passion; Mark, on the resurrection; and John on the ascension.[47] That we move from the humble to the sublime as we move through the *canonical* order of the scriptures was an argument found in virtually all patristic and medieval commentators on the gospels. Joachim's originality here is in changing the pedagogical order by which we ascend and by which faith is incrementally perfected.[48]

So far as Matthew in particular is concerned, Joachim agrees that the first evangelist wrote for and among the Jews. Because the scribes and Pharisees knew Christ only according to the flesh, rather than knowing the Son of God according to his divinity, it was not fitting that Matthew should write of the "divine signs of Christ" (*divina Christi sacramenta*).[49] That is why Matthew begins his gospel with a genealogy that traces Christ's origins back through David to Abraham.[50] These ideas are deeply rooted in the patristic tradition.

Much more daringly, Joachim interprets the relationship of the four gospels and the four creatures of Ezekiel's vision in terms of the history of salvation. "According to the spiritual understanding (*spiritalem intellectum*), we can assign the four gospels to the four times (*temporibus*)."[51] Thus Matthew, which begins with allusion to Abraham, corresponds to the Old (or First [*prior*] as Joachim puts it) Testament; Luke, which deals so much with the childhood and progress of Christ until he was twelve, corresponds to the teaching of the primitive church (this is the time which persists until Joachim's own day, he says); Mark, which deals with the time of Christ's preaching, corresponds to the spiritual teaching of which Paul spoke, which will persist until the end of the world; and John is the evangelist who hints at that ineffable wisdom we shall experience when we see the Divine *facie ad faciem*.[52] Clearly, each of the first three gospels corresponds to one of the three *status* and the fourth to the "time" of eternity. Joachim's treatment of the synoptic problem is an excellent example of his

capacity, indeed his tendency, to historicize traditional patterns and interpretations; and, as we shall, see, it is a tendency that is expressed over and
over in the *Tractatus.*

Persecution of Herod (Mt. 2:13–23)

As we recall, the early scholastic commentaries considered last chapter all
historicized the story of the Persecution of Herod—that is to say, all read
it as a type of historical development to come in the life of the earliest
church. The persecution of Jesus in his infancy represented, for these writ-
ers, the persecution of the church in its infancy.

Joachim accepts this reading of the story but expands on it considerably. For Joachim, the story is historically applied not just to the persecution that had occurred in the ancient church but to the persecution that
would occur at the time of the Antichrist. Indeed, he several times identifies Herod specifically as a type of Antichrist.[53] Just as Herod had persecuted the head of the church, Christ, so the Antichrist would persecute
his members, the church, in a crisis Joachim believed to be imminent. Just
as Christ, who is truth, reigns in the church of the humble, so the Antichrist has reigned and will reign "in the synagogue of the proud" (*in synagoga superborum*).[54] Herod's infanticide is not just a symbol but a *prophecy,*
according to the typical sense, of the persecution of the "church of the
humble" and of the just.

If we compare this reading with the one represented by the exegetes
considered last chapter, it is clear that both regard the pericope as having
a historical meaning. But for the scholastic exegetes considered, that
meaning resides in the *past.* For Joachim, the passage has that past historical meaning, but an even fuller, more "spiritual" meaning that refers to
the *future*—in fact, to the very near future. Few—very few—exegetes
before Joachim dared to read the gospels in precisely this typological-
prophetic sort of way. And, with equally few exceptions, few after him
would either.

The Temptation of Christ (Mt. 4:1–11)

Many patristic exegetes regarded this pericope as a timeless, allegorical
representation of the temptations to be endured by individual Christians
in all ages of church history.[55] Joachim also interprets the text in this
sense.[56] However, he regards it primarily as a type of the temptations and
persecution to occur after twelve hundred years of church history:

Therefore in the forty days (as in the forty years in which the sons of Israel remained in the desert), forty generations of years are designated, after the completion of which the Father of Lies will launch his temptations, more severe and bitter than those which came before.[57]

Joachim proceeds to establish parallels between each of the Devil's three temptations and those which the church as a whole, or especially its monks, will encounter in his own day. Thus Jesus' hunger after fasting for forty days and forty nights represents the hunger of the Christian people for miracles at the end of the twelfth century, a desire exploited by the wonder-working Antichrist. The devil tempting Jesus to jump from the pinnacle of the Temple represents the devil speaking through the mouth of the church's ministers, persuading the faithful to their ruin, or it symbolizes the devil suggesting to the monk in temptation that he leave his monastery. Again, the devil taking Jesus to the mountain and showing him the kingdoms of the world represents the devil tempting the servants of God with the spirit of ambition and the desire for the prelacy.[58] In short, where Joachim's patristic predecessors were prepared to view the account as an allegory of the temptations to be encountered by individual Christians in all ages of the church, Joachim interprets the account primarily as a type of the temptations to be endured by the entire church in the sixth *tempus* of its history. Again, Olivi would be influenced directly by Joachim's interpretation of the Temptation of Christ and, if anything, he heightened the negative assessment of ecclesiastical leadership found in Joachim's interpretation.

Conclusions

We should not conclude this analysis without noting several critical ways in which Olivi's gospel commentaries differ from the *Tractatus*. We can begin with the most fundamental difference. Olivi commented on the entire text of each of the four gospels, Joachim on only a fraction of them. This basic fact makes it all the more apparent that the *Tractatus*, if indeed it influenced Olivi's gospel commentaries, did so in ways that cannot often be described in terms of direct material influence. Second, Olivi spends the bulk of his commentaries transmitting inherited opinion on the literal meaning of the gospel or considering theological *quaestiones* raised by the scriptural text. Joachim spends very little time discussing the opinion of the fathers and much more rarely than Olivi asks such theological *quaestiones*. Third, and very importantly, Olivi almost always explicitly states that his typological reading of the New Testament is given in the non-literal, *spiritual* sense of the gospel.[59] Joachim does not always make clear how his own typological readings are related to the traditional four levels of medieval exegesis. When he does allude to such matters, he usually announces that such readings are given in the "typological" or "typical sense" (*sensus typicus*) of the text. Fourth, Joachim was especially concerned in the *Tractatus* with the interconnected future of the Jews, Latins, and Greeks. When Olivi considers the gospels typologically, he is preoccupied with the way in which it prophesies the rise, persecution, and eschatological triumph of the Franciscan Order. Finally, it should be noted that while in his Apocalypse commentary, Olivi frequently invokes the name of "Abbot Joachim," he never does so in his gospel commentaries. If he is referred to at all, it is as one of a number of anonymous *quidam* cited throughout the text.[60]

In sum, even if Olivi did not directly know the *Tractatus,* he had so mastered Joachim's hermeneutics and exegetical strategies that it can be said that Joachim's gospel commentary did exercise a profound, if indirect, influence on Olivi's Matthew commentary (and, for that matter, on Olivi's other gospel commentaries). It was in the use of assumptions and interpretive methods found in the *Tractatus,* combined with a number of elements of Franciscan mythology, that resulted in a set of gospel commentaries that are, in critical ways, much different than those produced by Olivi's mendicant contemporaries. It is to an analysis of those elements of Franciscan mythology that we now turn.

CHAPTER THREE

Franciscan Apocalyptic, 1240–1300

By the early to mid-1240s, some members of the Franciscan Order had begun to appropriate elements of Joachite apocalyptic thought. They did so in order to interpret the significance of the rise of their order in history, to attempt to foresee its role and destiny in the years to come, and to try to understand the special status of its founder. An exhaustive analysis of this development is neither necessary nor possible here. Nonetheless, we do need a sketch of the overall evolution and an examination in some detail of those elements of Franciscan apocalyptic which Olivi accepted and which influenced his interpretation of the gospels.

BEFORE BONAVENTURE

Two figures central to the spread of early Franciscan Joachism are Hugh of Digne (d. 1257) and John of Parma, minister general between 1247 and 1257. The evidence for Hugh's Joachism comes from the late 1240s. In his *Cronica,* Salimbene informs us that a group of Franciscans and laymen in Hyères would convene on holy days in the room of Brother Hugh in order to hear the latter expound the doctrines of Abbot Joachim. Hugh was, Salimbene adds, a "great Joachite" (*magnus Ioachita*) who owned "all of the books of the Abbot Joachim."[1] We know from Salimbene, in fact, that Hugh was one of those who owned the *Tractatus.* About what Hugh actually said in these sessions, however, we know remarkably little. Marjorie Reeves has argued that the conversations "turn entirely on Joachim's prophecies of the days of crisis and Antichrist, and not at all on the ushering in of the third *status.*"[2] She has also claimed that Hugh and his group did not know, or at least did not exploit, the Joachite prophecy of two future orders, as both Franciscans and Dominicans soon would.[3] Both of these assertions may be true. However, David Burr has reminded us that Reeves bases these proclamations on a single episode from Salimbene, who may not have recorded everything he knew about Hugh's Joachism.[4] It is, therefore, difficult to say very much at all about how Hugh interpreted Joachim or what he found interesting about him.

We know only slightly more about John of Parma's apocalyptic interests. Before moving to Paris in 1245, John served as *lector* in Naples, where Joachite ideas may have entered the Franciscan Order.[5] As Reeves has pointed out, however, "once again it is difficult to discover the precise content of his Joachimism."[6] He was apparently among the first to identify Francis as the Angel of the Sixth Seal of the Apocalypse.[7] Angelo da Clareno's assurances that John agreed with Hugh on apocalyptic issues might be more helpful if we knew more about Hugh.[8] In fact, the only really useful piece of evidence for John's Joachism is a joint letter issued in 1255, in the heat of the secular-mendicant controversy, by John and Humbert of Romans, master general of the Dominicans. In each generation, the letter tells us, Christ has raised up different ministries for the repair of the human race. Now, in the "last days at the end of the ages," he has raised up two orders to save it. The letter proceeds to describe the two orders in imagery which strongly suggests Joachite influence.[9] Again, however, we must be cautious, since, as Burr has reminded us, John was only the co-author of this letter and we have virtually no other evidence for John's Joachism.[10]

Shortly after issuing this letter, John was seriously compromised by the scandal of the eternal gospel. In 1254 Gerard of Borgo San Donnino, a young Franciscan friar at the Franciscan house in Paris, published his infamous *Introductorius in Evangelium aeternum*. In this work, Gerard announced that the spirit of life had passed from the two canonical testaments to the three major works of Joachim of Fiore. He also proclaimed that these three works would form the canonical scriptures for the coming third *status* of history. His order had been entrusted with the eternal gospel and would proclaim it in the new age to come.

Subsequent events are well known. Gerard's *Introductorius* was condemned at Anagni in 1255 and the young friar was himself imprisoned.[11] The whole series of events compromised John of Parma, who was soon forced to resign as minister general. In any case, Gerard's Joachism was so bizarre and singular that we probably cannot generalize from his case.

If Gerard's Joachism tells us little, a pseudo-Joachite commentary on Jeremiah may allow us to begin to describe the influence of Joachim on Franciscan apocalyptic in more detail. There has been much disagreement among scholars about the date, origins, and significance of this pseudepigraphical work. Reeves has argued that, in the later Middle Ages, this was "the book most usually attached to Joachim's name."[12] Until the nineteenth century, it was accepted as authentic. Reeves suggests that it was written before 1248 and probably even before 1243,[13] a view which has now won general acceptance. There is less agreement about its authorship. The early view, that it was produced by a Franciscan,[14] has been challenged by Reeves, who suggests that it originated in a Cistercian or Florensian context.[15] This argument itself has not gone unchallenged.[16] The latest contributions to the scholarship, by Stephen Wessley and Robert Moynihan, have noticed that the work exists in two versions, a shorter and a longer one, and Moynihan has suggested that Joachim himself wrote an original version.[17] In the absence of a critical edition, no definitive judgment can be made on many of these questions; the debate is likely to continue.

Far more certain is the sharp emphasis the commentary places on the arrival and role of two new orders. This is a theme to which the author of the *super Hieremiam* returns over and over, usually in ruminating on the significance of scriptural pairs like the raven and the dove, Esau and Jacob, Martha and Mary, and so forth. For example, the apostolic pair of Peter and John are symbolic, respectively, of the "order of preachers" and of the "order of minors."[18] Thus, it is clear that the *super Hieremiam* is one of the earliest "Joachite" documents to celebrate the arrival of two new orders, whether or not its authorship is mendicant.

BONAVENTURE

To this point, we have learned remarkably little about early Franciscan apocalyptic. We learn a lot more when we turn to Bonaventure's *Collationes in hexaemeron*. Delivered to the Franciscan brethren at Paris in the spring of 1273, the *Collationes* are an unfinished meditation on the meaning of the Genesis story of the six days of creation. The work survives in two forms, both *reportationes* by listeners, and there are some significant differences between them.[19] Nonetheless, the two documents tell us quite a lot about Bonaventure's apocalypticism and, in particular, his attitude towards Joachim.

Reeves has described Bonaventure as a Joachite *malgré lui*, and there does seem to be some truth to the characterization.[20] Bonaventure did avoid invocation of Joachim's third *status*. Nonetheless, it is certainly true that Bonaventure's theology of history resembles Joachim's in a number of important ways. Like Joachim, Bonaventure divided all of salvation history into two periods of seven ages each, the first running from Adam to Christ and the second from Christ to the final judgment.[21] Both attempted to work out a series of parallels or concordances between the two time periods.[22] Like Joachim, Bonaventure was convinced that he was living in the decisive time of transition at the dawn of the sixth age and, again like Joachim, he expected the second period to conclude with a seventh age of spiritual fulfillment within history.[23]

For Bonaventure, both positive and negative apocalyptic signs were evident at the dawn of the sixth age. The major positive sign of the sixth age was the appearance of St. Francis. Bonaventure repeatedly identifies him as the Angel of Apocalypse 7:2.[24] For Bonaventure, Francis heralded the arrival of a new contemplative order which would achieve new heights in piety, the practice of the apostolic life, and the understanding of the scriptures. Scholars are divided on the question of whether Bonaventure intended to identify this order with any existing religious institute, though almost all agree at least that Bonaventure saw considerable continuity between the Franciscan Order and the contemplative order to come.[25]

Of the major negative apocalyptic signs of the sixth period, none so agitates Bonaventure as the use of Aristotelian philosophy. The use of Aristotle in theology had led, in Bonaventure's mind, to all sorts of anti-Christian conclusions and errors (like the postulation of the eternity of the world), and Bonaventure dedicates much of the *Collationes* to solemnly registering, describing, and denouncing them.[26] In the battle with the Antichrist to come, presumably quite soon, a doctor or prelate would actually become a mouthpiece of error.[27] Some will stand strong against the Antichrist but will do so at the cost of their reputations.[28] The temptations will be so seductive and the tribulation so grievous that even the elect will be led into error.[29] Like Joachim before him and Olivi after him, Bonaventure saw the sixth period as a time of unprecedented temptation, decline, and persecution.

The sixth period would finally yield to a seventh of enlightenment and peace. Bonaventure prefers not to talk about this period in terms of Joachim's trinitarian pattern, nor does he identify this period, as Olivi later would, with the Joachite third *status* of the Holy Spirit.[30] Nonetheless, he does describe the period in terms that seem reminiscent of Joachim's third *status*. For one thing, Bonaventure expected in the seventh period an even fuller understanding of the scriptures than that found in the sixth, and he describes it in terms redolent of Joachim's *intellectus spiritualis*.[31] Bonaventure also predicts that believers will enjoy a sort of rapturous, ecstatic form of knowledge, one anticipated by Francis's experience on Mt. Alverna.[32] In short, in the seventh period, the church militant will be conformed to the church triumphant as much as is possible *in via*.[33]

David Burr has remarked that, "Once Bonaventure had offered Franciscans his vision of an apocalyptic Francis, they must have found it hard to ignore."[34] While some Franciscan commentators on the Apocalypse found it easier to ignore Bonaventure's periodization,[35] Olivi seems to have been among those most profoundly influenced by it and by Bonaventure's vision of an apocalyptic Francis. Nowhere does this influence seem to be more apparent than in Olivi's commentary on the Apocalypse.

OLIVI'S APOCALYPSE COMMENTARY

Olivi's *Lectura super Apocalypsim* was written in 1297, one year before its author's death. This fact should not, however, lead us to conclude that Olivi turned to apocalyptic concerns only in his declining years. Both the interest in apocalyptic ideas and the same apocalyptic themes are present in Olivi's early writings as well as in his later efforts. To be sure, there are some elements of his apocalyptic thought which underwent development over the course of his career,[36] but the major difference between the Apocalypse commentary and the earlier works is the richness of detail of the later commentary. As will be evident when we turn to the Matthew commentary, the basic historical patterns had been present at least from the late 1270s. Indeed, Olivi saw in the gospels a prophecy of church history very much like the one he perceived in the Apocalypse.[37]

Though Joachim's *Expositio* had a major influence on the *Lectura super Apocalypsim*,[38] Olivi structured the Apocalypse differently than Joachim. Where Joachim divides the book into eight visions, Olivi divides the book into seven.[39] Both, however, see church history unfolding in terms of seven ages. However, where Joachim saw the first seven visions as a *continuous* prophecy, Olivi sees the seven visions primarily as a *recapitulative* prophecy, though he does allow that there is a sense in which they can be taken as continuous as well.[40] For Olivi, each of the seven visions recapitulates the history of the church in seven ages. Olivi also insists that this is the literal meaning of each of the seven visions, except the first.[41] The first is literally about the seven churches to whom the letters are sent and only mystically about church history.[42] Olivi's *Lectura*, like Joachim's, thus marks a decisive break from the spiritualizing interpretation which dominated exegesis of the Apocalypse from the fifth century to the twelfth.

The seven periods of the church in Olivi's Apocalypse commentary are not unlike Joachim's, nor unlike those found in many contemporary mendicant commentaries.[43] In the first period, the apostles were persecuted by the Judaizers, the first of the hostile "carnal" forces the church would encounter in each of its ages.[44] The second period witnessed the emergence of a new Christian hero, the martyr, and a new enemy, the pagan Roman empiren[45] and was brought to a close by Constantine. The third period saw the growth of heresy, a threat countered by the rise of great doctors of the faith.[46] The chief enemies of the church in the fourth period were the lax and the hypocritical, who were opposed by the anchorites such as Anthony.[47] In the gospel commentaries, Olivi frequently draws explicit parallels between some of these early periods and his own. For example, Francis and his order are placed in the role of Christ and his apostles, while enemies of evangelical poverty are cast as scribes and Pharisees. Similar parallels are drawn in the Apocalypse commentary between the third and fourth periods and the sixth.[48] The difference is that the threats present in the sixth period of church history are more insidious than those encountered in the earlier periods.

In the Apocalypse commentary and elsewhere, Olivi puts himself at the end of the fifth period and the beginning of the sixth.[49] The long fifth period began with the rise of the Frankish empire. It was largely a period of decline or *condescensio*, in which the church gained members, wealth, and power but at the cost of rigor and purity. So ubiquitous and cancerous is the decay by the end of the fifth period that Olivi refers to the church in his own time as "infected . . . from head to toe and almost made into a new Babylon" (*a planta pedis usque ad verticem est fere tota ecclesia infecta et confusa et quasi nova Babilon effecta*).[50] Fortunately, the progressive deterioration so evident at the end of the fifth period has already begun to be offset by the signs of restoration and enlightenment of the beginning of the sixth. After centuries of condescension and laxity, at least a small remnant of Christians is again pursuing apostolic poverty and perfection in all its fullness.[51] At the same time, the dawning sixth period has witnessed a new illumination of the intellect, particularly with respect to the spiritual understanding of scripture.[52]

Quite clearly, Olivi's description of the first five periods of church history and the dawning sixth period resembles Joachim's in several significant respects.[53] It seems natural, then, to inquire if Olivi was interested in describing world history and the age to come in terms of Joachim's Trinitarian scheme of three successive *status* of Father, Son, and Holy Spirit.

The answer to this question has been a matter of protracted debate. The root of the disagreement can be traced to Raoul Manselli's desire to disengage his hero Olivi from the taint of Joachite heterodoxy. Manselli has argued that "Olivi considers Joachim an authority like all the others" and greatly muted his dependence on the three-*status* scheme of world history, his use of *concordiae*, and other characteristic features of his thought.[54] Of Olivi's relation to the three-*status* scheme appropriated to the three persons of the Trinity, Manselli has asserted: "Sia ben chiaro che *nulla di tutto questo e in Olivi*" ("It is quite clear that none of this at all is in Olivi").[55]

To subsequent interpreters of the *Lectura super Apocalypsim*, these claims have seemed somewhat dubious. With all due respect to the Italian scholar's great contributions to Olivi studies, the evidence presented over the past two decades has rendered his position on Joachim's influence increasingly vulnerable. David Burr's unparalleled familiarity with Olivi's writings has led him to state that, "In reality, Olivi looks upon Joachim as something more than one more authority,"[56] and there is ample evidence in many of Olivi's works to support such a thesis. Indeed, even a casual reading of the Apocalypse commentary would drive one to agree with Burr's conclusion that the three-*status* scheme "so pervades [the Apocalypse commentary] that it hardly seems necessary to give an example."[57] Throughout the commentary, Olivi makes reference to the third general *status* of world history. He correlates it either with the sixth and seventh periods of church history together or more exclusively with the seventh. In both cases, he describes the Christian life present in the third general *status* in terms of a this-worldy, Spirit-given, affective, and clear understanding and experience of faith and practice.[58] In sum, the influence of the three-*status* pattern in the Apocalypse commentary is clear and pervasive, and it would be misleading to minimize the degree of Joachim's influence on it.

One of the principal ways in which Olivi's Franciscan presuppositions govern his use of these Joachite historical patterns is in the eschatological role he assigns to Francis as a herald of the sixth period or third *status*. To be sure, Francis is not the only initiator of the third *status*. Olivi also rewards Joachim with that honor.[59] However, as David Burr has noted, Joachim "is dwarfed in significance by St. Francis, the principal *renovator* of evangelical perfection."[60] Throughout his works and especially in the Apocalypse commentary, Olivi sees Francis as a figure sent by God to revive the apostolic and evangelical life. As an index of Francis's eschatological importance, Olivi, like Bonaventure, identifies him with the angel bearing the seal of the living God (Apoc. 7:1) and with the angel with a face like the sun (Apoc. 10:1), as well as with the prophets Enoch and Elijah.[61] Even more importantly, he is frequently compared to Christ himself. Olivi underscores Francis's conformity to Christ not only by emphasizing the obvious parallel of Francis's stigmata but also by suggesting the possibility that Francis, like Christ, may rise from the dead to strengthen his disciples in a time of tribulation.[62] Though Olivi concedes that throughout salvation history there have been prophets and messengers sent to bring God's people back to fidelity, his frequent comparisons to Christ and his apocalyptic identifications elevate Francis far above Anthony, Benedict, and others who have occupied this prophetic role. As Burr has so nicely put Olivi's attitude toward the founder of his order, "In the twilight of history, as a deteriorating world staggered toward Antichrist and judgment, God had sent a new order to renew the life of Christ and his apostles."[63]

The new life and wisdom initiated by Francis do not, of course, go uncontested. Like Joachim and many mendicant contemporaries, Olivi pictures the whole of church history in terms of a continuing battle between the forces of light and darkness. He characteristically describes this struggle in terms of the assault of the "carnal" church or of "carnal" men upon their "spiritual" counterparts. By "carnal" church, Olivi did not mean to imply the existence of a separate church but to identify that element of the visible church which is Christian in name but not in fact.[64] According to Olivi, the carnal church in its various personifications has resisted the growth of evangelical perfection throughout church history. But its resistance has grown especially fierce in the thirteenth century, that is, in that age when evangelical perfection has begun to be practiced in all of its fullness by at least a small number of Christians.

The attack of the carnal church upon the spiritual is a two-pronged one. On the one hand, the assault is being furthered by those who have maligned evangelical poverty. Those outside the order (Olivi is thinking of the secular clergy here) have attacked the revival of evangelical poverty by arguing that Christ and his apostles had common possessions. To underscore the dangers this persecution has posed to his young order, Olivi sometimes draws parallels between it and that endured by the apostolic church. Just as Christ and the apostles of the early church were resisted by the scribes and Pharisees, so Francis and his apostles have been opposed by their present-day pharisaical counterparts. In the infancy of the order, Olivi notes at one place, "the new Herod of carnal doctors" was seeking to kill it.[65] Spiritual men also have had to face the twisted arguments and false interpretation of scripture not only of prominent extramural enemies but of those who were once considered champions of evangelical perfection. Indeed, some masters and religious (Olivi may well be thinking of Thomas Aquinas here)[66] have taught that to have possessions was more perfect than not to have them.[67] Finally, the carnal element of the church has infiltrated the Franciscan Order itself and threatens to ravage it from within by denying the necessity of *usus pauper*.[68]

At the same time as carnal masters pursue their attack on evangelical poverty, ostensibly Christian scholarship is being tainted by acceptance of philosophical error. Like Bonaventure, Olivi regarded as a major negative apocalyptic sign the acceptance at Paris of Aristotelian philosophy as interpreted by Islamic philosophers. By their uncritical endorsement of pagan philosophy, Parisian clerics had been subtly enticed into all kinds of anti-Christian error, including the denial of creation, of free will, and so on.[69] What is worse, those who invoke Aristotelian philosophy had used it to attack evangelical poverty.[70] Olivi is so alarmed by this threat that he designates it the temptation of the "mystical" Antichrist, one which predisposes its victims to ensnarement in the sect of the "great" Antichrist.[71]

In his *Lectura super Apocalypsim,* Olivi makes it clear that the forces of evil in the fifth and sixth periods will be led by a first or "mystical" Antichrist and a second or great Antichrist and identifies these with the last two heads of the dragon. Although Olivi's remarks on these two Antichrists are often tentative and cautious, it is clear that the mystical Antichrist will precede the great. The reign of the mystical Antichrist will last until the destruction of the corrupt church (which Olivi designates as Babylon) at the end of the fifth period. Members of the spiritual church may then rejoice but not for long, since the destruction of the mystical Antichrist inaugurates the reign of the great.

Olivi also makes it clear in his Apocalypse commentary that the persecution by each Antichrist involves the working in concert of a pseudopope and a secular leader.[72] The pseudopope, Olivi predicts, will err against evangelical poverty and perfection and may also be schismatically rather than canonically elected. At one point, Olivi even suggests that the pseudopope will be a Franciscan, as he designates him an "apostate from the state of . . . the highest religion" (*apostata a statu . . . altissime religionis*).[73] Thus, where papal support for evangelical poverty once shielded the order from its opponents, the Franciscans would now be vulnerable to their adversaries. True Christians will be faced with physical torture, twisted scriptural interpretation, spurious philosophical argumentation, false piety, and corrupt secular and spiritual authority. Even the elect would barely be saved from error, and those who follow Christ's life will be compelled to relive his suffering and cross.[74] Only when the great Antichrist is destroyed by Christ (Olivi does not say how) would the true followers of Christ be permitted to participate fully in the peaceful, contemplative religion of the third general age or seventh period.

CONCLUSION

In his gospel commentaries, Olivi indirectly borrowed from Joachim and, in particular, from the *Tractatus* the *formal* notion that the gospels were, in part, prophetic and apocalyptic books and, like Joachim, he assumed that they could be interpreted to reveal the future of salvation history. From the Franciscan apocalyptic tradition in the thirteenth century he borrowed the *material* content of the prophecies he saw inscribed in the text of the gospels. In particular, he saw in the gospels prophecies of the rise of the new evangelical order in the Franciscans and of its founder, as well as the tribulations the order would be forced to endure by its detractors. Nonetheless, while it is true that these elements of Franciscan apocalyptic were borrowed by Olivi rather than invented by him, he was the first to apply them systematically in his interpretation of the gospels. His ingenuity, in short, was to have Franciscanized the methods and contents of the *Tractatus super Quatuor Evangelia,* to have given Franciscan content to the hermeneutic he had inherited from Joachim. This will become clear in a later chapter, where we discuss Olivi's Matthew commentary. Before proceeding to the Matthew commentary, however, we need to place it in historical and exegetical context. Of particular importance to this context is the immediate and fierce threat to self-understanding and existence the Franciscans faced, first, from the secular clergy and, later, from the Dominicans.

CHAPTER FOUR

The Franciscan Order under Attack, 1250–1325

One of the qualities which makes Olivi's gospel commentaries unique is the degree to which they are influenced by and reflect three disputes over Franciscan poverty. Olivi's position on these issues deeply influenced his interpretation of texts which seemed to suggest that the apostles owned property. Even more striking is the way in which Olivi's apocalyptic sensitivities encouraged him to see in the texts of the gospels a prophecy of the persecution of the Franciscan Order by its adversaries.

THE SECULAR-MENDICANT CONTROVERSY

The dispute began at the University of Paris as a conflict of interest over theological chairs, pupils, legacies, and ecclesiastical jurisdiction.[1] By 1253 the mendicants had taken three of the twelve chairs of theology at the University, and they were preparing to take a fourth. Particularly galling to the seculars was that former colleagues (such as Alexander of Hales and John of St. Giles) took the mendicant habit and then continued to teach at their orders' respective friaries. In so doing, they cut even further into secular control of the professoriate. The secular monopoly of student clientele was also broken by the friars' success in attracting sizeable numbers of young recruits to their own schools. Other members of the parochial clergy resented the presence of the friars because their popularity as preachers and confessors drew parishioners away from local parish churches. Dying penitents often chose to be buried in the friars' churches, depriving parish churches of mortuaries and legacies. Finally, many bishops were opposed to the presence of unknown persons working in their dioceses, since they had no authority over them.

As is well known, the prominent theologian William of St. Amour was among the first and most vociferous spokesmen for the secular cause. The timing of his first attack was no coincidence. In 1254 Gerard of Borgo San Donnino published his *Introductorius.* William quickly exploited Gerard's colossal blunder. Armed with a list of thirty-one errors extracted from the *Introductorius,* William and three colleagues set out for the papal curia. Once there, they convinced the pope that the friars were a serious threat to ecclesial order. Innocent IV soon published the bull *Etsi animarum* (November 1254) rescinding all privileges enjoyed by the friars at secular expense.[2] The secular clergy had struck a decisive first blow.

Their success was, however, somewhat short-lived. Innocent soon died, only to be succeeded by the former cardinal-protector of the Franciscans. Upon ascending the throne of Peter, Alexander IV immediately began to act on behalf of the friars, first annulling *Etsi* with his own *Nec insolitum* and then ordering the restoration of fraternal privileges at the University with his *Quasi lignum vitae* (April 1255).[3] Undaunted by this display of papal authority, William soon attacked the friars with a number of *quaestiones disputatae,* which were in turn answered by Bonaventure in the latter's *Questiones de paupertate evangelica.*[4] However, William saved his fiercest fire for a much more fully developed polemic, the famous *De periculis novissimorum temporum* (spring 1256). In this tract, William denounced the friars as the pseudo-prophets and false brethren whom Paul had said would appear in the last days (2 Thess. 2:3–12; 2 Cor. 11:13). He also denied that the pope could override the rights of the secular clergy and bishops in their own dioceses and went to great length to argue that the friars' way of life was unscriptural.[5]

The young Dominican master Thomas Aquinas was, along with Bonaventure, among the first to respond to William's disputed questions and to the *De Periculis*. Thomas first composed three *quodlibets* and then in the autumn of 1256 wrote his longer *Contra impugnantes Dei cultum et religionem*, a detailed, point-by-point criticism of William's *De Periculis*.[6] Meanwhile, the Franciscans presented their longest and weightiest response to date, the *Manus quae contra Omnipotentem tenditur*, probably written by Thomas of York.[7] Partly as a result of these and other efforts of the now-united mendicant orders, a commission of four cardinals was appointed to examine the *De Periculis*. The commission included the Dominican Hugh of St. Cher and the cardinal-protector of the Franciscan Order, John Gaetani. Given the composition of the commission, it is not surprising that the four cardinals returned a negative verdict and condemned William's work.[8] In 1257 William fell ill and returned to Burgundy. While there, he received a letter from the pope forbidding him to teach or to return to France.

An uneasy peace lasted for about ten years after William's departure from Paris. The calm was shattered in 1267, when Clement IV renewed a number of the friars' privileges against the authority of local bishops. The new protagonist on the scene for the secular clergy was an old friend and ally of William. In the summer of 1269, Gerard of Abbeville issued his *Contra adversarium perfectionis Christianae*, a long-suppressed response to Thomas of York's *Manus quae*.[9] A significant part of this work was intended to show that Christ and the apostles did not practice or recommend renunciation of dominion as a way of perfection. Like William before him, Gerard attempted to show that renunciation of dominion had no basis in scripture. Indeed, Gerard was able to identify a set of gospel texts which seemed to indicate that Christ and the apostles used money and held dominion over property. For example, the episode in which Jesus heals Peter's mother-in-law begins "when Jesus entered Peter's house" (Mt. 8:14–17). This clause, which troubled Olivi greatly, seems to imply that at least Peter continued to hold dominion. The way in which the gospels refer to the use of boats by Christ and the apostles seems to imply that none of them relinquished ownership (Mt. 14:13, 24–34; 15:39). Several passages in John refer to the apostles "buying bread" (4:8, 6:5). Gerard and other masters were able to point out that Augustine had argued that Christ's instructions on the first missionary journey (Mt. 10:1–23) represented nothing more than temporary precepts, rescinded at the end of the journey. The prohibition to the apostles to take money with them on their preaching tour was intended to show them that they had a right to maintenance from their hearers.[10] (Olivi was to reject this idea with tremendous vigor.) Most difficult of all for the Franciscan apologist to account for was the bag of money which Judas carried (Jn. 13:28–29). As Malcolm Lambert has said of this problem, "Judas's bag was the classic example which, it was believed, exploded the Franciscan thesis of the absolute poverty of Christ and the apostles."[11]

Bonaventure's *Apologia Pauperum* was the first and most effective mendicant response to the *Contra Adversarium* of Gerard.[12] After the publication of the *Apologia,* Bonaventure left the literary side of the conflict to Aquinas and to the Franciscan John Pecham. Thomas drew up two more treatises and Pecham one.[13] After the publication of these works, the debate continued during the years 1269–1272 in the form of further disputed questions and quodlibets. Gerard drew up a list of erroneous statements in the *Apologia* and answered a similar list of an anonymous Franciscan with his *Replicationes.*[14] However, neither he nor William of St. Amour had much more time to wage literary war; both died in 1272. Bonaventure and Thomas would die two years later. Once the principal protagonists disappeared from the scene, the fervor of the remaining participants began to subside.

Nonetheless, there were sporadic outbursts from both sides for the next five years. More ominously, the united front the mendicants had presented against the seculars began to splinter badly over the issue of poverty and perfection during and even preceding this period. Finally, in August 1279 Nicholas III issued his bull *Exiit qui seminat.*[15] Unlike earlier clarifying bulls, *Exiit* was intended for secular (and Dominican) as much as for Franciscan consumption. Nicholas explicitly forbids his readers ever to open the question of Franciscan poverty again. Though not immediately effective, the bull did largely succeed in silencing the secular enemies of the mendicants. The long conflict with the secular clergy was over, and the mendicants emerged with a decisive triumph.

For our purposes, it is critical to remember that Olivi was in Paris as a student during the second phase of the secular-mendicant controversy. He was in the city in 1269 when Gerard published his *Contra Adversarium* and Bonaventure his *Apologia.* His presence in Paris in those years undoubtedly exposed him to the arguments of the order's adversaries and forced him to reconsider the biblical and theological foundations of the life and apostolate of the Friars Minor. Ten years later he was asked again to ponder such matters when he made his contribution to the papal commission gathered at Soriano to prepare *Exiit*. As we shall see in the following chapter, he was still considering the attacks of the secular clergy on the evangelical foundation of the order's life and apostolate when he wrote his gospel commentaries.

DOMINICAN-FRANCISCAN TENSIONS, 1240–1280

With a logic peculiar to the first century of Franciscan existence, once the mendicant orders seemed assured of victory over the secular clergy in the mid- to late-1270s, they began to turn on one another. To be sure, the tension did not begin in the 1270s. Indeed, it is possible to see the secular-mendicant controversy as a temporary cessation of hostilities between two antagonists compelled by circumstances to join forces against a common foe. Once victory was achieved in the 1270s and early 1280s, the mendicant orders were free to return to the mutual reproaches of the 1240s and early 1250s.

The sources of the tension in those early years are fairly easy to identify, thanks to the joint encyclical issued in 1255 by John of Parma, the Franciscan minister general, and Humbert of Romans, the Dominican master. Both orders were in competition for recruits from the same pool of young men and for space and buildings in the same cities. Some brothers would try to discourage recruits from joining the rival order by dwelling upon its relative lack of perfection. When one order would arrive first in a city, it would often do what it could to prevent the other from establishing itself. If one order heard of its rival's interest in a local building, it would try to acquire it first. Some brothers would disparage the other order in the hopes of attracting bequests. Sermons were sometimes thwarted by members of the rival order. Having compiled this list of underhanded behaviors, John and Humbert condemn them and exhort the brothers to fraternal amity.[16]

The secular-mendicant controversy put an end to much (but not all) of the inter-order bickering.[17] Evidence of the resumption of the quarrel in the late 1260s and early 1270s comes from England. Sources from this period indicate that the Dominicans were weary of being compared unfavorably to the Franciscans because they received money. They were anxious to show that the Franciscans also accepted money and to prove that, on this score, there was no difference between the two orders.[18] Among those making such charges was the Dominican provincial Robert Kilwardby and among those answering them was the Oxford regent master John Pecham. Like other Dominicans, Kilwardby seems to have questioned the Franciscan claim to observe evangelical perfection, noting that Christ had carried a purse. He and other Dominicans also seem to have wondered aloud whether the Franciscans were without possessions.[19] As David Burr has put it, "If any single motive for Kilwardby's attack emerges . . . it is the Dominican's desire to defend his order against what he interprets as arrogant Franciscan claims to superiority."[20]

Soon the respective leaders of the two orders once again felt compelled to issue a joint letter. In 1274, the Dominican master John of Vercelli and the Franciscan minister general Jerome of Ascoli published a letter demanding an end to the mutual disruption of ecclesiastical functions and invidious comparisons.[21] Once again, this tactic failed to end the hostilities. Indeed the conflict only intensified after the 1270 and 1277 Parisian condemnations of the use of Aristotle in theology and the subsequent controversy over Thomism.[22]

Thomas Aquinas himself had entered the fray well before his death in 1274. In both his *Summa* and in his quodlibetal questions, Thomas had criticized the Franciscan position regarding vows. In both works, Thomas asks whether someone vowing obedience to a rule sins mortally if he transgresses any part of it. He answers affirmatively. According to Thomas, the Order of Preaching Brothers follows the wisest course in vowing to live "according to" the rule rather than in vowing observance of all its parts. Under the terms of this vow, one sins only by transgressing against the precepts of the regular life (poverty, chastity, and obedience). Unfortunately, the Franciscan vows "to observe the rule throughout my whole life."[23] Thus, a Franciscan brother violating any part of his rule would find himself, in Thomas's words, "in the snares of mortal sin" (*in laqueum peccati mortalis*).[24]

One of the most important responses to Thomas's critique of the Franciscan vows occurs in William de la Mare's *Correctorium fratris Thomae*.[25] William begins by contesting the notion that the Franciscan vower is bound equally to all parts of the rule. No author, he argues, intends to produce such a rule. Francis intended to produce a rule consisting of both precepts and admonitions. Those vowing to observe it, he argues, are bound only to those things which are expressed in it in terms of a precept or inhibition (*praeceptorie vel inhibitorie*). One sins only when failing to observe precepts or in doing those things which the rule inhibits.

William's answer was to be quite influential. In attempting to quell Dominican (as well as secular) criticism of the Franciscan rule in *Exiit,* Nicholas III would argue very similarly.[26] William's influential answer in the *Correctorium* was also particularly important, as we shall see in the next section, in connection with Olivi's views on *usus pauper.*

Olivi was well aware of Thomas's attack on the Franciscan rule. However, it is not this assault that he answers in the Matthew commentary but his interpretation of what was for Olivi and his fellow Franciscans almost certainly the most important precept of the Apostolic Discourse ("Take no gold, or silver, or copper in your belts," Mt. 10:9). Thomas's controversial discussion of Matthew 10:9f. occurs at the end of the *prima secundae* of the *Summa Theologiae,* directly before his famous treatise on grace (Qq. 109–114). In Question 108, Thomas pauses to consider the issue of the content of the New Law (*de his quae continentur in Lege Nova*). In the second article of this question he asks whether the New Law is adequate, as the Old clearly was, in terms of prescribing specific actions to be observed (*utrum lex nova sufficienter exteriores actus ordinaverit*).[27] Does the New Law teach us exactly how to act or is its content less explicit than that?

Generally, Thomas is opposed to the idea that the New Law prescribes certain specific kinds of behavior. To be sure, there are exceptions to this general principle. The New Law does lay down commands with respect to those behaviors which pertain to the essence of virtue and to the sacraments. It certainly commands the performance of the latter and prohibits murder and theft.[28] For the most part, however, Thomas regards the New Law inaugurated by Christ as a "law of perfect freedom" (*lex nova dicitur lex perfectae libertatis*).[29] Under the terms of this law, the human agent is free to act under the inspiration of the Holy Spirit without reference to an inventory of commands. Indeed, this is what is new about the New Law for Thomas. The gospel, Thomas concedes, certainly *seems* to establish a large number of commands to be followed. For example, it appears to command the perfect to "keep neither gold, nor silver, nor money in your belts" (Mt. 10:9–10). Put in context, however, it is clear that the command was not intended to be of permanent ordinance, as it does not pertain to the essence of virtue (*ad necessitatem virtutis*).[30]

Thomas proposes two ways of understanding what appear to be the *precepta* of Matthew 10:9–10. First, they may be understood not as commands but as "concessions" (*concessiones*) or privileges allowing the disciples to accept food and necessities from those to whom they preached. Indeed, that is why Christ said, "The laborer deserves his food" (Mt. 10:10). Far from being a sin to carry one's means of living while preaching, it is an act of supererogation to preach without requiring support from those to whom one preaches. This is what Paul did.[31] Thomas explicitly assigns this interpretation to Augustine and, in fact, Augustine does interpret the text this way in his *De Consensu Evangelistarum*.[32]

Second, the *praecepta* may be understood as *temporary* ordinations (*statuta temporalia*) which were intended gradually to train the disciples, "as if children still under Christ's care," to relinquish care for material things. For those who had not yet achieved the perfect freedom of the Spirit, Christ set up fixed forms of life (*determinatos modos vivendi*), especially since the Old Law was still in force (*adhuc durante statu veteris legis*). Once the disciples were adequately rehearsed in these precepts, Christ rescinded them: "Now let him who has a purse take it and likewise a bag" (Lk. 22:35). Having achieved the perfect freedom of the Spirit, the disciples were then left completely to their own counsel in things which did not belong to the essence of virtue (*in his quae secundum se non pertinent ad necessitatem virtutis*). Thomas assigns this second interpretation to "the exposition of other saints."[33] These are ideas to which, as we shall see in a later chapter, Olivi was furiously opposed and to which he addressed an extremely angry exegetical response. But this was not the last threat Olivi would perceive. The third was in some ways the most dangerous, because it came from within.

RESTRICTED USE OF GOODS AND THE *USUS PAUPER* CONTROVERSY

The roots of the *usus pauper* controversy[34] lie in the profound transformation of the Franciscan Order from a small band of itinerant preachers to a large, powerful, and even wealthy order exercising important functions on behalf of the pope and secular administrations. Over the course of the fifty or so years between Francis's death and the composition of Olivi's Matthew commentary, the order grew phenomenally in numbers. In 1210 there were around twelve Franciscans. Forty years later, there were perhaps thirty thousand.[35] This kind of expansion alone was a significant factor in compromising the original rigor of the order. Perhaps even more significant was that popes, kings, and governments all recruited the friars to serve in a variety of positions which either encouraged them or forced them to use worldly power and enjoy higher living standards.

Once Franciscans started assuming positions in ecclesiastical, royal, or city government, the order came to be viewed as a road to worldly advancement rather than renunciation. Further, the gifts of generous benefactors brought the order into even more intimate contact with the wealthy and powerful and, for a variety of reasons, these gifts were not always easy to refuse. The result of all these developments was a somewhat understandable decline in standards. Since many of the order's new functions were either approved or ordered by the pope, it was clear that some adjustment in the observance of restricted use of goods (*usus pauper*) would have to be made.[36]

All these developments helped to give rise to the *usus pauper* controversy. Properly speaking, however, the *usus pauper* controversy that began in about 1279 did not start over the issue of how restricted Franciscan observance should be, or even over the issue of whether Franciscans were obligated to observe restricted use of goods.[37] All Franciscans in 1279 were in agreement that they were obligated to observe restricted use, and the debate over the appropriate level of observance was not new. As David Burr has proven, the distinguishing characteristic of the *usus pauper* controversy was whether the observance of restricted use was imposed upon members of the order by their vow. In Burr's words, the "most characteristic element [of the *usus pauper* controversy] was not a debate over whether Franciscans were obligated to live modestly, or even over how modestly they were obligated to live, but a debate over the source of their obligation in this regard."[38] The debate began because Olivi argued that *usus pauper* was included in a friar's vow to observe the rule, while his opponents insisted that their vows obligated them only to renunciation of dominion (*abdicatio dominii*).

Olivi's views on *usus pauper* were almost certainly produced as part of the larger conflict with Brother Ar. in the late 1270s and early 1280s. His views were thus hammered out in response to the positions and criticisms of adversaries.[39]

By 1283, Olivi's views on *usus pauper* had been examined by the Parisian commission of seven theologians. They denied that *usus pauper* was in any way included in the vow and said that to affirm the opposite was erroneous.[40] As Olivi himself notes, the commission was quite ambiguous or even silent about what precisely they found objectionable in his view.

Perhaps they themselves did not know. The problem was a very new one. Nonetheless, the commission is, as Burr has put it, "quite sure that, for whatever reason Olivi may be wrong, he is definitely wrong."[41] Recently, David Burr has offered two hypotheses which go a long way both toward explaining why the commission of seven found Olivi's views so dangerous, why the controversy surfaced when it did, and why it became so heated so quickly.[42]

By the time Olivi wrote his Matthew commentary, the author could have felt—and clearly did—that evangelical perfection was being assaulted from without and from within. He has the assaults of all of these enemies in mind as he interprets the gospels, and his exegesis of at least many parts of the gospel is directed against those who have perverted the true meaning of evangelical perfection. One cannot understand Olivi's gospel commentaries until one realizes that the commentary is, in part, an answer to William of St. Amour, Thomas Aquinas, and Brother Ar. and his associates. So much is all the more clear when Olivi considers both the renewal of evangelical perfection and the assaults upon it in terms of his apocalyptic theology of history.

CHAPTER FIVE

Olivi's Gospel Commentaries in Context

aving examined the scholastic, apocalyptic, and Franciscan sources which influenced Olivi, we are now ready to turn to his Matthew commentary itself. We must begin by discussing briefly the life of its author, its date, overall structure, and the sources on which it depends, because it is clear that his own life, and especially his vicissitudes, also had a deep impact on the sort of Matthew commentary he produced.

OLIVI: LIFE AND VICISSITUDES

Petrus Iohannis Olivi[1] was born in 1247 or 1248 in Serignan, just outside of Béziers in southern France. He entered the

Franciscan Order in 1259 or 1260 at the age of twelve.[2] Olivi himself informs us that he performed his novitiate at Béziers.[3] Once he completed his term as a novice, Olivi probably spent the next two or three years in a provincial house of studies.[4] By 1268 at the latest, he had arrived at the Franciscan *studium* in Paris to begin his advanced theological education.[5] Little though it is, that is all we know of the first two decades of Olivi's life.

These years in Paris must have had an important influence on the mind of Olivi. It is, therefore, unfortunate that we know so little about them. To start with, it is unclear how long he remained in the city. Olivi himself nowhere tells us. Perhaps four years would be a fair guess, though there is little in the way of solid evidence to support us in this conjecture.[6]

The question of how far Olivi advanced in his education is also difficult to answer conclusively. It is certain that he did not become a master. Why he failed to achieve the *magisterium*, however, is less clear.[7] Whether or not he taught at Paris as a bachelor is also somewhat unclear, though he likely did not.[8] Regardless of whether or not he became a bachelor, Olivi was sent back to southern France by his superiors upon completion of his term of study in Paris. We have evidence that by the late 1270s at the latest (and probably a bit earlier), Olivi was serving as a *lector* in one or more of the convents in his native province. Certainly before the fateful year 1283, Olivi served in houses in Montpellier and Narbonne.[9] During the mid- to late-1270s and early 1280s, Olivi, like other *lectores* in the order, taught theology to an entire convent of friars, and perhaps helped to prepare those who were to proceed to higher education as well. He also began writing voluminously. These were the years in which, among numerous other theological, disciplinary, and polemical writings, Olivi produced several of his biblical commentaries, including the Matthew commentary.[10] In short, these were years of extraordinary fecundity for Olivi. In terms of sheer volume, it was a period of remarkable productivity in the history of thirteenth-century scholasticism.

It was not, however, a period without adversity for Olivi. In his *Historia septem tribulationum ordinis minorum,* Angelo da Clareno supplies us with evidence that Olivi's encounters with those in authority began during the generalate of Jerome of Ascoli (1274–79).[11] Sometime during those five years, Jerome ordered Olivi to submit a number of questions which he had written on the Virgin Mary. Having examined the questions, Jerome found them offensive and burned them at some sort of meeting, perhaps a provincial chapter in Montpellier.[12]

There is other evidence which suggests that this was not the only issue on which Olivi was questioned during Jerome's tenure as minister general. In later works, Olivi refers to having answered Jerome (or perhaps his predecessors) on questions on marriage, baptism, and the relation of existence to essence.[13] This would not be the last time that Olivi would be questioned on these issues.

Though his writings had been scrutinized, the damage done to Olivi's reputation was hardly severe. He continued to teach and write. What is more, he was even consulted in the summer of 1279 during deliberations for the preparation of Nicholas III's *Exiit qui seminat*, the celebrated bull which greatly helped to silence the secular clergy's criticism of the mendicants. Olivi's career was flourishing and his prospects bright. He was, as Burr has put it, "a recognized scholar, and still not really behind schedule for the *magisterium*."[14] Four years later, disaster struck.

This second sequence of difficulties seems to have originated in a protracted feud with another Franciscan *lector* from Provence. In his *Letter to R.*, Olivi identifies his adversary only as "Brother Ar."[15] There has been significant debate about the identity of this obscure figure.[16] However, Gratien de Paris has pointed to a fourteenth-century report by Raymond of Fronsac that Olivi had quarrels "with brother Arnold Galhardi and many other good brothers, who attacked his erroneous sayings."[17] Unfortunately, we know nothing about Arnold Galhardi except his name. Nevertheless, he was probably the adversary in question. Given the obscure quality of the evidence, however, we shall refer to Olivi's detractor only as "Brother Ar."

What caused the quarrel between the two *lectores* is still an open question.[18] It remains possible that the dispute began because of Brother Ar.'s sincere reservations about Olivi's doctrinal positions (or, perhaps equally likely, less noble personal hostilities). Whatever his motives, Brother Ar., sometime after October 1279, sent to Bonagratia a list of nineteen questionable propositions culled from Olivi's writings.[19] Olivi retaliated by assembling a list of the same number of suspect propositions from the writings of Brother Ar. He then sent this list to the minister general.

We do not know what Bonagratia did with this list. However, he apparently sent Brother Ar.'s to Olivi's provincial and asked that Olivi respond to its charges. Olivi answered with his so-called *Attack*, a series of thirty-two articles aimed at Brother Ar. and an additional five directed at Brother Ar.'s associates.[20] Olivi then sent this work to Bonagratia and included an explanation of the nineteen articles taken from his works. He evidently hoped that both his and Ar.'s theses would be examined by the minister general and that, having been analyzed, his would be vindicated.[21]

They were not. Bonagratia responded with a letter censuring Olivi's theses and ordered that Olivi surrender his writings.[22] Unfortunately for Olivi, he was not through yet. The entire Olivi case was probably discussed during the General Chapter held in Strassburg in Pentecost 1282.[23] As a result of these discussions, Bonagratia decided to appoint a commission of seven Parisian masters and bachelors to discuss those things which "sounded bad" (*sonare male*) in Olivi's works.[24] In 1283, this commission drew up on a *rotulus,* or long parchment roll, a list of propositions from these writings, each of which they marked with what they considered to be the appropriate critical verdict.[25] In addition to this document, the commission drew up a second document, the so-called *Letter of the Seven Seals,* containing a list of propositions which stated in positive fashion the "correct" position on the Olivian theses condemned in the *rotulus.*[26] Bonagratia then ordered that Olivi's writings be collected and interdicted. He further directed that the *rotulus* and the accompanying letter be read publicly in all of the convents in Provence and announced that no one should contradict the positions stated in the *Letter of the Seven Seals.*[27] The outcome of the commission's deliberations could hardly have been more dire for Olivi. His hopes for the *magisterium* had now surely been dashed. Doubtless far more disturbing was that he had been branded a falsifier of the Catholic faith.

Olivi's subsequent behavior indicates that he was indeed anxious to destigmatize himself. In the fall of 1283, he was called to Avignon, where he was ordered to assent to the *Letter of the Seven Seals.*[28] Olivi did so, but not unconditionally.[29] But the Avignon hearing did not silence Olivi. He believed that he had been treated very unfairly, having been condemned without a hearing. Now he wished to confront his censors. He applied to his provincial minister for permission to go to Paris. It was denied. Meanwhile, deprived of both his writings and the *rotulus,* he was unable even to draw up a letter of protest.[30]

Olivi's fortunes soon changed. Sometime between January and May 1285, he gained access to the documents required for the letter that he had until then been unable to write. The result was an *apologia* written from Nîmes sometime in 1285.[31] In this document, Olivi lodges complaints against both the commission's procedures and its conclusions, and he defends himself at length on many of the specific issues on which he was censured. He closes by imploring the judges to repair the wrong they have done, or at least to favor him with a written reply.[32]

The commission did not reply. Nevertheless, the letter may have played some role in Olivi's imminent rehabilitation. At the General Chapter at Milan (May 1285), the assembled brothers chose Arlotto of Prato as the new minister general. Arlotto, inauspiciously enough, was a member of the commission which had censured Olivi two years earlier. Nonetheless, he may have read Olivi's *apologia;* perhaps he decided on his own to give Olivi a hearing. In either case, the new minister general summoned Olivi to Paris so that he might respond personally.[33] However, Arlotto soon died. The sources disagree on what action, if any, he took. It is possible that Olivi finally did get a hearing before at least some members of the commission.[34]

Regardless of what occurred at Paris, Olivi's rehabilitation was soon completed at the General Chapter of Montpellier (1287). Here Olivi was asked to clarify his opinion on *usus pauper* and perhaps on other matters as well.[35] His explanation of *usus pauper* was accepted by the whole chapter, and there were more fortuitous developments to come. As one of his first acts, the new minister general, Matthew of Aquasparta, appointed Olivi *lector* in the order's *studium* at the convent of Santa Croce in Florence.[36] Olivi was now restored to full respectability as a teacher in one of the order's most important convents.

In 1289, Olivi was called back to southern France by the new minister general, Raymond Gaufredi, who appointed him *lector* to the order's *studium* at Montpellier.[37] Olivi's return to southern France coincided with an escalation in the dispute over poverty. While his return may have contributed to the new agitation, both it and the new commotion over poverty are probably attributable to the same cause, the accession to minister general of one who sympathized strongly with the cause of the rigorous.[38] In any case, the zealous in southern France apparently became more vocal in their demands concerning *usus pauper;* it is hard to be more specific about what the dispute entailed. More certain is that the less rigorous members of the order resisted the new demands. A serious quarrel ensued. It was not long before Pope Nicholas IV considered the whole matter grave enough to warrant his intervention. In 1290 he wrote Raymond and, according to the *Chronica XXIV generalium,* demanded an investigation of schismatic brothers who think they are "more spiritual than the others."[39] The inquisitor of Provence did indeed carry out an investigation and a number of southern French brothers were punished in 1292.[40]

The sources disagree on how deeply Olivi was involved in the new disturbance or if the punishment were intended for him. A number of sources affirming his involvement, produced by members of the community in the fourteenth century, are quite tendentious, and it seems likely that Olivi was not one of those targeted for the 1292 condemnation.[41] Nevertheless, before escaping censure, Olivi was required to appear before the General Chapter at Paris in 1292. He was again asked to explain his position on *usus pauper*. Olivi seems to have provided basically the same explanation he gave at Montpellier and, again, his position was accepted by the chapter.[42] Those on whom censure fell this time were to the left of Olivi.[43]

In the six years that remained to him, Olivi managed to avoid further ecclesiastical censure. Indeed, Ubertino informs us that Olivi spent the last years of his life venerated by both clergy and people.[44] There is evidence that he kept busy with affairs in the order and with scholarly projects up until the time of his death.[45] Among other things, Olivi finished his Apocalypse commentary in 1297. It was to be among the last scholarly projects of Olivi's life, perhaps *the* last. Having completed his life's work, Olivi died on March 14, 1298 at the convent of Narbonne.[46]

The Gospel Commentaries: Order and Date

When and where exactly in this narrative Olivi's gospel commentaries— at least the latter three—were written is somewhat in doubt, though it is certain that he delivered them while serving as *lector* in Narbonne or Montpellier or Florence. Whatever doubt there may be about the precise date of Olivi's gospel commentaries, however, there is no doubt about the order in which they were written. Olivi refers often to his Matthew commentary in his John commentary[47] and even more copiously to it in his Luke commentary.[48] Therefore, the John and the Luke commentaries were written after the Matthew commentary. Since the Luke commentary also contains many references to the completed John commentary,[49] it is clear that the John commentary was written before the one on Luke.

The commentaries on Mark and Luke were conceived as a single project. In them, Olivi intended to comment on those parts of the gospels of Mark and Luke which differed from Matthew.[50] Indeed, one constantly runs across comments like this in the Luke commentary: "I intend almost everywhere to omit the things which I have written on more diffusely on Matthew and John."[51] The Mark and Luke commentaries were composed at roughly the same time, though the very short commentary on Mark was completed before the lengthier one on Luke.[52] Thus the commentaries were written in the following order: Matthew, John, Mark-Luke.

So much for the order. What can be said about their date? Thanks to some very clever sleuthing by David Burr, we are able to say with some confidence that the Matthew commentary was written either in the academic years 1279–80 or 1280–81, probably the former.[53] At the very least, then, it is clear that the John commentary was written sometime after 1280 and the Mark-Luke commentary sometime after that. Given the fact that many of the references in the later commentaries are to works completed by Olivi early in his career, or to works not dated or datable, it is difficult to say more than that. The John commentary seems early—perhaps it was written between 1281 and 1283—while the Mark-Luke commentary seems later—it was probably written after 1287—but these impressions should be taken only as that—as impressions. Because Olivi's apocalyptic thought does not, with one exception, develop in great detail over the course of his career, the question of precise dating is not crucial for our purposes.

The Gospel Commentaries: Form and Structure

However much they differed from contemporary mendicant efforts, Olivi's gospel commentaries were hardly distinguishable from them in terms of outward form and structure. That this should be so is hardly surprising. While a student at Paris, Olivi heard lectures on the gospels and on other books of the Bible, and he absorbed from these lectures the methods and, to some degree, the conclusions of his mendicant teachers. In their overall design and organization, then, his gospel commentaries follow the pattern established by his teachers and contemporaries at the University of Paris.

Thirteenth-century gospel commentaries have come down to us in two forms. Some are finished products, so that the manuscripts and editions we have depend, ultimately, on a manuscript written and finished by the author himself. Others come down to us in the form of student notes or *reportationes*. Thomas Aquinas's Matthew commentary, for example, has survived in this latter form.[54] Olivi's gospel commentaries lack all the characteristic marks of a *reportatio* (for example, they never say *"Magister dicit"* or *"Petrus Iohannis legit"*), and they contain the characteristic first-person marks (*"puto," "credo,"* etc.) of a manuscript written by the author himself.

Olivi's gospel commentaries consist, in standard fashion, of a prologue and one chapter of exposition for each chapter of the gospel under consideration. Medieval exegetes also attempted in their prologues to explain the structure of the biblical book as a whole. Thomas Aquinas sees the Gospel of Matthew, for example, unfolding in terms of three large movements: Christ's entrance into the world, his progress through it, and his departure from it.[55] Olivi sees two large patterns in the same gospel. The first is much like the one given by Thomas. The second, which he attributes to Chrysostom, is in fact taken from Pseudo-Chrysostom's *Opus Imperfectum in Matthaeum.*[56] According to Pseudo-Chrysostom, the Gospel of Matthew unfolds in seven stages as a revelation of Christ's nativity, baptism, temptation, teaching and miracles, passion, resurrection, and ascension.[57] Combining these larger divisions with the more precise ones Olivi gives in the course of his commentary, we can reproduce a detailed outline of the Gospel of Matthew as Olivi would have seen it:[58]

OLIVI'S OUTLINE OF THE GOSPEL OF MATTHEW

I. Birth and Infancy (Chaps. 1–2) *(Ingressus Christii in Mundum)*
   A. Genealogy (1:1–17)
   B. Conception and Birth (1:18–25)
   C. Adoration (2:1–12)
   D. Persecution and Flight (2:13–18)
   E. Re-presentation (2:19–23)

II. Baptism (Chap. 3) *(Progressus Christi per Mundum)*
   A. John Prepares Way of the Lord (3:1–12)
   B. John Baptizes Christ (3:13–17)

III. Temptation (4:1–11)
   A. Narration of Perfect Mode of Penitential Preparation (4:1–2)
   B. The Hostile Temptation (4:3–10)
   C. Final Triumph of Christ (4:11)

IV. Twelve-Part Teaching of Christ (4:12–25:46)
   A. Preaching, Miracles, Call of Four Disciples (4:12–25)
   B. Doctrinal Instruction of the Disciples (5:1–7:28 = Sermon on
       the Mount)
   C. Confirmation of Doctrine through Miracles (8:1–9:38)
   D. Instruction of the Disciples for Preaching Mission and for
       Perfect Mode of Following a Rule (10:1–42)
   E. Blindness and Unbelief of the Jews, Especially the Pharisees
       and their Confutation (11:1–12:50)
   F. Instruction of the Crowds in Parables (13:1–52)
   G. Jesus' Provident Governing of the Crowds (13:53–16:12) in
       Seven Ways
   H. Secret Revelation of the Glory of Christ (16:13–17:27)
   I.   Revelation and Commendation of the Humility and Piety of
       Christ (18:1–35)
   J.   Explication of the Evangelical Counsels (19:1–20:34)
   K. Regal Dignity of Christ (21:1–22:45)
   L. Judicial Equity, Severity, and Power (23:1–25:46)

V. The Passion (Chaps. 26–27)   (*Exitus Christi a mundo*)
   A. Those Things Preceding the Passion (26:1–50a)
   B. The Passion (26:50b–27:50)
   C. Those Things Following the Passion (27:51–66)

VI–VII. Resurrection and Ascension   (*Reditus Christi ad Patrem*)
       (Chap. 28)
   A. The Clarity of the Resurrection Shown to the Disciples
       (28:1–10, 16–20)
   B. The Blindness of Error Remains with the Jews (28:11–15)

When we examine contemporary mendicant commentaries on the gospels, it is evident that there is nothing particularly novel about the way in which Olivi structures the gospel. A casual inspection of any of Thomas's or Bonaventure's commentaries will demonstrate that Olivi's mendicant contemporaries divided the biblical text in similar ways. Like most contemporaries, Olivi regards much of the gospel (perhaps as much as three-fourths) as a record of Christ's teaching. Even his miracles are ordinarily regarded by Olivi less as a sign of extraordinary authority or of his divine origin than as a confirmation of the truth of his teaching.

There are several other respects in which, structurally at least, Olivi's commentaries resemble others produced in the second half of the thirteenth century and the first half of the fourteenth. After presenting his outline of the gospel, Olivi turns to a detailed, massive commentary on every line and indeed every word of the gospel. Like Thomas on Matthew or Bonaventure on John,[59] Olivi includes hundreds of theological *quaestiones* on a wide range of topics raised by the text.[60] Like these exegetes, he almost always comments on the literal meaning of the gospel. Again, like his contemporaries, he often will comment on the other meanings in the text, allegorical or mystical, moral and anagogical. Like them, he almost nowhere offers an interpretation of the text which systematically provides meanings on all four of these standard levels of medieval exegesis.[61] As will become clear, Olivi distinguishes himself from his contemporaries above all in those interpretations of the text which he calls "mystical" or "allegorical," where he tends to read the gospel typologically or prophetically.[62] While his spiritual readings of the gospels are in many cases strikingly original, many of his literal readings are quite derivative. Olivi himself usually acknowledges their paternity. But in what form did he find them?

PATRISTIC AND CAROLINGIAN SOURCES

The greater part of the gospel commentaries are made up of literal interpretation of the gospel in which Olivi offers to his auditors standard readings of the text which he usually explicitly assigns to one of his Greek or Latin predecessors.[63] The most frequently quoted authors are Jerome, Chrysostom, and Augustine. Others, including Origen, Hilary of Poitiers, Bede, Rabanus, and Remigius, are also cited frequently.[64] The question thus arises, did Olivi read and cite from the complete commentaries of these exegetes or did he have available some sort of *florilegium* of patristic authorities?

The answer is that he had a chain of excerpts provided him by Thomas Aquinas's *Expositio continua* on the four gospels, better known as the *Catena Aurea*.[65] Olivi's dependence on the *Catena*, especially in the Matthew and John commentaries, is extensive, as the following transcription will demonstrate. The commentaries of both scholastics are on Matthew 15:39 ff. ("After sending away the crowds . . . ") and 16:2 ff. ("When it is evening . . . ").

Olivi, *Mtt.*, 105ra ff.

Dicit ergo *dismissa turba.* CRISOSTOMUS. Sicut post miraculum quinque panum Dominus turbas dimisit, ita et nunc nec recedit pedes, sed navigio, ne turba eum sequatur.

Et venit in fines Magedan. Marc. 8 dicitur *venit in partes Dalmanuta.* Sed dicit AUGUSTINUS quod idem locus per utrumque nomen significatur. Unde et dicit quod plerique libri habent Magedii. Est autem *Mageda* secundum RABANUM regio circa *Gerasam.*

Et accesserunt ad eum Saducei temptantes an scilicet posset facere signum quod querunt ut signum de celo. Secundum REMIGIUM hoc est illud quod Iohann. 6 post miraculum de quinque panibus refertur, ubi dicunt Christo, *Quod ergo tu facis signum ut videamus et credamus tibi.* Et ubi dicunt ei, *quia Deus dedit patribus panem de celo,* scilicet manna et ideo dicit REMIGIUS quod hic petunt a Christo signum de celo, id est, quod faciat ut uno die vel duobus pluat manna ut totus populus pascatur.

Thomas, *Catena*, p. 247:

CHRYSOSTOMUS In Matt. Sicut post miraculum quinque panum, Dominus turbas dimisit, ita et nunc; nec autem pedes recedit, sed navigio, ne turba eum sequatur. . . . AUGUSTINUS De Cons. evang. Marcus autem dicit, quod in Dalmanutha; nec est dubitandum eumdem locum esse sub utroque nomine: nam plerique codices non habent, etiam secundum Marcum, nisi Mageddan. RABANUS. Est autem Mageddan regio contra Gerasam. . . . (248) *Et accesserunt ad eum Pharisaei et Sadducaei tentantes et rogaverunt eum ut signum de caelo ostenderet eis.* REMIGIUS . . . Quod autem signum postularent, Ioannes manifestat: refert enim post refectionem de quinque panibus, turbam accessisse ad Dominum et dixisse: *Quod signum facis. . . .* Ideoque et hic dicunt: Ostende nobis signum de caelo; idest, fac ut uno vel duobus diebus manna pluat, ut totus populus pascatur, sicut multo tempore factum est in deserto. . . .

It should be noted that Olivi does not cite every authority contained in the *Catena* but chooses selectively. Once he chooses, though, Olivi almost always follows his authorities closely, often verbatim. This is evident from the excerpts above. Where his authorities disagree, he is usually prepared to say which he prefers. Finally, Olivi does frequently cite the *Glossa*

Ordinaria in his commentaries, but in these cases he is quoting it indirectly from Thomas's *Catena* rather than independently.

We may conclude with a brief discussion of Olivi's reliance in his gospel commentaries on another widely used contemporary source. For historical and etymological data, Olivi made direct and frequent use of the *Historia Scholastica* of Peter Comestor (whom Olivi refers to as *Magister Historiarum*).[66] Comestor's *Historia* was full of information regarding the history, language, politics, and topography of ancient Palestine. Olivi frequently has recourse to it for this kind of information.[67]

Though the emphasis in this book is on what made Olivi's gospel commentaries unique and different, it is clear that, in many respects, they were very much *like* his contemporaries' gospel commentaries. They were delivered in similar academic settings, they have the same outward scholastic form, they ask almost identical *quaestiones,* and they depend on the same traditional patristic sources. Where Olivi's commentaries really differ is in the Joachizing and Franciscanizing of the text of Matthew, a topic to which we now turn.

CHAPTER SIX

The New Evangelical Order and Olivi's Matthew Commentary

ʰaving examined early scholastic commentaries on Matthew, Joachim's historicizing reading of the gospels, and at least some elements of Franciscan apocalyptic, we are now ready to turn to the content of Olivi's gospel commentaries. Our examination of Joachite and Franciscan apocalyptic is important here because the uniqueness of Olivi's gospel commentaries is traceable to the influence of Joachite hermeneutics, of historicizing readings of the gospel possibly inherited from Joachim's *Tractatus,* and to the incorporation of certain elements of Franciscan apocalyptic. A final factor, of course, is the ingenuity of Olivi himself, because it was Olivi who blended these influences in novel and inventive ways to produce a fresh way of interpreting the gospels. Few, if any, of Olivi's mendicant contemporaries interpreted the gospels as a prophetic genre. It was Olivi's conviction, derived from Joachim, that the gospels were on one level prophetic, and that they prophesied among other things the rise of and resistance to the new evangelical order that made his commentaries unique.

ECHOES OF JOACHIM

In his Matthew commentary, Olivi interprets the accounts of Christ's nativity typologically. That is, he views these accounts not simply as historical reports of the birth of Christ but as prophecies of the creation of a new, evangelical religious order and of the dawn in his own day of a new age in salvation history. In each instance, the parallels with Joachim's *Tractatus* are quite close. In a number of instances in the Matthew commentary, Olivi seems to be recasting a historicizing interpretation found also in Joachim's *Tractatus.* In these cases, Olivi's originality consists in supplying a peculiarly Franciscan content to the prophecy whose broad outlines are traceable to Joachim. In some cases, that Franciscan content— implying as it does the superiority of the fifth and sixth periods of church history and of the Franciscan Order—is really quite daring, so daring, in fact, that the investigation which led finally to Olivi's condemnation singled these ideas out as particularly objectionable.

ADORATION OF THE MAGI (MT. 2:1–12)

Such is certainly the case with Olivi's interpretation of the Adoration of the Magi (Mt. 2:1–12). In the *Tractatus,* Joachim had interpreted the appearance of the star as a herald of the rise of the spiritual understanding of scripture that coincides with the birth of Christ.[1] The wise men are said to see the star in the East because in the birth of the church the apostles in Palestine first handed on the spiritual understanding of the scriptures.[2] The journey of the wise men to the West signifies that the fuller understanding of the scriptures was to be given more fully and openly (*plenius et apertius*) to the Latin doctors such as Ambrose, Jerome, and Augustine.[3] Joachim also interpreted the twelve days of the journey of the Magi as a prophecy of the fuller spiritual understanding to be given at the dawn of the third *status* of history:

> I believe that just as Christ appeared to the Magi after twelve days, so this revelation of truth ought to be completed in spirit after twelve hundred years.[4]

Following Joachim or at least his exegetical strategy closely, Olivi also interprets the star as a harbinger of the spiritual understanding of scripture. He too interprets the Magi's twelve-day journey as the pilgrimage of humankind to increasing enlightenment. First, Olivi says, the journey under the star represents the "great plenitude of illumination" (*magnam plenitudinem illuminationis*) to occur after twelve generations of church history with the conversion of Constantine, the condemnation of the heretic Arius, and the rise of many great doctors of the faith.[5] But Olivi also interprets the twelve days of the journey as a prophecy of the decisive transformation to occur at the dawn of the sixth period of church history. However, here his Franciscan presuppositions lead him to furnish the prophecy with a significantly different content:

> And again after twelve centuries, namely in the beginning of the thirteenth, an evangelical rule and its renovator appeared, sealed with the wounds of Christ, in whose end and apostles something great is believed to have arisen regarding the second conversion of the gentiles and also of the Jews.[6]

It takes very little insight to see in this text and its references to an evangelical rule, its renovator, his apostles, the stigmata, and so forth multiple allusions to Francis, his rule, and his order. Structurally and hermeneutically, Olivi's interpretation is very much like Joachim's, even if (as is sometimes hard to believe) he did not know the *Tractatus*. It is in the details that the two exegetes differ, and in Olivi's eagerness to infuse his Joachite hermeneutic with elements drawn from Franciscan myth. Olivi's interpretation here (and his commentary in general) reads very much like an "updating" or "modernizing" of the *Tractatus*, one that has taken into account the important evolution in religious life that had occurred in the first half of the thirteenth century. Like Joachim, Olivi would regard the nativity accounts and, for that matter the accounts of the Temptation and the Passion, not merely as historical records of Christ's life but as prophetic of the fate of the mystical body of Christ. As is the case throughout Olivi's commentaries, Olivi's inventiveness resides in the way he "Franciscanizes" readings found also in the *Tractatus.*

In his later gospel commentaries, Olivi would continue to interpret the infancy accounts as types of the birth of the evangelical order. In his Luke commentary, for example, Olivi states that the birth of Christ "designates the rise of the contemplative and evangelical status at the end of time."[7] And, again in the Luke commentary, glossing Luke 1:26 ("In the sixth month the angel Gabriel was sent . . ."), Olivi says, "Typically (*typice*) under the opening of the sixth seal, evangelical religion, like a most pure virgin, will conceive Christ and the spirit of Christ."[8] This text is especially interesting because it is one of the very rare instances in Olivi's gospel commentaries in which he seems to follow very closely Joachim's interpretation of the same pericope in the *Tractatus* but also, and explicitly, his teaching on the senses of scripture. Usually Olivi merely states that his prophetic interpretations are given in the mystical or allegorical sense of the text, but here, apparently following Joachim, he specifically invokes the "typical" sense of the text.

HEALING OF JAIRUS' DAUGHTER (MT. 9:23–26)

Throughout the Matthew commentary, Olivi perceives and underlines parallels between the person and work of Christ and the person and work of Francis. This we see, for example, in his interpretation of the Healing of Jairus' Daughter (Mt. 9:23–26). Ancient tradition at least as far back as Hilary of Poitiers had interpreted this tradition allegorically. Hilary, for example, viewed the episode as an allegory of the healing of the sick and nearly moribund synagogue by the spiritual ministrations of Jesus.[9] Some of Olivi's mendicant colleagues, including Thomas Aquinas (who had an uncommon appreciation for Hilary) also followed this line of interpretation quite closely.[10] Olivi reports and approves this line of interpretation: Christ, he says, appeared at the end of the age of the synagogue in response to prayers that he might heal it.[11]

Olivi also interprets the passage typologically and sees a concord between this act of healing and the rehabilitation of the carnal church at the end of the ecclesiastical age. Just as Christ appeared at the end of the first age, so "another Christ" will appear again in the form of Francis at the close of the second *status*. Indeed, at a time when the synagogue has been revived, with all its corruption, carnality, and the pollution of idolatry, not to mention the "vain teaching of fools" (*vana doctrina stultorum*), another Christ will come, as the first had, to revive the contemplative life.[12]

SIGNS OF THE KINGDOM (MT. 11:2–6)

Another way in which the Joachite corpus, hermeneutically at least, influenced Olivi's Matthew commentary is in Olivi's fondness for finding prophecy in places where the sacred text implicitly or explicitly arranges itself numerically. Throughout the commentary, Olivi finds in those texts which arrange themselves in groups of seven a prophecy of all of church history, including the renewal of evangelical poverty in the sixth period. In Matthew 11:2–6, for example, the imprisoned John the Baptist sends his disciples to ask Christ if he is the Messiah who is to come. Jesus tells the disciples of John to tell the Baptist what they hear and see:

[1] the blind receive their sight
[2] the lame walk
[3] the lepers are cleansed
[4] the deaf hear
[5] the dead are raised
[6] the poor have good news brought to them
[7] and, blessed is anyone who takes no offense at me.

Jerome offered an influential reading of this passage in which he emphasized that it was the poor and marginalized who were healed and evangelized, for "everyone who can be saved is equal."[13] Among Olivi's contemporaries, this reading is closely followed. Interestingly, Bonaventure does not historicize the text but he certainly does Franciscanize it, paying special attention to the verse "*pauperes evangelizantur*" and delivering a short excursus on ten *dignitates paupertatis*.[14] In short, neither Olivi's patristic authorities nor his scholastic contemporaries found in Jesus' answer anything but a literal description of miraculous occurrences connected with Jesus' ministry in the first century.[15]

Because the text arranges itself in terms of seven, Olivi finds in Jesus' answer not only a record of deeds accomplished in Jesus' own lifetime but a prophecy of his work over the course of seven periods of church history. Thus the restoration of sight to the blind represents the illumination of the world in the apostolic church of the first ecclesiastical period. The cleansing of the lepers symbolizes the healing of Constantine's leprosy and the expurgation of the idolatry of the gentiles in the third period. In the fourth period, hearts slow of hearing the divine call were stimulated by the life of the anchorites and the decrees of the general councils of the fathers.[16]

Olivi then turns from prophecy already consummated to prophecy just now being fulfilled. In the raising of the dead and the evangelizing of the poor, Olivi finds a prophecy of the *condescensio* of the corrupt fifth period of the church and of the mendicant renewal of apostolic perfection in the sixth:

> In the fifth time, when failings of mortal sins had proliferated, the life of the saints was necessary, as were the institutes of divine religious orders, in order to rescue those drowning in the waters of secular wickedness. In the sixth age, evangelical poverty is preached.[17]

Quite clearly, the most important exegetical principle involved here is a numerological one. Joachim did not interpret this passage in the *Tractatus*, so there can be no question of direct material influence. However, Olivi did borrow from the Joachite corpus in general the notion that numbers such as six or seven could be taken as indicators of prophetic content when it came to interpreting the gospels. In his case, though, the prophecy had distinctively Franciscan content.

The Seven Parables of Matthew 13

Though Olivi did not see special apocalyptic significance in the overall sevenfold division of the gospel (as he did in the sevenfold structure of the Apocalypse), he does on occasion see long sections or even chapters of the gospel in terms of his apocalyptic theology of history. Probably the best example of this occurs in his interpretation of Matthew 13, a chapter which consists of seven consecutive parables and a number of explanatory glosses made by Jesus.

To be sure, contemporary scholastic commentators were willing to read the entire chapter as a whole, and many insisted that the seven parables were intended to make a single point. Thomas Aquinas, for example, read the whole sequence as an illustration of the impediments to growth and dignity of the teaching of the gospel. For Thomas, the Sower and the Wheat and Tares represented the impediments to evangelical teaching, the Mustard Seed and the Leaven its growth, and the Hidden Treasure and the Pearl its dignity.[18]

In his Matthew commentary, Olivi reads the sequence of seven parables as a unit as well. However, he reads the whole sequence, as well as each individual parable, as a prophecy of the history of the church in seven ages:

> Note that all of the parables [i.e., each individually] describe the course of faith and of the church or New Testament. In addition, [as a group] the first two have to do with the beginning of the sowing of faith and of the church. The next two, namely, the Mustard Seed and the Leaven, have to do with its expansion. The last three have to do with its end. The first two of these deal with the renovation of evangelical poverty and perfection and the last with the final conversion of the world.[19]

The sequence of seven parables and what it reveals may therefore be illustrated as follows:

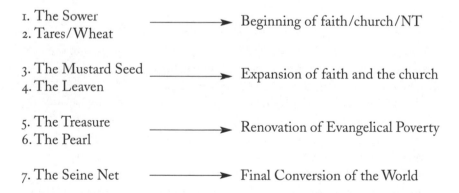

1. The Sower
2. Tares/Wheat   ⟶   Beginning of faith/church/NT

3. The Mustard Seed
4. The Leaven   ⟶   Expansion of faith and the church

5. The Treasure
6. The Pearl   ⟶   Renovation of Evangelical Poverty

7. The Seine Net   ⟶   Final Conversion of the World

This is the largest complete segment of the four gospels which Olivi sees in terms of his apocalyptic thought. Why Olivi tended to interpret this chapter as a prophecy of church history must, I think, be explained in terms of his debt to Joachim's hermeneutics. Joachim died before he commented upon Matthew 13, so, again, there can be no question of direct material influence. What is more, Joachim nowhere in the *Tractatus* interpreted an entire chapter of one of the gospels as a prophecy of the future of the church. Nonetheless, the kind of historicizing exegesis cultivated in the *Tractatus* and throughout his work must have encouraged Olivi to see prophetic meaning in pericopes or parts of the gospel which arranged themselves in groups of sevens. Indeed, if there is any consistent exegetical principle evident in Olivi's apocalyptic interpretations of the gospels, it is an apocalyptic-numerological one.

The actual content of the prophecy has several interesting connections with the *Lectura super Apocalypsim*. As we have seen, Olivi divided the Apocalypse into seven visions, while Matthew 13 is naturally divided into seven parables. Olivi interpreted each of the seven visions of the Apocalypse as a recapitulation of church history, and he interprets each parable in the same way. He was also willing (though less anxious) to see the sequence of seven visions as a whole as a continuous prophecy of church history, and he interprets the sequence of seven parables in precisely the same way. Nonetheless, there is a critical difference between the Matthew and Apocalypse commentaries. Olivi explicitly states that the prophecy of church history is the *literal* meaning of each of the seven visions of the Apocalypse except the first. Here he explicitly states that it is the allegorical or mystical meaning of each of the seven parables of Matthew 13. As we can recall, in the *Tractatus* Joachim usually notes that such meanings are given in the "typical sense" of the gospel text. Olivi, however, never uses this kind of terminology in the Matthew commentary.

For the Franciscan Olivi, the fifth and sixth parables in the sequence would be of natural interest, since they represent his own time, the fifth and sixth periods of church history. Remarkably enough, the narrative in both parables (the Hidden Treasure and the Pearl) results in the complete alienation of goods by their protagonists (13:44, 46), as Olivi himself is anxious to note.[20] The fact that these two parables were the fifth and sixth in the sequence of seven was, in Olivi's eyes, no accident. Both parables center upon the complete renunciation of goods, that is, on the characteristic mark of the Franciscan Order. Thus, for Olivi, the Franciscan renewal of evangelical poverty and perfection is inscribed allegorically into the very structure of the Matthean discourse.

Interestingly enough, Olivi also perceives in these two parables a prophecy of the carnal opposition to this renewal. Why, Olivi finds himself wondering, is the treasure for which all is sold hidden in the field? "The treasure is said to be hidden in the field," he answers, "because it is very remote from the notice and experience of carnal men."[21] Who these "carnal men" might be is unclear. Olivi might have in mind the secular clergy, the order's Dominican enemies, or even Franciscan opponents of *usus pauper*. As will be evident in the following chapter, Olivi sometimes leaves several clues which make it clear which element of the "carnal church" he has in mind when he interprets the gospel. Here he is content to read the fifth and sixth parables as a prophecy of the renewal of evangelical perfection and of its opposition by the carnal church and to let his reader draw more specific conclusions.

The Parable of the Sower (Mt. 13:3–9)

As I have suggested, Olivi reads not only the entire sequence of Matthew 13 but each individual parable as a prophecy of church history and the renewal of evangelical poverty by Francis and his own order. Indeed, Olivi regarded the parables of the entire gospel, and not just those of its thirteenth chapter, as particularly important epitomes or similitudes of the entire course of salvation history. In the first chapter of the commentary, Olivi remarked of the parables: "God distinguishes the times and states of the people of God according to a certain order and number. . . . Thus, as will be clear below, Christ distinguishes in a variety of ways the times of the church or of the people of God under the mystery of different parables."[22] The words "*or of the people of God*" are important, since Olivi would see in several parables in Matthew a *concordia* of Old and New Testament history. Indeed, he does so with the first parable in the sequence of seven.

Patristic and Carolingian exegesis of the Sower (Mt. 13:3–9) did not develop much of an allegorical tradition of the parable, in large part because the Matthean Jesus provides an explanatory gloss of the story (Mt. 13:18–23). The inclusion of this gloss prompted Hilary of Poitiers to remark that there was nothing left to clarify in the parable and to proceed with his commentary without further remark.[23] Not all of his patristic contemporaries were so reluctant to discuss the parable further, though all hew very close to the letter of Jesus' gloss. Jerome, Chrysostom, and subsequent medieval exegetes all agree that the sower is either Christ or the preacher and that the four kinds of soil represent different types of hearts: those susceptible to devils, the shallow, the worldly, and the pious.[24] This basic reading was to be very stable throughout the Middle Ages and is the one favored by all of the mendicant commentators under consideration here.[25] Olivi also explains the traditional literal reading of the parable at some length.[26]

In his literal reading of the parable, Olivi is quite impersonal and dependent upon his customary sources. But his presuppositions about the Bible as a whole, and the nature of the parables in particular, did not permit him to rest content with communicating the inherited literal meaning of the story. In his allegorical interpretation of the Sower, Olivi correlates the different sowings described in the parable not with the purchase they find in different types of souls but with the spiritual harvest they yield in successive periods of Christian *and* Jewish sacred history:

> Note that in this parable the course of the world from Adam until Christ, and also from Christ until the end of the church, can be mystically revealed. In the first time, there was an unrestrained wandering that was vulnerable to devils which finally slid into idolatry, the worship of demons. In the second time, there were the superficial Jewish people, glib at promising everything: 'We will do whatever the Lord has said.' Nonetheless, they were always stiff-necked and, as a sign of this, they received the Law in tablets of stone. To be sure, for a time they put their trust in God. But in times of any temptation whatsoever, they withdrew from him. This was the case in every temptation from the departure from Egypt and afterward. In the third time a multitude of riches divided them into two kingdoms. They also had a deceitful contingent of pseudo-prophets promising peace and even the good things of this world. There were also many wicked deeds done in order to exterminate the true prophets and, in the end, the head of the prophets, Christ. In the creation of the first man, therefore, God had gone out to sow his seed. Although in this way it had been destroyed, finally in the Virgin and in the church of the apostles it returned abundant fruit. . . . After Christ there was in the Gentile church, first, a wandering of pagans vulnerable to demons; second, a stubborn stony soil of heretics who quickly entered the faith and more quickly deviated from it; and, third, the churches became wealthy and there was worldly involvement in riches, simony, and litigation. However, Christ had gone out to sow the seed of evangelical life, which in Francis and his Rule began to return a more abundant fruit, which will be perfected at the end of time.[27]

Olivi's debt to Joachim's apocalyptic thought is almost nowhere so well expressed as in his interpretation of this parable. Though not the more common "double-seven" form found throughout his works, this *concordia* of four periods of Old and New Testament history is clearly indebted to Joachim.[28] However, Olivi does depart from Joachim in one important respect here. Olivi explicitly states that the tour of salvation history given in this parable is revealed only in the mystical sense of the text. As has already been mentioned, Joachim argued that concordances between Old and New Testament history were given in the literal sense of the Bible. Indeed, he calls them "letter-to-letter" comparisons.

The Transfiguration (Mt. 17:1–13)

A similar hermeneutic and similar results are at work in Olivi's interpretation of the Transfiguration (Mt. 17:1–13). The first few words of the pericope did indeed tempt Olivi to find in it a prophecy of church history: "Six days later, Jesus took with him Peter and James and his brother John" (17:1). As always, that number is an indicator of prophetic content to come, and so Olivi interprets the pericope in its allegorical sense as a prophecy of the transfiguration of the mystical body of Christ to occur after six periods of fifty years and then, more fully, in the sixth period of ecclesiastical history. After three hundred years and the sacrifice of the martyrs,

> the church was led to a high mountain apart from the synagogue. Then Christ under Constantine took all of Europe, Africa, and Asia, as he did Peter, James, and John, showing himself to be the light of the world and the Lord of the Roman Empire. Then the saints who were joined to Christ in martyrdom appeared white as snow. . . . And then with Christ appeared the law of the ecclesiastical councils and statutes issued from the holy bishops as if from Moses; so did the zeal of the anchorites, as if from Elijah. After this, however, the cloudiness of the faith resulting from the excess of his light darkened the church, driving out from the elect the Arians and other heretics who had failed to understand the eminence of Christ. As a result, the elect entering this cloud were afraid. But then, through the doctors, the voice of the Father was heard: "This is my beloved Son," for then the mystery of the generation of the Word became singularly clear

and Jesus alone appeared as the highest God and equal to the Father. Finally, when the Eastern Church had split from the Latin, Christ and his church descended to a lower state. That is why it is said that until Christ suffers and rises again in his mystical body, this vision is to be silenced.[29]

The descent referred to is the eclipse of the brilliance of Christ's mystical body by the luxury and cupidity of the carnal church of the fifth period. The light that had been extinguished could only be restored by Christ or by *alter Christus* or by another Elijah:

> Then the solar clarity of Christ will appear to the whole world far more clearly. Then it will be known that Elijah was to come twice: first, as who comes before and introduces to the world the life of Christ, as John prepared the way of Christ. As a sign of this he is borne among his brethren, as Elijah, in a chariot of fire. Secondly and literally, as one who will restore to Christ the tribes of Jacob.[30]

Few other passages in the gospel commentaries express so clearly Olivi's veneration of Francis or his conviction of his significance in salvation history. Like John the Baptist, Francis introduces the life of Christ into the world at a time of appalling decay and idolatry, and like Elijah calls the people of God back to fidelity and piety. However, this part of Olivi's interpretation of the Transfiguration is rendered in terms of his familiar seven-period scheme of church history. In Peter's offer to build three dwellings, one each for Christ, Moses, and Elijah (Mt. 17:4), do we find a suggestion of the three-*status* scheme:

> The staying on the mountain of the church ought indeed to have been threefold as a mystery of the blessed Trinity: namely of the married signified in Moses, who had a wife; of the clerics signified in Christ, who was the Word and wisdom of the Father; and of the religious, whose duty is to serve the ardor of the Holy Spirit and the holy solicitude designated in Elijah.[31]

Notice that Olivi does not use the word *status* in this text, nor does he explicitly correlate the different persons of the Trinity with a different age in history here. The threefold *ordo* described is of course the one *Joachim* corrclated with the three-*status* scheme of world history. But here, if that connection is to be made, it is by the reader. Olivi does not make it except by implication.

This is as close as Olivi comes to invoking the Trinitarian three-*status* scheme of salvation history in the entire *Lectura super Matthaeum*. In this respect, the Matthew commentary is less completely "Joachimized" than the Apocalypse commentary. In the Matthew commentary, Olivi does refer, like Joachim, to a final, this-worldly age of sabbatical peace and contemplation, but he never refers to it as the third general *status* of history. He prefers to speak in terms of the more respectable and safe sevenfold pattern and to avoid the dangerous implications of describing an age which unfolds primarily under the aegis of the Holy Spirit.

In his later gospel commentaries, however, Olivi would be far less reluctant to invoke the three-*status* scheme in the most explicit terms. There are numerous examples, but we will confine ourselves only to an examination of Olivi's interpretation of the Wedding at Cana (Jn. 2:1–12), where the influence of the *Tractatus* also seems quite plain. Joachim interpreted the pericope as a symbol of the transformation of the understanding of the scriptures to occur at the dawn of the second and third *status* of world history. Olivi also talks about the transformation of the literal understanding of the Old Testament to its spiritual understanding. But he then proceeds to say: "In the present time you may perceive similar things if you have eyes to see."[32] Indeed, this is the "singular time of the life of Christ or of evangelical perfection and of the contemplative life."[33] This time, he concludes, "is properly appropriated to the Holy Spirit" (*tempus proprie Spiritui Sancto appropriatur*), just as the second time was to Christ and the first to the Father.[34] In short, Olivi's later gospel commentaries are replete with references to the three-*status* scheme, especially in instances, such as this, where Joachim himself used it in the *Tractatus*.

CHAPTER SEVEN

Franciscan Persecution and Olivi's Matthew Commentary

O ne of the qualities that makes Olivi's gospel commentaries unique is the degree to which they are influenced by three disputes over Franciscan poverty. Olivi's position on these issues deeply influenced his interpretation of texts which seemed to suggest that the apostles owned property. Even more striking is the way in which Olivi's apocalyptic sensitivities encouraged him to see in the texts of the gospels a prophecy of the persecution of the Franciscan Order by its adversaries.

ECHOES OF JOACHIM

The Infanticide of Herod (Mt. 2:13–18)

If Olivi unearths in Matthew many prophecies of the rise of evangelical poverty and the appearance of Francis, he finds even more of the persecution of the followers of Francis and of his way of life. Again, at the beginning of the Matthew commentary, there are uncanny parallels between Olivi's interpretation of the narrative of Christ's nativity and Joachim's, as in the case of the Infanticide of Herod (Mt. 2:13–18). To be sure, Olivi does differ in certain details. For example, Olivi contends that Herod represents the devil rather than (as Joachim had suggested) the Antichrist. Several of Olivi's mendicant contemporaries such as Hugh of St. Cher and Thomas Aquinas also identified Herod as a symbol of the devil. However, each of these Dominicans interpreted Herod's infanticide morally. Hugh, we recall, argued that Herod represents the devil, "who is troubled when Jesus, that is salvation, is born in the heart of a human being."[1]

Olivi eschews the moral interpretation found in contemporaries for the typological reading paralleled in the *Tractatus*. Olivi explicitly invokes the principle of "head-and-members" for his interpretation of the pericope: "Here is begun the first persecution of Christ and the church or of the head and members."[2] Herod, Olivi asserts, represents "the devil ruling in the world and all the hypocritical and carnal leaders who were, are, and will be (*fuerunt, sunt et erunt*) in the people of God from his [i.e., Herod's] time until the end of the world."[3] In his later Apocalypse commentary, Olivi would identify Herod as the persecutor of the infant Franciscan Order. Here, however, Herod is a type for carnal persecuting leaders in all ages, not just in the late fifth period of church history and not just of Franciscans. If the secular masters were undoubtedly among those "carnal leaders" whom Olivi had in mind when contemplating the significance of Herod in this early commentary, they were hardly the only ones. In any case, Olivi's systematic and historicizing use of the principle of head-and-members would lead him time and again to interpret texts of Christ's persecution as types or prophecies of the trials and temptation to be endured by the Franciscan Order (or, more broadly, of those committed to evangelical perfection) in the fifth and sixth periods of church history.

The Temptation (Mt. 4:1–11)

Olivi again explicitly invokes that principle in his interpretation of the Temptation of Christ (Mt. 4:1–11). According to Olivi, after forty generations (symbolized by the forty days of Christ's fasting in the desert), "Satan will be released to tempt Christ most bitterly in his members."[4] Like Joachim, Olivi departs from the exegetical tradition in regarding the story not only as a historical account of the temptation of Christ or a timeless moral message about the temptation of individual Christians. Both emphasize that it is also (on some non-literal level) a prophecy about the temptation of the entire church at a *particular moment* in its history.

In details, Olivi's exegesis is less indebted to Joachim's than in his appropriation of the idea that the account can be taken typologically. Both exegetes agree that the first temptation is a prophecy of how the devil will exploit the desire of Christians for miracles. But Olivi departs somewhat from Joachim especially on the second temptation; his exegesis there is conditioned by his own special social context and presuppositions. In the devil taking Jesus to the top of the temple, Olivi sees a prophecy of the devil leading his members to the top of the carnal church (*ad culmen totius carnalis ecclesie*).[5] This interpretation, which hardly reflects optimism in the powers of resistance of the ecclesiastical leadership in times of temptation, furnishes evidence that, as early as the Matthew commentary, Olivi feared that the corruption of the fifth and sixth periods would reach the highest levels of the church. The theme is pursued perhaps less vigorously in the Matthew commentary, but it is there nevertheless. This is not a position he embraced only at the end of his life or only in the Apocalypse commentary.

As in the later commentary, Olivi nowhere in the Matthew commentary states or even suggests very clearly who he has in mind. There is in the Matthew commentary no suggestion that the corruption he fears will extend to the papacy. Again, Olivi does not state that the corruption he envisages has extended to the leadership of his own order or would soon do so. However, as further evidence will suggest, it is difficult to believe that he did not have his own order in mind when he interprets the significance of corrupt and hypocritical leaders, the scribes and Pharisees in the Gospel of Matthew. And there is almost no doubt that he was thinking of enemies in the secular clergy and in the Dominican Order.

PERSECUTORS OF EVANGELICAL POVERTY AND PERFECTION

The Incarceration of John (Mt. 11:1–11)

It seems likely that Olivi was thinking of either the Dominicans or the secular clergy in his allegorical interpretation of the incarceration of John (Mt. 11:1–11). Olivi here attempts to establish a concord between the persecution of the Baptist and the persecution of Francis and the way of life he represented. For Olivi, the incarcerated Baptist represents the "understanding of the truth that is imprisoned under the figures of the law and prophets." This understanding of the truth became doubtful, Olivi goes on to state, only because of the jealousy and rivalry of the disciples of the law ("For John came neither eating nor drinking, and they say, 'He has a demon'" [11:18]).[6] Therefore, two scribes and Pharisees are sent from John to ask Christ if he is the one to come (Mt. 11:3). Since by his works ("the blind see . . .") Christ shows himself to be the true understanding of the law and prophets, John is vindicated as an angelic messenger sent "to prepare the way of the lord."[7]

After furnishing this initial interpretation, Olivi offers a second, typological reading which views the imprisonment of John and the questioning of his witness to Christ as a prophecy of the persecution of Francis and the skepticism concerning the way of life he inaugurated:

> You may consider a similar allegory for the end of the ecclesiastical age (*pro fine temporis ecclesiastici*), in which another John has appeared. In him the understanding of the secrets of the gospel clearly shone, in order that the spirit of Christ (or Christ in his spirit or the perfect life of Christ) might be introduced. This understanding in the times of the church *and of several preceding religious orders* was hidden; and because of the jealousy (*emulatio*) of certain Judaizers, this understanding will appear doubtful at the end.[8]

Olivi then proceeds to develop a typological reading for the scribes and Pharisees sent out to question Christ as types for those contemporary detractors, members of the sect of the Antichrist, who disparage this understanding of the gospel as represented in Francis and his followers. Just as the scribes and Pharisees obscured the truth represented by John, so "two disciples will be sent out [from the sect of the Antichrist], imbued with magisterial knowledge and hypocritical, superstitious religion."[9] Olivi typically abstains from categorically identifying the detractors he has in mind here. However, the fact that he identifies them as possessors of "magistral knowledge" and his earlier remark that the truth was hidden by several "preceding religious orders" certainly makes it possible that he has in mind either members of the secular clergy or the Dominicans whom he elsewhere accuses of using their knowledge in the service of carnal attacks on the truth of the gospel represented in his own order. In any case, Olivi predicts that such attacks will ultimately be frustrated. Just as John was vindicated by Christ, so the "evangelical understanding and its precursor, sealed with the passion of Christ, will be shown to be such as it is said among the people that among those born of women there has been none greater than he."[10]

This is a good example of the influence of Olivi's own polemical social context on his interpretation of the gospels. This interpretation has no precedents in the patristic or mendicant tradition, and it has no source in Joachim either.[11] The most important influence on his exegesis of this pericope is his own unique social context. It was that context, rather than an ancient or medieval source, which encouraged him to see in the imprisonment of John at the end of the time of the law a *concordia* for the persecution of Francis and his order at the end of the ecclesiastical age.

Peter's Confession

The special features of Olivi's own social context also encourage him to read the Confession of Peter at Caesarea Philippi (Mt. 16:13–23) in a similar way. As Olivi himself notes, Origen had argued in his Matthew commentary that Christ put this question to the disciples in order that we might learn from their answer (i.e., "Some say . . . others say . . .") that "there were at that time among the Jews various opinions concerning Christ."[12] Olivi's own context prompts him to establish a concord between Christ's time, or his first advent in the flesh, and the time of Francis and his successors, when Christ came in the spirit:

> Note for the mysteries of this final time that just as in the first advent of Christ, which was in the flesh, there were among the people various opinions concerning the person of Christ, but the disciples truly and solidly confessed the truth and the church of Christ was founded upon them; so in his second advent, which is in the spirit, there are and will be various opinions concerning the life of Christ, but in the disciples solidly confessing its sublimity the spiritual church will be founded. Against this the gates of hell, that is the infernal sects of the Antichrist, will not prevail. . . . Note that from the time that they are solid in this confession, the life of Christ (or Christ in the spirit of his life) will openly tell them that not only he but they must go to Jerusalem and be reproved by the scribes and leaders of the carnal church.[13]

Quite clearly, Olivi identifies those who hold "various opinions concerning the life of Christ" with his and the order's opponents in the various poverty controversies of the thirteenth century. Did he have anyone else in mind? In his discussion of this text, David Burr has pointed out that,

> In his early works, Olivi never says precisely where these scribes and elders will be encountered, but it seems likely that here, as in the Revelation commentary, he assumes that they will eventually dominate the church hierarchy and the Franciscan order. One could deduce as much from the model provided by Christ's passion, from the weight of persecution and subtlety of temptation constantly identified with the spirituals' 'passion' in the dawning sixth period, and from Olivi's anticipation of a future domination by Antichrist. After the great Antichrist the church will be ruled by good shepherds, but before him spiritual men must face increasing persecution by their own leaders.[14]

As Burr points out, Olivi in this passage never states explicitly who he has in mind. Occasionally, however, one can deduce the likely suspects from the wider context of Olivi's thought.

Franciscan Poverty, Possession, and the Secular-Mendicant Controversy

Throughout the Matthew commentary, Olivi is unusually alert to proof-texts that can be used for and against Franciscan self-understanding. He is especially sensitive to those texts which could and had been used by the secular clergy to argue that Christ and the apostles had, in fact, possessed property. Among the most difficult of these to deal with was the seemingly unambiguous reference in Matthew 8 to "Peter's House." Olivi goes to great and ingenious (or tortured) lengths to prove that the text does not mean what it appears to say. His sensitivity to the implications of such narratives becomes especially marked when we compare him to Bonaventure and Thomas. Both Bonaventure's Luke commentary and Thomas's Matthew commentary were delivered as lectures in Paris when the dispute was at its height.[15] Nonetheless, the controversy seems not to have influenced Thomas's Matthew commentary at all, and it affected Bonaventure's Luke commentary much differently than Olivi's.

"Peter's House" (Mt. 8:14–15)

The pericope begins, "Jesus went into the house of Peter." Perhaps not surprisingly, no patristic or Carolingian commentator was deeply troubled by the implications of this verse. Olivi's predecessors usually interpreted this text in one of two ways, one literal and one allegorical. Pseudo-Chrysostom simply explains that Jesus entered the home of Peter in order to take food and because he wished to do honor to the apostles.[16] Anselm and Bede allegorize the pericope. According to these exegetes, Peter's house represents the Law and his mother-in-law the synagogue. Jesus' cure of the febrile mother-in-law represents the healing of the sick and carnal Jewish synagogue.[17] In neither case is poverty, perfection, or the religious life seen as an issue raised by the text. No patristic or Carolingian exegete regarded Peter's apparent ownership of property as a difficulty requiring explanation.

Interestingly enough, most of Olivi's mendicant contemporaries perceived no problem either. The friars under consideration here simply interpret the text in one of the two ways established by the Latin and Greek fathers or in very similar ways. Thomas, who was so influentially involved in the controversy, follows Chrysostom's reading closely.[18] Hugh and Alexander allegorize the pericope as the cure of carnal concupiscence by the entry of Christ into the conscience.[19] More remarkably, Bonaventure picks up this reading from Hugh with no apparent anxiety about the first verse of the pericope.[20] Clearly, the verse poses some threat to the key Franciscan claim that the apostles owned nothing individually. As we have seen, secular masters themselves had used the verse in an attempt to explode the truth of that claim. Glossing this text in the heat of the secular-mendicant controversy, the author of the *Apologia Pauperum* puzzlingly overlooks the grave implications of these words in his Luke commentary.

Olivi is hardly unaware of the danger. He clearly recognizes that the passage implies that Peter retained dominion over the house in which the cure occurs. Indeed, virtually all of Olivi's interpretation of the pericope is an attempt to resolve this difficulty. Olivi's first tack is to check the parallel passages in Mark and Luke. Perhaps Matthew has made an error of fact? Unfortunately, this maneuver fails. After comparing the parallel passages, Olivi concedes that all three evangelists represent the house in question as Peter's.[21] But how could this be? Had not Matthew earlier stated that Peter and Andrew "left everything, even their nets" (Mt. 4:18–22)?[22]

Olivi is stymied. His next approach is to look more closely at the preceding context of the pericope, and he has more success with this strategy. Olivi notices that Matthew reports that Jesus "entered Capernaum" just before the cure of Peter's mother-in-law (Mt. 8:5). He then points out that the first chapter of the Gospel of John states that Peter was from Bethsaida (Jn. 1:44). His conclusion is that Peter would not have owned a house in a city other than his native one. The house in Capernaum, therefore, could not be his. The evangelist, he reasons, must have called the house in question "Peter's house" because it belonged to the apostle's wife.[23]

In order to appreciate the significance of Olivi's interpretation of these two pericopes, we need to consider his Matthew commentary in relation to the gospel commentaries of the two principal apologists for the mendicants. Unlike Thomas and Bonaventure in their gospel commentaries, Olivi is determined to make the gospel advocate key mendicant claims regarding the poverty of Christ and the apostles in the context of opposing claims. To be sure, Bonaventure was anxious to show that the Gospel of Luke, in Dominic Monti's words, would "confirm the friars in their belief that they were indeed living out the way of life specifically proposed by Christ himself."[24] Yet there is a significant difference between the two commentaries. Bonaventure's Luke commentary was not (again I use Monti's words) "directed against outside assailants."[25] Olivi's was. Bonaventure was searching for texts which could be used for and by the young friars he was teaching. Olivi was anxious about and especially sensitive to texts which could be used against the friars. That is why Bonaventure is not apparently worried about the mention of Peter's house, while Olivi evidently was. Bonaventure's commentary was offensive in nature, Olivi's defensive. Bonaventure is preoccupied with proposing constructive and positive readings of the text, Olivi with discrediting damaging and obnoxious ones.

The difference between the principal mendicant apologists and Olivi can be put in terms of generic differences as well. Bonaventure and Thomas were both quite willing to prepare separate polemical tracts for use against their respective orders' detractors. However, neither would allow ecclesial disputes to contaminate the academic purity of their biblical commentaries. Unlike his Franciscan master, Olivi permitted the arguments of detractors to polemicize a genre ordinarily untouched by the scandal of ecclesial conflict. In Bonaventure and Thomas, the *apologia* and the *postilla* were separate genres. In Olivi, they are one. In Olivi's gospel commentaries, the *postilla* becomes a vehicle for the apologetic defense and justification of his disparaged order. Bonaventure and Thomas kept affairs of convent and chapter separate from those of the classroom. In his gospel commentaries, Olivi mingled them.

John the Baptist and Jesus (Mt. 4:12–17)

The influence of the secular-mendicant controversy on Olivi's gospel commentaries is evident even in Olivi's reading of those parts of the gospel not obviously connected with the issues of poverty and the religious life. As will become apparent, Olivi regarded the attack of the seculars as diabolically inspired. However, he hardly considered the secular clergy an intrinsically evil society of clerics. Clearly, he is convinced that the secular clergy had and still has an important role to play in salvation history. However, he was equally persuaded that they misunderstood their role in relation to the new and more perfect orders. For Olivi, their role is transparently reflected in the text of the Gospel of Matthew. In pondering the relationship of John the Baptist to Jesus, Olivi perceives a model for the relationship of the seculars and mendicants. Just as John had to decrease in order that Jesus might increase, so too the secular clergy must now diminish in the presence of the new order of evangelical perfect. This, incidentally, is an idea that is ubiquitously present in Joachim's *Tractatus*,[26] and it is found elsewhere in Olivi's Matthew commentary as well.[27]

This line of thought is present in Olivi's interpretation of Matthew 4:12–17, where it is reported that Jesus began to preach after John was arrested. No later than the fourth century, exegetes began to ask why Jesus began to preach only after the imprisonment of John and why John did not stop preaching after the initial appearance of Christ. Jerome offered an important mystical interpretation of the text which asserted that Christ began to preach as soon as John was delivered to prison "because when the Law ceased, the Gospel commenced."[28] "Chrysostom" asserted that Christ waited until John's arrest so that the Baptist's preaching would not seem to be superfluous. Both of these answers were popular among Olivi's contemporaries.[29]

Olivi begins by arguing that John did not cease preaching immediately upon Christ's advent so that Christ and his status might receive fuller clarification. The more clear (*clarius*) is placed next to the less clear (*minus clarum*) so that the preeminence of Christ and his status over John and the prior status might appear more clearly. Olivi adds that it was also to avoid the disorder and chaos of sudden change, for "it is useful for the prior state to be abolished and obscured little by little."[30] At this point, it is not completely apparent that Olivi is thinking of the relationship of John the Baptist to Jesus in terms of the relationship of the secular clergy to the Franciscan Order. Three later reasons leave much less doubt:

> The fourth reason is to show that in the church it is sometimes useful for there to be at once several states and doctors, though they be far apart in perfection.
> Fifth, in order that an example might be given that those holding some prior and more imperfect state ought to prefer the following state to their own and to direct its disciples or those coming to him as to the better, just as John did when he sent his disciples to Christ.
> Sixth, so that we might also be given a notable example of transferring ourselves from prior imperfect states to new more perfect ones . . . as certain of John's disciples transferred to the discipleship of Christ.[31]

The references to disparity in perfection, to directing disciples to a better, more perfect discipleship, and to the possibility of transferring to new, more perfect states all seem to include hints of the secular-mendicant controversy. The mendicant claim to imitate the perfection of Christ, the scramble for young recruits joining the new orders, and the example of secular masters such Alexander of Hales and John of St. Giles are all suggested by this text. Clearly, Olivi saw in John the Baptist the paradigm for the contemporary behavior of the less perfect secular order. Having completed their preparatory role, they should be prepared to accept the invitation to join the new more perfect order.

Laborers in the Vineyard (Mt. 20:1–16)

In some of Olivi's interpretations of the parables, the detractors of evangelical perfection are not difficult to identify. The parable of the Laborers in the Vineyard (Mt. 20:1–16) had been historicized in the Greek tradition as far back as the third century. Origen interpreted the day of the laborers as the history of the world until the coming of Christ, so that the different calls by the landowner in the parable marked the major ages in the history of Israel. The interpretation he cultivated may be illustrated as follows.[32]

Call	Matthew	Age in Salvation History
First	20:1–2	Adam to Noah
Second	20:3–4	Noah to Abraham
Third	20:5	Abraham to Moses
Fourth	20:5	Moses to Christ
Fifth	20:6–7	Christ to Present

Origen also interpreted the murmurers (20:11–12) as discontented Jews complaining that the gentiles were offered the grace of the gospel. This historicizing reading was popular among patristic successors of Origen such as Jerome and Hilary.[33] Most of the mendicant commentators under consideration here follow the patristic figures closely.[34] Olivi also follows Origen and his successors closely.[35]

This part of Olivi's interpretation is highly dependent upon the long patristic tradition inaugurated by Origen. Far more inventive is that Olivi projects a *concordia* between these five periods of Old Testament history and five periods of New Testament history and pauses several times to make explicit comparisons between the ages:

> The first call was made by Christ and the apostles. The second call, around the third hour, was made from the time of the general councils, which took place after Constantine. Just as from the time of Moses the Law was produced, so from that time came the ecclesiastical decrees and regular statutes. The third call, around the sixth hour, represents the times of Augustine and Gregory the Great, when first in the Greek and then in the Latin church there flowed rivers from the mouths of the doctors, as if from the mouth of Solomon. The fourth call, around the ninth hour, was after the schism of the Greeks from the Roman church and after the mutilation of many churches by the Saracens. At this time, too, the monastic life in regions of the West began to proliferate. Finally, many kinds of religious orders, both military and monastic, began to rise. The fifth call, around the eleventh hour, was begun by the Least of All the Lesser Ones, honored . . . with the wounds of Christ and honored by the marks of an evangelical rule, which it is fitting to withhold from the multitude of

murmurers until that judgment is pronounced by him who said, 'I choose to give to this last as I gave to you.' And then again it will be clear that the first will be last and the last first.[36]

As with his interpretation of the Sower, Olivi states that the historical reading of the parable is given in the allegorical sense of the text.[37] Yet there are two interesting differences as well. First, Olivi develops his *concordia* from an exegetical tradition which had already historicized the parable. His originality, therefore, resides in the unique historical content he gives to the parable, rather than his decision to historicize it. Throughout the gospel commentaries, Olivi would "add" a concord of New Testament history to those pericopes in which the fathers historicized in terms of Old Testament history.

Second, the polemical social context in which Olivi wrote influenced the way in which he interprets the Laborers much more than it does in his reading of the Sower. As usual, Olivi discreetly resists identifying the "multitude of murmurers" objecting to the late arrival of Francis and his order (those laborers who arrive in the eleventh hour of the day). In this case, however, there is evidence in other parts of the commentary which may help to identify the group in question. As we shall see in the next chapter, Olivi in the Matthew commentary argues that whenever something new appears, there are always groups ready to point to their own primacy and antiquity.[38] It seems possible and perhaps probable that Olivi is referring to the secular clergy here. Clearly, Olivi takes satisfaction in the reversal promised by Jesus. Those who were first on the scene, such as the seculars, will be last in the eschatological judgment; those who came in the eleventh hour of salvation history, such as the Franciscans, will be first.

The Wedding Banquet and the Secular Clergy (Mt. 22:1–14)

It seems as if he has the secular clergy in mind when Olivi discusses those invited to the feast in the parable of the Wedding Banquet (Mt. 22:1–14). This parable had been historicized by Origen as a narrative depicting the persecution of God's servants by the unbelieving Jews. Origen's interpretation of the parable was widely influential in the ancient and medieval period; subsequent exegetes tended to differ only in details.[39] It was widely agreed that the first group of servants sent represented the prophets calling Israel to fidelity to God. The second group of slaves represent the apostles calling Israel to faith in Christ. The mistreatment and slaughter of the servants illustrates the persecution of the early apostles; some commentators specifically mention the stoning of Stephen (Acts 7:54–60). The king's anger and decision to "burn their city" (Mt. 22:7) represents the destruction of Jerusalem, divine punishment for rejection of the proffered grace. Most of Olivi's contemporaries followed their ancient predecessors very closely.[40]

Olivi himself offers the traditional interpretation of the parable.[41] However, a number of his remarks indicate that he was thinking of the story as a parable of the contemporary persecution by the secular clergy. First of all, Olivi represents the first invitation as a "call to evangelical perfection." Those to whom the invitation is extended are asked "entirely to relinquish and to renounce all the carnal and earthly things that are most dear to them" (and, Olivi adds, "their own vicious wills"). One enters the banquet hall by means of "highest poverty."[42] Second, Olivi states that those who reject the invitation are in a "prior" and "inferior" *status*.[43] Third, the invited guests are angry at the servants because "they appear superior to those who are called." Perhaps most tellingly, Olivi attributes their anger to the fact that the servants sent by the king "assume for themselves the office of mediators and preachers."[44] This text makes it likely that Olivi was interpreting the parable in terms of recent events in the order's history. After all, one of the main reasons the secular clergy objected to the mendicants was their usurpation of functions traditionally reserved for the secular, parochial clergy, namely confession and preaching. The words *assumebant sibi officium mediatorum et predicatorum* thus neatly summarize the principal complaint of the Franciscans' detractors. Olivi seems to be suggesting that just as the carnal persecutors of Christ rejected his invitation and judged his teachings erroneous, so today their carnal successors reject the invitation of the new preachers of the way of perfection.[45] Like those who killed the apostles of Christ, the secular clergy persecute the latter-day apostles of *alter Christus*.

DOMINICAN-FRANCISCAN TENSIONS AND THE MATTHEW COMMENTARY

The Apostolic Commission (Matthew 10), Thomas Aquinas, and Olivi on Poverty

Olivi launches a fierce and lengthy polemic against Thomas Aquinas when he comes to comment on Matthew 10:9–10: "Take no gold, nor silver, nor money in your belts." His commentary on these verses is actually a long, vigorous, and at times vituperative response to two of Thomas's *quaestiones* on poverty.[46] As we saw in an earlier chapter,[47] Thomas interprets this command either as a "concession" allowing the disciples to accept food and means or as a temporary statute.

For Olivi, one should be especially on guard against Thomas's arguments (*precipue sunt cavenda*).[48] Olivi first responds to the argument that the injunctions of the Apostolic Discourse might be interpreted as "concessions." Olivi is quite appalled by Thomas's line of argumentation here. His first objection to the argument—one which he repeats over and over again—has to do with Thomas's (in his mind) nonchalant dismissal of "the explicit words of sacred scripture."[49] And these are not just any words of scripture; they are express commands (*precepta*) of Christ himself. Olivi notes that the text in Matthew begins with the words *Iesus precipiens eis* (Mt. 10:5) and ends *cum consummasset Iesus precipiens duodecim discipulis* (Mt. 11:1), while the parallel text in Mark begins *precipit eis ne quid tollerent in via* (Mk. 6:8).[50] Olivi's point is that the *precepta* of Christ can only be read with strict literalism. There are no hermeneutical options with *precepta*. They leave the reader with one choice, obedience or disobedience. They do not permit of modification or adaptation. To assert that a strict command is a "concession" is to distort the clear literal meaning of the words of Christ. Consequently, Olivi marvels that Thomas dares to contrapose "a few words of a single saint" against the most explicit words of sacred scripture (*expressissima verba Scripture sacre*).[51] For Olivi, Thomas's appeal to Augustine counts for very little when assessed in relation to the lucid clarity and preeminent authority of the sacred text.

Olivi's response calls out for several remarks. First, the "concessions" argument must have been particularly exasperating coming from the pen of Thomas. Among other things, this was an argument used by Gerard of Abbeville and other secular masters against the mendicant orders.[52] Now it was being used by one friar against his mendicant confederates. The Old Enemy had put the same deceptively obnoxious words against evangelical poverty in the mouth of a former ally.[53]

Second, and more importantly, it seems clear that the two friars differ over the interpretation of Matthew 10:9–10 because of a more fundamental split on the content of the Christian gospel, at least that part of it described by both Thomas and Olivi as the "New Law." It is hardly insignificant that Thomas treats the disputed Matthean text in the context of a consideration of the content of the New Law. Quite clearly, he is convinced that the New Law includes very few prescriptions for the conduct of the Christian life. Equally clearly, he is persuaded that Matthew 10:9–10 is not one of these, as it pertains neither to the performance of the sacraments nor to the height of virtue. Olivi, on the other hand, is convinced that the New Law contains a modest number of commands which are of eternal (not temporary) ordinance. Commands given by Christ to the disciples are binding on all those successors of the disciples who profess poverty in their vows. This is obvious, Olivi remarks, in the sarcastic tone which pervades his response, "even to the blind and deaf."[54] Olivi could not believe that the commands of Christ to the disciples pertained to anything but the highest virtue. Their observance therefore represented the peak of evangelical perfection. Thomas, on the other hand, was persuaded that Matthew 10:9–10 was simply not part of the *nova lex*.

Third, Olivi's disparaging reference to Augustine's "concessions" interpretation as the "few words of a single saint" should not blind us to the fact that Olivi was quite distressed that Thomas was able legitimately to claim the authority of Augustine for his position. Nor should it conceal the fact that Olivi thought it very important to bring the weight of patristic authority to his side, including that of Augustine:

> I am astonished that an intelligent man would wish to reduce a few words of a single saint against the most explicit words of sacred scripture and of all the other saints, against the express sayings of the Roman popes, against the message, life, and Rule of such a man as St. Francis, sealed with the wounds of Christ, against other words of Augustine himself, and against the light of irrefragable reasons.[55]

This impressive catalogue of offenses calls out for several comments. First, Olivi initially prunes the authority of Augustine to that of an anonymous "single saint." Yet he is apparently so reluctant to forswear his authority that he finds himself appealing to other, presumably contradictory words of Augustine (now named) just a few lines later. Second, Olivi puts the life and rule of Francis in company with patristic and papal authority. Thomas might be forgiven for not recognizing this generous estimate of Francis's significance for the passage in question. (However, as we shall see momentarily, Olivi later chides Thomas for ignoring the example and teaching of Dominic as well.) Finally, where he was forced to concede that Augustine had supported the "concessions" argument, he flatly denies that any saint had stated that the commandments of the Apostolic Discourse were rescinded at the passion. "No one of sane mind" would assert this.[56] Indeed, the saints "teach the very opposite."[57] Olivi is able to point out that Bede had asserted that it was the permission to *use* money in Luke 22:35, not its prohibition, that was of temporary ordinance. According to Bede, Jesus permitted the apostles to carry money during the time of persecution at and after the passion. However, "when the madness of the persecutors had subsided," the old requirements were to obtain. Indeed, the commands of the Apostolic Discourse were virtues to which, according to Bede, "one must always and with all one's might cling."[58] Olivi proceeds to quote several other Greek and Latin fathers to support his position as well.[59] In short, despite his confidence that the literal meaning of "the most explicit words of sacred scripture" is on his side against Augustine, and despite his insistence on adhesion to that literal sense, he is obviously quite anxious to have the principal Greek and Latin fathers, including Augustine, vindicate his position here.

Still, the authority of the fathers for Olivi is clearly secondary to the transparent clarity of the literal sense of scripture, and especially of a *praeceptum Christi*, which in this case unambiguously forbids successors to the apostles to carry money or goods. For Olivi, that *praeceptum* was religious law, and for those who had bound themselves by vows to that law, its observance was compulsory. (And here, whether one was a Franciscan or Dominican would be completely irrelevant.) Olivi finds himself appealing over and over again to the clear literal meaning. For Olivi, to finesse or domesticate the literal meaning of the text is to go "expressly against the counsels of Christ" (*expresse contra consilia Christi*).[60] To suggest that any apostle or Christ carried gold or silver or provided for themselves is (besides being insulting to Christ and the apostles) "nothing other than violently to twist a repugnant scripture to his own position."[61] The will of the Deity for the apostles and their successors had been clearly revealed in these commands. The obligations of the *nova lex*, at least here, were quite clear. For his part, Thomas would certainly have agreed that strict adhesion to the *nova lex* was obligatory for those who had vowed to observe it. Where he parted company with Olivi was on the issue of the content and essence of the New Law.

Later in the *Summa*, Thomas returns to the issue of poverty once again. This time, the issue is considered in relation to an explicit discussion of the different forms of religious life (*de differentia religionum*).[62] In the seventh article of Question 188, Thomas asks whether having possessions in common diminishes the perfection of a particular form of religious life (*utrum habere aliquid in communi diminuat perfectionem religionis*).[63] Thomas provides a carefully nuanced answer to this question. Here the nature of his response makes it clear that his own thinking had indeed been shaped by the controversy with the Franciscans over the relative merits of each order. His argument is intended to undermine the idea that there is a simple correlation between an order's poverty and the degree of its perfection.[64] Thomas argues that the perfection of a religious institute should instead be measured in terms of how its poverty corresponds to the common end (*finis communis*) of all religious orders and to the special end (*finis specialis*) of the particular order in question. The common end of all religious institutes, he asserts, is "to dedicate oneself to the service of God" (*vacare divinis obsequiis*).[65] There is a wide variety of "special ends." Some orders are ordained to warfare, others to hospital service, and still others to contemplation. The perfection of all of these orders cannot be assessed in relation to the ideal of absolute poverty. It must instead be judged with respect to their "special ends." In this context, military and hospital orders would be imperfect if they *lacked* common possessions. In fact, orders dedicated to the corporal works of the active life should have "an abundance of common riches" (*abunduntia divitiarum communium*).[66] Those ordained to contemplation would need fewer possessions but should nonetheless store a moderate quantity in order to prevent solicitude for the morrow.[67] A religious order, in Thomas's view, is not more perfect insofar as it has greater poverty but "insofar as its poverty is better proportioned to the common and special end" (*magis proportionata communi fini et speciali*).[68] Thomas concludes: "Poverty is not perfection, but an instrument of perfection, and the least among the three principal instruments of perfection."[69]

Olivi's response to Thomas again demonstrates that their disagreement over poverty is also rooted in a deeper conflict over the meaning of the *nova lex,* this time on what the New Law has to say about the principal aims of the religious life. More precisely, the two friars disagree on the weight given to a religious institute's "special end" as a factor determining its level of poverty or the degree of its perfection. Olivi defines the principal end of a religious institute quite differently than Thomas. For Olivi, the principal end of a religious institute is, he asserts, "the love of God and of neighbor and the spiritual salvation of one's own soul and then of the souls of others."[70] He goes on to state quite categorically that "the temporal and corporal struggle against the infidel and the corporal defense, rescue, or feeding of the faithful is not the proper end of a religious institute."[71] The principal end even of the military and hospital orders, he maintains, is the salvation of their own members' souls and the spiritual, not the corporal, worship of God.[72]

Thomas would not have disputed the assertion that military defense and corporal care are not the primary aims of a religious order. As we have seen, Thomas argued that the common end of all religious institutes was "to dedicate oneself to the service of God." However, in Olivi's mind, Thomas had collapsed the common and special ends of a religious order to such a degree that he seemed in danger of making its "special end" the sole criterion of the importance and appropriate level of its poverty. Olivi distinguishes the two ends more sharply than Thomas and makes the "principal" end of an order more important in the determination of the importance of poverty. The poverty of any religious institute should, he argues, be adjusted to its *proprius finis*, not to its *finis annexus*, to its spiritual rather than its temporal end. Consequently, an institute is not more perfect "as its poverty is better proportioned to the common and special end." So to suggest is *mira falsigraphia*.[73] For Olivi, the "special end" of an order does not enter into the judgment as a criterion at all. An institute is more perfect simply as its poverty is better proportioned to the proper end of all religious orders. Thus, the closer to the ideal of absolute poverty, the more perfect the institute. Again, "no one of sane mind" would say that an order that has kingdoms and castles (Olivi is thinking of the military orders) was more virtuous than an order of mendicants.[74]

> Who indeed—until now—has heard in the New Law riches commended in this way, so that some religious institute (*aliqua religio*) is said to be imperfect, not only if it does not have riches, but indeed unless it has abundant riches?[75]

To Thomas's contention that a hospital order should have an abundance of possessions, Olivi indignantly replies: "Is this the teaching of Christ or Paul? Did any saint ever say this? God forbid!"[76] And to Thomas's comment that poverty is the least of the three principal instruments of perfection, Olivi responds: "*Mira res!* This fellow degrades poverty below all else," while Christ "extols it above all else." He is, moreover, sure that Dominic would never have said this.[77]

Having presented the differences between the two friars on this critical Matthean text, we should not proceed without noting one important way in which this dispute conceals the very significant extent of their agreement on the nature of the religious life. The polemical context in which Olivi responded to Thomas did not allow him to recognize, or perhaps to acknowledge, their similarities, but they are there nonetheless.[78] Perhaps the most important way in which they agreed is that neither thought of the religious life in terms of a vow to do a certain number of things.[79] Olivi later opposed members of his own order and three popes in refusing to specify all of the precise requirements of *usus pauper* as set out in the Franciscan rule. Indeed, this was an impossibility. There was an "indeterminacy" on many issues regarding Franciscan use of goods. Neither gospel nor rule could always give one precise instructions on what one could and could not do. Thus Olivi was closer to Thomas than to many members of his own order here (another reason that the dispute cannot be seen exclusively in Dominican-Franciscan terms). Nonetheless, both gospel and rule made *some* requirements very clear. Both clearly proscribe possession of goods. There was no ambiguity or "indeterminacy" here. For Olivi this was one of the few *precepta* of the gospel on which there was blinding clarity. Part of the vigor of his response might be attributed to Olivi's conviction that Thomas was muddying one of the few *clear* requirements of the gospel, as well as one of the most significant for the observance of evangelical perfection.

Finally, it should be noted that Olivi's attack on Thomas arises not only out of current inter-fraternal tensions but out of Olivi's own special attitude towards the use of Aristotle in Christian theology and toward Paris and its University. While it is simplistic to portray Olivi as a plain anti-Aristotelian, he was convinced that the incautious use of Aristotle would lead inevitably to error. According to Olivi, the source of almost all of Aristotle's errors lies in his overvaluation of sensible things and in his fidelity to the data of sense experience. Those who rely incautiously on Aristotle share these flaws and can be expected not only to fall into doctrinal error but to attack evangelical poverty as well. For Olivi, Paris was the symbol of the uncritical use of Aristotle. Not surprisingly, it had produced a variety of forms of doctrinal error and a breed of worldly clerics ignorant of the value of evangelical poverty. As a Parisian master celebrated for his use of Aristotle and now intent on attacking Franciscan poverty, Thomas corresponded perfectly to the prototype Parisian cleric in Olivi's mind. What is more, Olivi's apocalyptic program encouraged him to view Thomas and his fellow Parisian masters as part of the sect of the Antichrist.[80] Thus, Olivi must have regarded Thomas's attack on poverty as the inevitable assault of the carnal church upon the spiritual and evidence that the carnal church was infiltrating the world of ostensibly Christian scholarship.

One of the reasons that the contrast between Thomas and Olivi on poverty is so interesting is that it involved questions of abiding interest in the history of Christian theology, ethics, and biblical interpretation. What is the content of the gospel? What is required of the Christian? Does the gospel teach us how to act? Or is its content more nebulous than that? Are the commandments of Christ intended to be observed literally? Must all Christians observe the *precepta Christi* literally, or only those who would be perfect? What is the relation between the Bible and its authoritative interpretation?

Although the polemical context in which Olivi wrote did conceal some of the ways in which he agreed with Thomas, the two mendicant thinkers split on this issue largely because of a fundamental disagreement on the content of the gospel or the New Law. Thomas states his position on this issue nowhere more clearly than in one of the *quaestiones* we have been analyzing: "What is primary in the New Law is the grace of the Holy Spirit" (*principalitas legis novae est gratia Spiritus sancti*).[81] For Thomas, the New Law is a law of liberty: *lex Evangelii lex libertatis*.[82] Indeed, that is precisely what makes it different than the Old Law. "The Old Law," Thomas declares, "left human freedom with only a few things to decide."[83] Under the New Law, there are many things which neither contradict nor are in accordance with the life of faith working through love. To use a term Thomas did not use, they are *adiaphora*—matters of indifference. Neither commanded nor forbidden by the lawgiver Christ, they are works which leave the individual free to decide to do or not to do them.[84] The New Law compels one to do nothing except that which is necessary to salvation and to avoid nothing except that which is repugnant to it.[85] Carrying money or food is, in Thomas's mind, neither necessary nor repugnant to salvation. And it certainly did not form the essence of the *nova lex*. Consequently, it may be left to the individual either to observe or to ignore the command *Nolite possidere*.

Although Olivi did not generally think of the vowed life or the gospel in terms of obedience to a catalog of commandments, there can be no question that he does think that there were a modest number of precepts, stated with lucid clarity, in the New Law. Moreover, he was convinced that strict observance of them was the revealed will of the Deity *at least for those who would be perfect*. For those vowed to religious perfection, the gospel requires the meticulous observance of the *precepta Christi*. For those who would be perfect, the New Law is, in part, a morality of code. Evangelical perfection consists in the willingness to obey perfectly the master who lays down a rule. Moreover, these precepts are not merely broad guidelines to the Christian life, *except* for those who are not vowed to perfection. For those vowed to perfection, the command to carry no gold nor silver is a clear, concrete, and possible moral and disciplinary law. It was not intended to provide an occasion for individual deliberation. In fact, the command leaves no doubt as to what is required. That is why Olivi almost monotonously insists that the "most explicit words" of sacred scripture be taken in their literal sense. That is also why he argues that the interpretation of any father, even one of such authority as Augustine, counts for little if the *praeceptum* is, as he believes it is here, eminently clear. For Olivi, what is required for following the divine law on poverty is not, as for Thomas, an ethic of deliberation, but a morality of imitation: "We used to have no other principle except the counsel and example of Christ."[86]

The differences I have outlined here have something to do with the fact that Thomas was a Dominican and Olivi a Franciscan. But what makes the debate of perennial relevance is that it involves a dilemma which has always divided Christians of good faith. Indeed, this is the kind of dilemma seen in slightly different form in virtually all of the major Western religious traditions. How does one deal with the detailed legislation handed down by the founder of a religion? How, if at all, do evolving contexts change the way in which religious law is to be interpreted? What is the relationship between righteousness or perfection and the religious law? Can the religious law be obeyed literally? Should it be? What authority do the great interpreters of the law have? These questions divided two of the most powerful thinkers of the High Middle Ages; it should come as no surprise that they continue to split religious communities today.

THE OPPONENTS OF *USUS PAUPER*

The Seven Evil Spirits (Mt. 12:43–45)

In his interpretation of the Seven Evil Spirits, Olivi launches a lengthy attack against those religious whose *tepeditas* in religious life makes them vulnerable to seven more serious evils. Olivi does not come right out and say, but it is clear that he is thinking about Franciscans who fail to observe *usus pauper.* (Thus, his concern here is not over the theoretical issue of whether *usus pauper* is part of the Franciscan vow but whether the vow is being taken seriously in practice.) How does Olivi let us know? First of all, he says, these pseudo-religious are held *in magna estimatione et veneratione;* indeed, they are regarded by others as saintly men (*ab aliis reputantur sancti*).[87] These are men who have status, eminence, and learning, but in reality, they are hypocrites. Having committed themselves by vow to a "high profession and state" (*alte professionis et status*)—a characteristically Olivian way of referring obliquely to the Franciscans—they prefer to remain quietly in a state of *accidia* and carnal leisure and to use their spiritual offices to traffic in superfluous temporal things.[88] To be sure, they abstain from the grossest sins. But this simply gives them cover to consume many things they deem necessary—things which a "zealous man would judge superfluous for himself."[89] From this reluctance to rise *ad alta* and their incompetence *ad profunda* follows a whole sequence of other sins. First of all, "implacable envy" (*invidia implacabili*), which leads the hypocritical wrongly to contemn and assault the innocent and spiritual.[90] (Here Olivi's own biography—especially the 1283 condemnation—seems especially relevant.) Indeed, the more spiritual and enlightened the elect, the more vehemently they are attacked.[91] Olivi then elevates these conditions onto the apocalyptic plane. Such men as he attacks here are latter-day Pharisees, precursors of the Antichrists and pseudo-religious who would fight against spiritual and evangelical men of whom Paul spoke. For Olivi, the closing words of the pericope—"So shall it be also with this evil generation"—have special meaning and the generation he has in mind is his own.

The Unmerciful Servant (Mt. 18:23–35)

The special importance of Olivi's own social context, particularly the disputes over poverty, may also be seen in his interpretation of the Unmerciful Servant (Mt. 18:23–35). Most exegetes made this parable a simple story of guilt and forgiveness.[92] Rabanus Maurus seems to have been the first exegete to have historicized the parable, making it an allegory of the relations of Jews and gentiles.[93] Olivi historicizes the parable as well but does so in ways conditioned by his own social context and in terms of his own theology of history. For Olivi, the giving of the ten thousand talents represents the creation, the inability to meet the debt symbolizes the fall, the servant begging for mercy signifies the desire of the patriarchs for mercy to be done in Christ, and the forgiveness of the king represents the mercy shown in Christ.[94] Olivi then leaps suddenly forward from the time of prophecy long fulfilled to prophecy just now being fulfilled:

> Fifth, [the cruelty of the unmerciful servant represents] the perversity of the shepherds in the final age of the church, who not only from impiety but also from cruel and presumptuous injustice are cruel to their simple sheep and the innocent.
>
> Sixth, [the distress of the fellow slaves represents] the piety and charity of spiritual men in the sixth time of the church who bear grief over the loss of the simple and over the impiety of those who rule and direct their vows to God (*regentium et ad Deum dirigentium vota sua.*).[95]

Who are those *regentium et ad Deum dirigentium vota sua?* Olivi never explicitly says. However, the facts that their offense occurs in the sixth time of the church (Olivi's time), that it involves the violation of religious vows, and that the *usus pauper* controversy was beginning at the time Olivi wrote the Matthew commentary makes it at least possible that Olivi had in mind his opponents in that controversy. Note too that Olivi links the cruelty of the unmerciful servant with the cruelty and presumption of the leaders (*rectores*) of the church, furnishing further evidence that Olivi felt less than sanguine about the possibilities for strong ecclesiastical leadership as early as the Matthew commentary. In any case, Olivi's interpretation of this parable is another instance in which there is no patristic or mendicant precedent for the kind of historicizing reading he furnishes. The decisive influence on Olivi's exegesis in this case was not literary but social, namely, the controversy over poverty within the Franciscan Order in the second half of the thirteenth century.

ANTICHRIST AND ANTICHRISTS

Matthew 24: The Apocalyptic Discourse

In his *Commentary on Matthew,* Olivi nowhere makes mention of a "mystical" Antichrist—one of the notions for which he is most noted and which he will develop soon after the Matthew commentary is completed. But buried in this long commentary are two remarks which furnish us with a short but, I think, fascinating and certainly clear look at the distinction in its embryonic form.

The pertinent remarks are found, not surprisingly, in chapter 24, Olivi's commentary on the so-called "apocalyptic discourse" of the same chapter of Matthew. Olivi's interpretation of this chapter is quite interesting in its own right, both for its reliance on, and independence of, established exegetical tradition, as well as its relation to Olivi's well-developed understanding of prophetic texts in general, of which, of course, this chapter in Matthew is one. In part, Olivi seems to be relying for his view of the whole chapter on traditions of interpretation which reach back at least to Jerome, who in his *Matthew Commentary* saw the discourse as a threefold prophecy of the destruction of Jerusalem, the coming of Christ in glory, and the destruction of the world.[96] Through Thomas Aquinas's *Catena Aurea*, Olivi was aware of this view of the chapter and, as a matter of fact, he cites it explicitly and assigns it to Jerome in one of his first comments in the chapter.[97]

Intriguingly, he cites it without comment and proceeds just lines later to supply his own, somewhat different view. From Jerome, he takes the general idea that the entire chapter looks forward prophetically to three ages and events. More specifically, Jesus' discourse, Olivi says, touches on several times (*plura tempora*) in a mixed way (*mixtim*), especially on three times to come: first, the time of Jewish captivity under the Romans, and third, the time of the final judgment.[98] If we pause here, we perceive that, in arguing that the discourse prophesies concerning these two times, Olivi stands squarely in the tradition represented by Jerome and picked up by many of his Parisian-trained confreres. But, departing from Jerome, Olivi also argues that the discourse prophesies concerning a second time, the age of the Antichrist.

Then, unlike almost any high-scholastic commentator, Olivi supplies hermeneutical justification for reading the chapter as a multiple prophecy:

> In order to understand this part, one should know that, just as the prophets under the Babylonian captivity comprehended three other captivities . . . and similarly, as the liberation of the people of God from the Babylonian captivity comprehended three liberations of the elect . . . so Christ in the Roman captivity which occurred around his time comprehends two subsequent captivities *more prophetico* . . . in certain places in the text, things are said that more properly look

to one of these captivities and at other places in the text look rather to another.[99]

Thus, Olivi concludes, those things said of the multitude of pseudochristians and of pseudoprophets and of their prodigies and of the danger of error to the elect and the cooling of charity have more properly to do with the time of the Antichrist.[100] In addition, some things are said which look forward to all three times and captivities.[101] Finally, and further complicating the theory, Olivi says that each of the three evangelists in whose gospels the discourse appears wrote "more directly" (*directius*) about one of the three captivities, so that each "specialized" in one of the three times, though all, he concludes, prophesied about all three times.[102] While some of Olivi's contemporaries (Thomas among them) do talk about the Antichrist in their commentaries, few, if any, develop this sort of brief prophetic theory to organize the text and to discipline their remarks in this way.

In any case, the point is that Olivi is confident that part of the text does refer to the time of Antichrist, and, in fact, he makes a number of remarks about *the* Antichrist—singular—in this chapter. In the course of his remarks on the times of Antichrist and of his temptations, Olivi pauses to ask the following *quaestio:* why does Christ not make explicit mention of the final temptation of the church *preceding* the temptation of the Antichrist and disposing the church to it? After all, the Antichrist cannot make himself adored unless the church is first in many ways "made prostrate and seduced and blinded." That preliminary temptation, Olivi suggests, will function to blind carnal Christians under the appearance of truth. The second temptation is the one that is "properly the Antichrist's" (*proprie Antichristi*). This temptation, Olivi says, ought to be preached openly by Christ (*aperte predicanda*), in part because the Antichrist and his minions will do things which will seem miraculous and supernatural and it is fitting that explicit mention be made of those, "lest such things," Olivi says, "be believed as if they were true."

However, the first, disposing temptation ought not to be preached except—and here is the crucial language—*mistice et oculte*. Nevertheless, anyone not wishing to go astray in the second temptation, Olivi recommends, "let him be aware of the first" so that he might understand what is that abomination sitting in the temple of God to damn the life of Christ, just as Caiphas condemned the person of Christ.[103]

Again, while discussing those parts of the chapter he takes to be refer-ring to the tribulations occurring in the first and third times, the destruc-tion of Jerusalem and the day of judgment, Olivi remarks that these texts refer also to the time and events of the Antichrist. He then goes on to add:

> the tribulations (*ista*) of that time [i.e., of the Antichrist] I believe are to be completed *dupliciter et sub duplici sensu*. First, namely, *mistice* and as it were through a certain conformity (*conformitas*) to the time of Christ condemned by the pseudo-scribes and pseudo-priests. Second, *literaliter* and *aperte* according to the type of Simon Magus, who said he was the son of God and of Nero.[104]

At least two elements of the texts here seem to invite comment. First, the essential distinction Olivi seems to want to establish is not a personal one, that is between individual Antichrist*s*. Rather the essential distinction is between two consecutive temptations, which in turn rests on a clear dis-tinction of two senses of scripture, but which reverse the usual order of interpretation, since the first is mystical and the second literal. Second, only the literal temptation is associated with a concrete individual, namely, *the* Antichrist, in the singular. The mystical temptation is impersonal or acephalous. Thus, in these respects, it becomes quite clear that at the time the Matthew commentary was composed, Olivi had not yet arrived at a distinction of dual individual Antichrists, though he speaks often of plu-ral antichrists, in the Johannine, small-a sense. Thus, at the time the Mat-thew commentary concluded, Olivi was thinking in terms of a single apocalyptic Antichrist and numerous antichrists bedeviling the church throughout her history.

Nonetheless, the hermeneutical theory that prophetic texts have a double or triple reference, the distinction of a precursory or preparatory temptation from the temptation of the Antichrist proper, and the iden-tification of the first temptation with Caiphas and the latter with Simon Magus and Nero—each of these three elements is a major motif in Olivi's fully developed distinction between the mystical and great Antichrists. Here in the Matthew commentary, then, we clearly see in larval form what will become the later mature doctrine. Olivi had only to work out all of the concrete implications of his own prophetic hermeneutic and especially of that notion of *conformitas* or, to put it in Joachite terms, *concordia*.

If we leap ahead to Olivi's commentary on the *Lucan* apocalyptic dis-course, we can see how he did so. Instructive here is a brief comparison with Bonaventure's overall view of the same chapter in *his* Luke commentary. Bonaventure divides the discourse into four parts, each of which has to do with things which are to come: first, what is to come *generaliter*, second, what is to come around the persecution of the apostles, third, what is to come in the destruction of Jerusalem, fourth, what is to come around the final judgment at the end of time.[105] Notable here is Bonaventure's belief that the discourse involves a grand chronological vault from about 70 C.E. to the end of time.

Olivi divides the chapter rather differently. The Lucan apocalyptic discourse, he says, has to do with three "final judgments," where "final" refers to the conclusion of some dismal preceding state. Thus the Lucan discourse refers first to the destruction of Jerusalem and the synagogue, second to the final desolation of the carnal church around the times of Antichrist, and finally to the judgment at the end of time. In his preaching, Olivi concludes "Christ comprehended these three final judgments *more prophetico*."[106] One part of the text of Luke has more to do with the first final judgment, another with the second, and another with the third, though, he adds, that part concerning the destruction of the carnal church is not so distinct from the others and especially from the third, as in Matthew 24 and in other sayings of the prophets.[107] Thus Luke "specializes" in the second final judgment during the time of Antichrist. (Interestingly, in his Matthew commentary, Olivi states explicitly that the "words of Luke more directly respect the temporal captivity of the Jews under the Romans.")[108] When we compare Bonaventure's treatment of this chapter with Olivi's, it becomes obvious that the major difference is that Bonaventure does not see it as a prophecy of the time of Antichrist, while Olivi sees it *primarily* as such a prophecy.

What is more, when we look past Olivi's introductory hermeneutical remarks, surely the most striking feature of the chapter, one which distinguishes this commentary not only from Bonaventure's *Commentary on Luke* but from his own Matthew commentary, is that Olivi is no longer speaking of *the* Antichrist in the singular. Again, two remarks in this chapter are worth noting. The first: glossing one of the first lines of the discourse, *multi enim venient in nomine meo, dicentes quia ego sum* (Lk. 21:8), Olivi declares that the *multi* here refer to the Antichrists, of whom, "as the learned believe" (*ut docti estimant*) there will be two. Both of these Antichrists, Olivi states, will declare themselves to be God. The first will call himself the messiah promised in the Law, the last one (*ultimus*) will call himself Christ, though whether the *ultimus* is the one who in

Ezekiel 38–39 is designated by Gog "is not," Olivi admits, "clear to me" (*non mihi constat*).[109] Leaving aside that unclarity, Olivi proceeds to declare that before the *ultimus Antichristus* there will be a "mystical Antichrist" (*mysticus Antichristus*) who with his pseudoantichrists, that is, his co-leaders, will publicly condemn the life and spirit of Christ, just as Caiphas with all his council solemnly condemned the person and teaching of Christ. The mystical Antichrist will seduce many with impressive cunning and power (*multa astutia et potentia*), and so Christ urges the elect to be vigilant, warning them *videte ne seducamini*.[110]

That is the first important remark in the chapter. Passing on to the next line of Luke, and the mention of the near approach of "wars and tumults" (21:9), Olivi observes that, in the Jewish-Roman War, certain preliminary battles of Vespasian paved the way for his son Titus finally to destroy Jerusalem. Just so, he argues, the onslaughts of the mystical Antichrist—whom he again, and not unimportantly associates with Annas and Caiphas, who persecuted the spirit of Christ and his elect—will precede the wars of the *magnus Antichristus,* in which the carnal church, almost like another synagogue, will finally be destroyed and the elect purged *ad plenum*.[111]

If we juxtapose Olivi's remarks on the Matthean apocalyptic discourse with the ones on the Lucan version, it is clear that the apocalyptic drama as envisaged by Olivi in the Matthew commentary does *not* change all that much in terms of structure or sequence of events in the Luke commentary. What does change is that Olivi has augmented or fleshed out the *dramatis personae.* What was in the Matthew commentary an anonymous temptation is given in the Luke commentary a concrete agent, and a distinction of activities has evolved into a distinction of persons. In terms of grammatical number, Antichrist—capital A—has now become plural; in terms of parts of speech, focus has shifted from verb to subject.

If that much can be accepted for the moment, we are still left with the difficult question of the meaning of that obscure adjective "*mysticus*." Olivi, of course, does not address the issue directly in the Luke commentary. Nonetheless, I think his language, while not transparent, is not absolutely cryptic either. The first thing to be said is that it is not clear that Olivi is thinking only, or even primarily, about a spiritual sense of scripture in using the adjective "*mysticus*." That is in part because Olivi does not unambiguously or consistently specify that, in speaking of the mystical Antichrist, he is thinking *mistice,* though in one of his remarks he indicates that he is interpreting *spiritualiter.* Perhaps a not unreasonable suggestion is that Olivi is thinking about a person to whose *identity* and *character* the elect will remain dangerously oblivious. The first, preliminary Antichrist, that is, is *mystical* because of the difficulty, almost the impossibility, of *recognizing* or *identifying* him as evil rather than as good. This theory seems to be strengthened somewhat when we consider Olivi's references to the *blinding* of the elect in the first temptation, to the cunning (*multa astutia*) of the mystical Antichrist, and to the activity of *deception* undertaken by his minions, whom Olivi pointedly designates *pseudo*-scribes and *pseudo*-priests. In other words the significance of the adjective 'mystical' is that it defines a particularly treacherous kind of tempter, one whose true identity will be cloaked, as Olivi implies by the repeated analogies to Caiaphas and by other language, by impressive priestly and magisterial credentials and authority. Thus, "mystical" seems to refer less to a particular layer of scriptural meaning than to a particular sort of tempter and temptation.

In the early Matthew commentary, then, Olivi nowhere makes explicit mention of a double-Antichrist. By the time he wrote the Luke commentary, however, he alluded to the idea often. Commenting on the narrative early in Luke where Jesus is "lost" for three days and found teaching in the temple, Olivi finds himself wondering why Jesus is found after an absence of "three days" (Lk. 2:46). The most popular Latin interpretation of this verse can be traced back at least to Ambrose, who argued that the length of the absence prefigured the time that Jesus would spend in the grave, presumed by everyone to be dead:

> He is found in the temple after three days as a sign that, after three days of victorious suffering . . . he who was believed to be dead should rise.[112]

Olivi himself discusses some of the traditional interpretations of the text before commenting that Jesus' absence for three days is a type of "the three years in which the Antichrist, not only mystical but open (*expressus*) will rule violently, so that the true Christ and God will seem to be absent from his church."[113] That is, Christ's absence from home is taken as a type of his apparent absence from his church at the time of the persecution by the Antichrist. Again, in his interpretation of the Good Samaritan (Lk. 10:30–37), Olivi finds himself interpreting the meaning of Jericho, the land in which the innocent man is beaten. Jericho, Olivi tells us, is a land of cupidity (*terrena cupiditatis*), which, around the time of the imminent advent of Elijah, "will be horribly rebuilt by the Antichrist—not only the mystical but the open."[114] In what is quite possibly his most unusual typological interpretation of the commentaries, Olivi sees in the polarity of Martha and Mary a prophecy of the opposition of the church occupied with temporal things and the church of evangelical poverty and in the complaint of Martha against Mary a type of the litigious character of the Mystical Antichrist.[115]

So much for Olivi's interpretations. What can we make of them, especially in relation to the Apocalypse commentary? The basic two-stage structure of dual temptations and of a tandem of tempters was securely in place by the time Olivi wrote his Apocalypse commentary, and this is a conception he certainly worked out, in part, in the course of his career as a commentator on the gospels. Still, the details *not* included in the Matthew and Luke commentaries are quite significant. In talking about the dual Antichrist, Olivi makes no reference, for example, to the activities of a pseudopope, nor to an apostate from the highest *religio,* nor does Olivi provide us with any chronological thoughts about the arrival of the mystical or great Antichrists, not even of the highly provisional sort we see in the Apocalypse commentary. His remarks on the double Antichrist are much less highly developed than in the later Apocalypse commentary. Second, Olivi nowhere implies in the Matthew or Luke commentary that the Antichrist will be an apostate "from the highest *religio*"—that is, a Franciscan. Nor does he talk about the persecution of the double Antichrist as involving the working in concert of a pope and king. His remarks in the later Apocalypse commentary are themselves cautious and provisional, but in the gospel commentaries they are almost cryptic. Nonetheless, the roots of the later system can be seen here in nuclear form.

The Passion of Christ and the Passion of the Church: Matthew 26 and 27

One of Olivi's most interesting historicizing uses of the principle of head-and-members occurs in his interpretation of the passion of Christ in Matthew 26 and 27. Olivi's typological interpretation of the passion is significant because it is one of the few instances in the commentary in which Olivi's historicizing interpretation is rendered in relation to large parts of the Gospel of Matthew, in this case two chapters. Olivi notes that over the course of these two chapters in Matthew, Jesus is betrayed and tormented in seven places by a variety of Jewish and Roman leaders (Annas, Caiphas, Herod, and Pilate) and one disciple (Judas). Again, there is a

deeper prophetic meaning to the narrative. Olivi regards the whole episode as a type of the sufferings of the church over the course of seven periods of church history:

> Observe how marvelously in the passion of our head, the passion of
> the entire church is allegorically exemplified. According to the seven
> openings of the seven seals, the church is to be battered about in seven
> spiritual wars. But in the sixth and seventh the image of Christ should
> be crucified, as the signs of the cross in Francis manifestly stretch
> forth. Thus all the humiliation and insults borne by Christ signify the
> various types of insults borne and to be borne by the entire church and
> its members over its whole career.[116]

Olivi proceeds to describe the meaning of each of Christ's seven sufferings
in relation to those of the church over the course of its history. Throughout his gospel commentaries, Olivi would interpret many of the sufferings of Christ as prophecies of the tribulations and temptations of his
mystical body.

Resurrection

Olivi's pessimism regarding ecclesiastical leadership is also reflected in one
of the more curious and daring passages in the gospel commentaries. At
the end of the Matthew commentary, Olivi finds himself trying to decide
what happened to those who rose out of their tombs after Christ's resurrection (Mt. 27:52–53). Jerome had asserted that these had first ascended
with Christ to heaven.[117] Olivi finds himself in agreement with this theory
but then proceeds to tell us that it is believed by "certain not unlearned
persons" (perhaps an oblique reference to Olivi himself) that there would
be two partial and exemplary resurrections before the general one. The
first occurred after the crucifixion of Christ. The second would occur "after
the crucifixion of his life and rule by the leaders of the heretical church,
or rather synagogue, which spiritually is called Sodom or Egypt."[118] The
crucifixion of "his life and rule" is, of course, a reference to the contemporary persecution of the Franciscan Order, and this text furnishes us with
further evidence that as early as the Matthew commentary Olivi was afraid
that carnal corruption would infect the leadership of the church (*a principalibus erronee ecclesie*). Olivi then goes on to explain the nature of the
second "partial and exemplary" resurrection:

I have heard that it has been revealed by a very holy man that this will be fulfilled in the angel of the sixth seal with certain of his confreres, so that he conform to Christ in his resurrection as in his passion; and so that the disciples of that time, nearly led into error, would have an instructor and comforter as the apostles had in the risen Christ.[119]

Olivi hastens to add that he leaves such matters "to divine judgment and counsel."[120] However, this reservation did not prevent him from repeating the thought, slightly modified, in his Apocalypse commentary (where he again proposes it without temerity of assertion). The 1318 commission gathered to examine Olivi's Apocalypse commentary showed little appreciation for Olivi's caution here and simply denounced this opinion as "a fantastic fiction unworthy to be written or told."[121]

THE END OF PERSECUTION AND THE *STATUS* TO COME

Miraculous Feeding of the 5,000 (Mt. 14:13–21)

In places throughout the commentary, Olivi holds out to those who have gone the way of the cross the prospect of an age of sabbatical peace and contemplation, in which the faithful will enjoy an affective experience of the faith and a deep understanding of the scriptures. Consider, for a second example, his interpretation of the Miraculous Feeding of the 5,000 (Mt. 14:13–21). No later than Hilary of Poitiers, the pericope was interpreted as an allegory of the multiplication of the letter of the Law (the five loaves being equated with the five books of the Pentateuch) into the heavenly food of the spiritual senses.[122] In his Matthew commentary, Olivi establishes a *concordia* between this multiplication of senses and the one which is to occur in the future contemplative age:

> Note for the mysteries that just as in the evening the five loaves and two fishes were broken and multiplied by Christ, so in the end of the synagogue Christ appeared and multiplied the five books of Moses, that is the Law, and two fishes, that is the prophetic and historical books (which were the spice of the Law) in the mystical senses; and it is believed that something similar is to happen at the end of the church with respect to both Testaments.[123]

Such texts seem to underline the discontinuity between the current age of carnal corruption and the future age of spiritual contemplation.[124] As was the case with Joachim, Olivi's language is probably more incautious than his actual intention. Olivi tells us relatively little in the gospel commentaries about the future age he envisages, though texts like the ones above do suggest a real novelty in the understanding and experience of the faith, even if one would hesitate to suggest a radical discontinuity. On ecclesiastical institutions, he is virtually silent. In any case, it is texts such as these which put him in bad odor with the investigating authorities in the fourteenth century.

Miraculous Feeding of the 4,000 (Mt. 15:32–39) and the Status of the Holy Spirit

On several occasions in the commentaries, Olivi describes the age to come in terms which suggest Joachim's third *status* under the aegis of the Holy Spirit. In his interpretation of the Miraculous Feeding of the 4,000 (Mt. 15:32–39), Olivi finds himself struggling with the verse which states that the crowds had been with Jesus "for three days" (15:32). What is the meaning of this three-day period and why were the crowds fed on the third day? Olivi suggests that, mystically, the triduum might signify the threefold time of nature, scripture, and grace. He then offers a second possibility:

> Or by the triduum is signified the time of the twofold letter, namely, of the Old and New Testament or of the Jews and gentiles. The third, however, will be a time of spiritual concord and understanding, in which the gifts of the Spirit will be poured out. . . .[125]

This exegesis certainly suggests the three-*status* pattern pioneered by Joachim. However, as is the case in the rest of the Matthew commentary, the pattern is only suggested here, not explicitly stated.[126] But there can be no doubt that Olivi borrowed the idea of a coming age of *intelligentia spiritualis* and more perfect state of the church from Joachim, even if he does not explicitly call it the *status* of the Holy Spirit here. Nor can there be any doubt that he borrowed from Joachim the notion that prophecies of that age could be found in the spiritual sense of the gospel. Indeed, he alone among his mendicant contemporaries would follow the Calabrian abbot in this.

The Triumphal Entry (Mt. 21:1–17) and "The End of the Ecclesiastical Age"

In his commentary on the Triumphal Entry (Mt. 21:1–17), Olivi finds himself asking why Christ wished to enter Jerusalem this time with such glory. He responds by asserting that it was so that a "notable clarification of his person, faith, and doctrine" would occur before his death.[127] Just as the mysteries of the faith were illuminated at the end of the Old Testament period, so would they be even more clearly revealed at the end of the New Testament period:

> There is always a solemn clarification of the truth at the end. Thus, just as the final end of the synagogue introduced the clarity of the New Testament, and the final end of the world introduces the clear vision of God, and the end of the church at the time of Antichrist introduces the clear contemplation of the faith, so it was fitting that the fruit of the teaching of Christ might more clearly shine at his end.[128]

Like Joachim, Olivi could be incautious about how he described the transition from the age of persecution to the age of contemplation. Here he describes it as the "end of the church," and he implies that the new age would be related to the first five ages of church history as the church was to the synagogue. As we shall see in our conclusion, it was precisely this suggestion which the 1318 commission assembled to investigate the Apocalypse commentary found so objectionable. It was not the only time in the commentary Olivi would make such a suggestion.

Conclusion

Olivi's gospel commentaries were influenced by exegetical assumptions and methods of exegesis, if not actual interpretations of texts, found in Joachim's *Tractatus super Quatuor Evangelia*. The most important assumption Olivi took from the *Tractatus* was that the gospels, as well as the Apocalypse, were texts capable of revealing the fullness of the divine plan for humanity and therefore ought to be interpreted typologically. He also followed Joachim closely in the latter's tendency to read the gospels in terms of the meaning of the Apocalypse and found that the revelation given mystically in the former was identical to that given literally in the latter. In a few instances, Olivi was also directly influenced by the *Trac-*

tatus's apocalyptic reading of certain texts, such as the Adoration of the Magi. From the wider body of Joachim's thought, Olivi borrowed and modified the notion that the sixth age heralded a new more perfect form of the religious life and a new spiritual understanding of scripture and the idea that these developments were prophesied in the text of the gospels. He also borrowed and modified the idea that the text of the gospels was capable of revealing the fullness of Old Testament history as well as that of the New and found "concords" of the two histories inscribed in various parts of the gospel. Like Joachim, Olivi would often historicize gospel texts given a historical reading by the fathers, but with peculiarly Joachimist and Franciscan content without precedent in the patristic commentaries.

Finally, Olivi's gospel commentaries differed from the *Tractatus* in a number of significant ways as well. Olivi was usually careful to insist that his prophetic readings of the gospel were given only in the spiritual or allegorical sense of the text, while Joachim insists that they are given in the "typical sense" of the text. Secondly, Olivi's prophetic readings constitute a slim fraction of the gospel commentaries, while they occupy virtually all of the *Tractatus*. Olivi was certainly very interested in them, but he was also interested in communicating inherited opinion on the gospel in a way and to a degree that Joachim was not.[129] Third, the three-*status* scheme of world history is much less in evidence in the early Matthew commentary than it is in the *Tractatus*. There is one brief allusion to it in Olivi's interpretation of the Transfiguration, and even this is not an unambiguous reference to the Trinitarian scheme of salvation history. Olivi does, however, invoke it more frequently and explicitly in the later gospel commentaries. Finally, Olivi always modifies the prophecies and historical schemes inherited from Joachim to include the decisive role played by Francis and his order in the unfolding of salvation history.

In the previous chapter, we saw that Olivi perceived in parts of the gospels a prophecy of the renewal of evangelical poverty in the fifth and sixth *tempora ecclesie*. In similar fashion he saw in the gospels a prophecy of the persecution to be suffered by the order in those ages, as well as prophecies of the age of sabbatical peace and contemplation. In both cases, Olivi furnishes us with a form of exegesis which distinguishes his commentary from those of his mendicant predecessors. None of the contemporaries we have examined was prepared to read the gospel typologically in so systematic or pervasive a fashion as Olivi. None would allow the abbot's *Tractatus* to influence his commentary in any way at all. Olivi's contemporaries would allow their social context to influence their exegesis of the gospels, but none would see both the champions of evangelical poverty and its detractors in terms of an apocalyptic program which was given allegorically in the gospels. Only Olivi would. It is this typological exegesis of the gospels which most sharply distinguishes his commentaries from any contemporary *postilla* and which makes them some of the most original exegetical efforts of the thirteenth century.

CHAPTER EIGHT

Papal Condemnation and Possible Consequences

A s noted in the introduction to this book, when Pope John XXII launched his campaign against the Spirituals, he also ordered an investigation of Olivi's Apocalypse commentary.[1] As we have already observed, this campaign resulted, finally, in the condemnation of Olivi's Matthew commentary in 1326.

Did this condemnation have a chilling effect on exegesis of the Gospel of Matthew for the remainder of the fourteenth century and, in particular, on Nicholas of Lyra? Given the evidence we have, it is difficult to answer that question. However, as we shall see when we examine his commentary on Matthew, Lyra certainly repudiated the Franciscanizing and Joachite options in favor of the non-particularizing, scholastic approach so popular in the first half of the thirteenth century. This may have been caused by the papal condemnation. On the other hand, it may merely have coincided with it.

THE CONDEMNATION PROCESS

The process against the commentary began when John appointed the Dominican cardinal Nicholas of Prato to handle the investigation. Nicholas in turn put together a list of doubtful propositions from the commentary and gave them to a single theologian to review. He then gave them to a commission of eight theologians. Since the report of this eight-man commission survives in the form of sixty articles, we are able to tell what they thought of the Apocalypse commentary.[2]

Twenty-two of the sixty articles center upon Olivi's comments regarding the "carnal church." Unfortunately for Olivi, the commission tended to identify the carnal church with "the Roman Church" or "the Catholic Church," and this distortion, whether intentional or not, was very damaging to Olivi's cause. Fifteen articles focus upon Olivi's comments regarding the superiority of the sixth and seventh periods of church history over the first five. In some of these articles, Olivi is attacked for suggesting that the spiritual men of the sixth and seventh periods will experience knowledge and virtue superior to that of the apostles. Others censured him for suggesting that the last two periods were related to the first five as the church was to the synagogue. In other articles, Olivi is censured for elevating Francis to a rank just behind Christ and his mother and for suggesting an exaggerated role for Francis and his order in church history.

Some four years after this commission completed its work, Pope John extracted four articles from the *Lectura super Apocalypsim* and submitted them to at least two, and probably three, scholars for analysis. One of these four articles dealt with the new experience of faith in the third *status*, when knowledge of the incarnate word will be known not by simple understanding but by "taste and touch." Another dealt with the idea that Francis is the revealer of the apostolic life in the sixth and seventh periods and its greatest observer after Christ and his mother.

Not surprisingly, those entrusted with the investigation of the Apocalypse commentary showed little appreciation for these ideas. None of the investigating theologians would accept the notion that the future state could be one which would surpass that of the apostles in virtue and knowledge. The commission of eight failed to see how the church guided by Christ could slide into the decay Olivi describes as characteristic of the fifth period of church history.[3] The second group of theologians consulted thought it blasphemous to place Francis before the apostles, and the commission of eight rejected the claim that the Franciscan rule is the same as the evangelical life observed by Christ. The commission of eight was also notably unenthusiastic about Olivi's contention that the Franciscans were different from other orders in piety or historical mission. As already noted, the commission of eight also dismissed the legend of Francis's resurrection as a "false and fantastic fiction" that Olivi might better have kept to himself. Olivi's prophecies concerning the eschatological conversion of the Jews, Moslems, and pagans the first commission dismissed as lacking scriptural or rational authority. In short, the investigating theologians found the Apocalypse commentary to be filled with erroneous, temerarious, and fantastic opinions worthy of denunciation. Once Pope John had secured the decisions of these theologians, he did indeed condemn the Apocalypse commentary on February 8, 1326.

For our purposes, the outcome of the investigation against the Apocalypse commentary is particularly relevant. Upon further reflection, it seems clear that the same charges which resulted in the condemnation of the Apocalypse commentary could have been brought against the earlier gospel commentaries. Indeed, we have evidence that one member of the second group of theologians consulted discovered the same errors in the Matthew commentary that he found in the Apocalypse commentary. In a document which has come to be known as the *Allegationes,* an anonymous member of the investigating team bolsters his case against the Apocalypse commentary by referring to several texts of the Matthew commentary, as well as to other Olivian works. The author of this work is responding to an anonymous attempt to furnish Olivi's words concerning the superiority of Francis and his rule and his criticism of the carnal church in the Apocalypse commentary with an *interpretatio benigna.* The commission member responds by arguing that Olivi meant what he appears to say in the Apocalypse commentary because he says the same things in his Matthew commentary.[4]

If the author of the *Allegationes* found the same errors in the Matthew commentary, why did the Matthew commentary not suffer the same fate as the Apocalypse commentary? There is no easy answer to this question. However, there is at least some evidence that the Matthew commentary was indeed condemned by Pope John. The author of the *Allegationes* begins his document against Olivi by announcing that he will put forth reasons for condemning "the aforesaid *postilla* [i.e., the Apocalypse commentary] *and other books of Peter of John.*"⁵ There is no *contemporary* evidence which suggests that the Franciscan Order or Pope John followed the author's advice.

There is, however, evidence from a source that comes to us from more than five decades after John's decision which does suggest precisely this result. In his *Directorium Inquisitionis,* the Dominican inquisitor Nicolas Eymerich informs us that John XXII condemned the Apocalypse commentary. Interestingly, he goes on to add the following remark:

> He also condemned the postil on Matthew of the same brother Peter of John, and also his postil on the canonical epistles, in which books, as in the postil on the Apocalypse, there are some very similar heresies.⁶

It is difficult ultimately to know what to do with this source. On the one hand, the fact that it is not a contemporary witness detracts from its historical value. However, we know from the author of the *Allegationes* that many of Olivi's books and many other treatises were analyzed in connection with the process against the Apocalypse commentary and that it was recommended that some of these be condemned. It is certainly possible that Nicolas accurately recorded which ones in fact were censured. In any case, if the Matthew commentary was condemned, Nicolas is sure that it was because it contains *haereses aliquae consimiles*. In Nicolas's eyes, the same errors which condemned the Apocalypse commentary doomed the Matthew commentary.

Did the Condemnation Affect Nicholas of Lyra on Matthew?

Nicholas of Lyra was the most prolific and influential biblical exegete of the late Middle Ages and, it has been argued, the greatest biblical commentator since Jerome. His reputation was securely established with the production of his *Postilla Literalis* on the Bible, a running commentary on both Testaments. Nicholas of Lyra (ca. 1270–1349) took the Franciscan habit at the house of Verneuil 1300 and later studied theology in Paris. By 1309 he had become regent master in theology at Paris. Ten years later, he was elected minister of province of Paris. In 1322, he began *Literal Postill on the Whole Bible,* which he presented, not insignificantly, to Pope John XXII in 1331.

The *Postilla* was the first biblical commentary to be printed.[7] In some printed editions, his commentaries are accompanied by the *Additiones* of Paul of Burgos (d. 1435) and the *Replicae* of Matthew Doering (d. 1469). In 1339, Lyra completed his *Postilla Moralis* (which was often printed with the *Postilla Literalis*), a shorter commentary which emphasized the moral and mystical meanings of the text and was intended as a practical handbook for preachers and teachers.

Unlike most contemporary Christian exegetes, Lyra was able to read at least some Hebrew, and he knew the Talmud, the Midrash, and the works of the medieval Jewish exegete Rashi (d. 1105), who influenced him deeply. He also had read the Jewish philosopher Maimonides. Nonetheless, Lyra engaged in Jewish-Christian polemic and wrote two tracts in which he criticized Jewish practice and belief. In addition to his exegetical and polemical writings, Lyra also wrote nearly 300 sermons, a commentary on the *Sentences* of Peter Lombard, and a number of other minor works on the eucharist, the beatific vision, and Franciscan poverty.

His great hermeneutical innovation was his teaching on the "double literal sense" (*duplex sensus literalis*), which held that citations from the Hebrew scriptures found in the New Testament had two literal meanings. The first and more perfect meaning referred to Christ, the second and less perfect to pre-Christian history.

Lyra's influence was enormous. Over 200 manuscripts of his *Postilla Literalis* exist. Since the late fifteenth century, it has been printed 176 times. It ranks, along with the *Glossa Ordinaria* and the *Sentences* of Peter Lombard, as one of the most influential theological works of the Middle Ages.[8] But, in many ways, he was far from the most original.

Lyra's Prologues to the Matthew Commentary

Lyra begins his commentary on Matthew by writing three prologues or short prefatory commentaries, one each on the vision from Ezekiel, the prologue to Jerome's gospel, and the prologue to the *Gloss's* commentary on Matthew. In each of these, he deals with the issues raised by Augustine, Jerome, and Gregory. He also depends heavily upon them for his own positions, often explicitly quoting them. Indeed, there is no subsequent part of his commentary that is more indebted to the opinions of the fathers.

After considering the gospels in terms of four Aristotelian causes,[9] Lyra turns to the questions of order, date, place of origin, and christological tendency. Not surprisingly, Lyra accepts the dominant Augustinian hypothesis that the gospels were written in the order in which they appear in the canon.[10] He also describes the principal christological tendency of each of the gospels in terms of Ezekiel's vision of four creatures. Matthew, he says, principally has to do with the humanity of Christ, John with his divinity, Luke his priesthood, and Mark his kingdom.[11] The idea that Matthew is primarily interested in the humanity of Christ is repeated several times throughout Lyra's prologues,[12] though Lyra also agrees with Jerome that Matthew's "principal intention" was to show that Christ was true man *and* true God.[13] Lyra also accepts the ancient position that Matthew was written in Judea and in Hebrew.[14] Like many of his contemporaries, Lyra was also convinced that Matthew wrote to combat early christological heresies.[15] In short, there is very little, if anything, that is novel in Lyra's prologues. His positions on the date, order, and character of the gospels all have their roots in the opinions of the fathers. Here, as throughout his commentary on Matthew, Lyra represents the established consensus of scholarly opinion and shows little inclination for exegetical novelty.

Like his contemporaries, Lyra attempts in his prologue (and at the beginning of each of the twenty-eight chapters) to explain the overall structure of the Gospel of Matthew. When we collate the remarks he makes in the prologue with those made at the beginning of each chapter, we can reproduce how Lyra would have seen the structure of Matthew.

LYRA'S OUTLINE OF THE GOSPEL OF MATTHEW

I. Part One (Mtt. 1:1–4:11). Christ Is Shown To Be Truly God and Truly Human

    A. True Humanity and True Divinity are Shown by Angelic and Prophetic Testimony (1:1–25)

        1. Genealogy (1:1–17)

        2. Conception (1:18–25)

B. True Humanity and True Divinity Are Shown by Heavenly Illustration and Regal Veneration (2:1–23)
1. Manifestation (2:1–12)
2. Persecution (2:13–23)
C. True Humanity and True Divinity Are Shown by Testimony of
John and God the Father (3:1–17)
1. Testimony of John (3:1–15)
2. Testimony of God the Father (3:16–17)
D. True Humanity and True Divinity Are Shown by Temptation
and Angelic Veneration
1. Temptation (4:1–10)
2. Angelic Veneration (4:11)

II. Part Two (Mtt. 4:12–28:20). The Redemption Accomplished
through Christ
A. The Giving of the Law (4:12–9:38)
1. Explication of the Law (4:12–7:29)
2. Confirmation of the Law through Miracles (8:1–9:38)
B. Promulgation of the Law (10:1–23:39)
1. Promulgation of the Law to the Jews (10:1–14:36)
a. Instruction of the Apostles (10:1–42)
b. Confirmation of Doubters (11:1–30)
c. Confutation of Detractors/Pharisees (12:1–50)
d. Parabolic Promulgation of the Law (13:1–58)
e. Confirmation of Promulgation of Law (14:1–36)
f. Christ Reproves Errors of the Jews (15:1–39)
2. Promulgation of the Law to the Gentiles (15:1–23:46)
g. Foundation of the Church of Gentiles (16:1–28)
h. Confirmation of Foundation (17:1–27)
i. Christ Teaches Virtues of Active Life (18:1–35)
j. Virtues of Contemplative/Religious Life (19:1–30)
k. Christ Teaches the Virtues of Prelates (20:1–34)
l. Reproval of the Synagogue of the Jews (21:1–23:39)
C. Judgment According to the Law of Christ (24:1–25:46)
1. Things Preceding the Judgment (24:1–51)
2. The Judgment (25:1–46)
D. The Passion, Death, and Burial of the Mediator (26:1–27:66)
1. Christ Seized for Interrogation by the Jews (26:1–75)
2. Condemnation by Execution by the Gentiles (27:1–66)

E. The Resurrection (27:1–28:20)
1. Manifestation of the Resurrection (28:1–15)
2. Publication of the Resurrection (28:15–20)

The conservatism of Lyra so evident here also appears in his actual interpretation of the gospel, to which we shall now turn.

"Peter's House" (Mt. 8:14)

One of the most difficult texts for Franciscan controversialists to deal with, as we have seen, was Matthew 8:14, which implies quite unambiguously, it seems, that Peter owned a house: *Et cum venisset Iesus in domum Petri, vidit socrum eius iacentem et febricitantem.*

In his extremely brief comments on the disputed verse, Lyra aligns himself with his non-controversial mendicant predecessors: he refuses to acknowledge that the apostolic ownership of property is even an issue in the interpretation of the text. In his *Postilla Moralis,* Lyra remarks that Peter's mother-in-law signifies sensuality that is cured by reason, represented by Christ.[16] In his *Postilla Literalis,* Lyra makes just one remark on the verse where Christ is said to have entered "the house of Peter":

> Our savior, because he had assumed a passible body for our salvation, occasionally would decline to the places of those familiar and devoted to him in order to have quiet after his labors: and in this way he came to the house of Peter.[17]

Few parts of Lyra's Matthew commentary illustrate more clearly how anxious Lyra was to avoid controversy in his gospel commentaries. So unconcerned is he with the problematic implications of the verse for Franciscans that he actually *repeats* the disputed words ("the house of Peter") in his own analysis. Not only does he not attempt to deny that Peter owned the house; he does not even acknowledge Peter's dominion as an issue requiring reflection, explanation, or defense. Again, his commentary represents a decisive rejection of the Franciscanizing form of exegesis found in Olivi and a return to the non-particularizing, dominant Parisian tradition of Hugh, Alexander, Thomas, and others.

The Temptation (Mt. 4:1–11)

Lyra's interpretation of the Temptation owes nothing whatsoever to the Joachite-Olivian reading and much to the dominant Parisian interpretation. It differs only in two ways. First, Lyra's interpretation is drastically shorter than that of contemporaries. Second, he declares that the purpose of the narrative was to demonstrate both the true humanity and the true divinity of Christ. Curiously, while never explicitly doubting the literal veracity of the narrative, Lyra does say that the *evangelist's* intention here was to demonstrate the truth of his humanity and divinity,[18] causing one to wonder whether Lyra meant that the narrative was authorially constructed, or absolutely literal, or something in between. In any case, like most of his predecessors, Lyra connects Jesus' fasting with that of Moses and Elijah,[19] and he distinguishes each of the temptations: the first was to lure Christ into carnal concupiscence, the second into pride or vainglory, and the third into concupiscence of the eyes.[20] Like his predecessors, Lyra also underlines the moral implications of the narrative: Christ shows us that "anyone who begins a new life, ought to offer himself to God through fasting and prayer."[21]

Once again, Lyra rejects the apocalyptic interpretation of Joachim and Olivi for the simple literal-historical and moral sense of the text. And again, his contribution was a concise summary of the dominant, non-particularizing Parisian tradition. The same can be said about his interpretation of the parables, even those which had been historicized in the tradition.

The Wedding Banquet (Mt. 22:1–14)

Like the representatives of the mainstream Parisian tradition, Lyra historicizes the parable. But he does not read the parable as a type or prophecy of the persecution of the Franciscans, as does Olivi. Like the majority tradition, Lyra identifies the invited guests as Jews given the Law, in which is found the promise of the incarnation of Christ.[22] The first group of servants represent the prophets sent to call them and to announce to them the things concerning Christ which were more obscurely put in the law; they exhort the people to expect the advent of Christ.[23] The invited guests' refusal to come to the banquet represents the Jews' rejection of the words of the prophets.[24] The second group of servants represent those who near the birth of Christ announced his advent, like John the Baptist and the disciples.[25] The meal that has been prepared is a symbol of the sacraments and teaching of the church, especially the sacrament of the eucharist.[26] The second refusal represents the Jews' rejection of the preaching of Christ and the apostles.[27] "The cause of this," Lyra declares, "was cupidity for temporal things" and worldly occupations impeding concern for the divine.[28] Though this remark seems to have a Franciscan edge to it, it too had deep roots in the tradition,[29] and it is clearly implied in the literal sense of the text. The killing and stoning of the servants represents the persecution of John the Baptist, James, Stephen, the other disciples of Christ, and even many prophets in the Old Testament.[30] The destruction of the city by the king represents the devastation by divine ordination of Jerusalem by the armies of Titus and Vespasian.[31] The final invitation to *quoscumque inveneritis* (Mt. 22:9) represents the calling of the gentiles after the rejection of the preaching of the apostles by the Jews,[32] and the filling of the wedding hall, the universal diffusion of the Catholic faith.[33]

Lyra's interpretation of the parable of the Wedding Feast again illustrates a number of principles of his exegesis. First of all, he is willing to historicize parts of the gospel, but he is willing to do so only where the dominant tradition has done so. Second, he refuses to historicize the gospel in the way that Joachim and Olivi do. He does not see this parable, for example, as a prophecy of events in the thirteenth or fourteenth centuries. Finally, he does not read the parable in terms of distinctively Franciscan values. Again, he avoids the controversial interpretations so characteristic of Olivi and allies himself with the majority, non-controversial Parisian tradition.

The Laborers in the Vineyard (Mt. 20:1–16)

The same sort of conservatism appears in Lyra's exegesis of another parable historicized by the tradition, the Laborers in the Vineyard. Lyra historicizes the parable as well, but along the lines established by Origen. The first call represents the course of the world from the time of Noah to Abraham; the second from Abraham to Moses; the third from Moses to Christ; and the last from the time of Christ until the end of the world—the time during which the gentiles were called through the preaching of the apostles and doctors.[34] Like most exegetes in the mainstream tradition, he identifies the murmurers as Jews complaining about grace being offered to the gentiles.[35] Again, he refuses to historicize the parable in Joachite or Franciscan terms. The historical reference of the parable has nothing to do with modern Franciscan controversy. The conflicts it describes are ones safely buried in the remote past.

Lyra's commentary on Matthew is a highly traditional and conservative effort, one whose similarities with the non-particularizing Parisian tradition are far more numerous than the differences. There is virtually no hint in his commentary that he is writing as a Friar Minor. Where the commentaries of Bonaventure, Pecham, and Olivi are littered with references to Francis and his rule, Lyra refers to the Franciscan rule only once. Moreover, he refers in the same sentence to the rules of Augustine and Benedict and he makes no distinctions of value among them. All, he says, are founded "on the perfection of charity."[36] This is a gospel commentary almost completely stripped of explicitly Franciscan language and values. It is also completely devoid of Joachite presuppositions and interest. Where Lyra historicizes the gospel, he does so in conformity with long tradition and without polemical references, even implicit subterranean ones.

Conclusion

Did Lyra's exegesis assume these characteristics because of the papal condemnation of Olivi? The evidence here, unfortunately, is virtually nonexistent. We can only know that Lyra was certainly aware of the papal condemnation, as well as that of Olivi at Marseilles in 1319. The difficulty is that we have no way of knowing whether Nicholas shied away from apocalyptic speculation or from celebrating his order in his Matthew commentary because of the hardened attitude of the papacy toward the Franciscans. Speaking of interpreters of the Apocalypse after the condemnation of Olivi, David Burr has observed: "None gives the Franciscan order the sort of apocalyptic role celebrated by Olivi. It is one thing to note these differences and quite another to say that they were a result of the Olivi process . . . there is little point in suggesting that the condemnation caused exegetes to eschew positions they never would have held anyway."[37] The same remark might be made about Franciscan interpreters of Matthew after the condemnation. The most we can say from this vantage point is that the condemnations and the de-Franciscanizing of the gospel occurred simultaneously. Whether the connection was co-incidental or causal is impossible to say. What is not in doubt is that, with Nicholas, the Joachizing and Franciscanizing of Matthew abruptly discontinues.

Conclusion

The Gospel De-Franciscanized

𝒯 he four gospels were not high on the agenda of exegetes for much of the early Middle Ages. It is only with the turn of the twelfth century that we see the gospels begin to receive serious, widespread, and sustained commentarial attention. That this intellectual development more or less coincided with the renewed interest in the eleventh and twelfth centuries in the "apostolic life" as portrayed in the gospels is almost certainly no accident. Nor does it seem accidental that most of the distinguished and influential commentators of the High Middle Ages were members of orders whose conscious aim was to reproduce in their own ways of life the primordial apostolic experience and religious passion they perceived represented in the gospels and in the ancient writings on them.

The earliest commentators we have examined in this study so revered the ancient commentarial tradition that, as we have seen, they stitched their own commentaries together with patches of excerpts from the patristic tradition. It was difficult for them to think of the gospels except *in sensu patrum*—in the sense of the fathers. Their scholarship was a work of compilation, not innovation. As a consequence, early twelfth-century commentaries on Matthew—above all the *Gloss*—were, by and large, syntheses of venerable authorities. Early medieval commentaries on Matthew were, for the most part, traditionalist and conservative in nature. Rarely does one encounter personal opinion, much less criticism, on the received wisdom of the fathers. The *Gloss*, we recall, was meant to be "ordered" well. The test of a good commentary was whether it accurately conveyed the "sense of the Fathers" on the verses in question. In this sense, "commentary" is something of a misnomer when applied to a project such as the *Gloss*. The *Gloss* has some features of a commentary. It was meant to be an explanatory treatise. But it was not written so much as compiled, and its producers were learned scholars rather than brilliant, innovative thinkers.

If such efforts were not meant to reflect individual opinion, even less were they intended to reflect ecclesiastical dispute or conflict. Commentators surely believed Matthew had contemporary application, but they were careful to keep that application general and somewhat imprecise. Few if any commentators viewed the genre as a vehicle intended for the expression of personal grievances, dissent, or alienation; fewer still intended their commentaries as thoroughgoing critiques of the contemporary church. Again, social context is relevant here. These commentators were produced in what was, by and large, a quieter ecclesial world— certainly a different ecclesial world—than those composed in the thirteenth century, which can be considered, from one point of view, as a century of intra-religious conflict. If in the thirteenth century, some commentators, like Olivi, felt that the barbarians had breached the gates, twelfth-century predecessors felt, by and large, that the enemies of the church were outside the church. It is not surprising that signs of conflict shine through some thirteenth-century commentaries. In the twelfth century, commentaries were somewhat colorless, and they were intended to be so.

That is not to say they were static. As we saw in our examination of the *Enarrationes in Evangelium Sancti Matthaei*, commentaries in the twelfth century *did* in fact reflect certain changes in the life of the church. For the most part, however, these were intellectual and theological changes. Above all, we see in the *Enarrationes* the beginning of the scholasticizing of the gospel commentary, first in Laon, then in Paris. This commentary is fit within a new scholastic framework, includes new technical terms, and introduces the theological *quaestio*. This is a development of some moment. It marks the beginning of the kind of commentary that would dominate professional exegesis for more than three centuries.

As we move into the early thirteenth century, and as the friars begin to dominate the universities and convents of Europe, we begin to perceive new changes. If it is true that, for the most part, commentators are still somewhat reluctant to let either their personality or contemporary church politics shine through their work, we do occasionally—rarely by later thirteenth-century standards and especially by the standards of Olivi's Matthew commentary—glimpse a new concern with thirteenth-century realities such as public preaching, pastoral care, and contemplation. Nonetheless, there is little that is daring or adventuresome in most of these remarks. Even the critical observations are relatively benign. There is little if anything eschatological, still less bitterly critical of the institutional church, and nothing that could draw the attention, much less the ire, of the papacy or even a provincial minister or commission of theologians. It is instructive to recall that the greatest of exegetes in the decades before Olivi was Hugh of St. Cher. He was made a cardinal.

The great exception to my remarks on the late twelfth and early thirteenth century is Joachim of Fiore. His *Tractatus,* as we have seen, did not circulate terribly widely in his own day or even in the following centuries. It is probably fair to say that it was the least influential of his four major works. Nonetheless, it represented an almost completely novel way of approaching and reading the four gospels. Hardly any contemporary was likely to regard the Gospel of Matthew, for example, as a book whose narratives prefigured both the negative and positive apocalyptic signs of the times in which he was writing. Joachim regarded it *primarily* as such a book. Unlike contemporary commentaries on the gospels, Joachim's *was* replete with eschatological speculation, fear of the imminence of the Antichrist, and bitter denunciation of ecclesiastical failings, as well as hope for the dawning of a new, more perfect contemplative and monastic age. In Joachim's commentaries all sorts of political and ecclesiastical events— the rise of heresy, the resurgence of Islam, the conflict of pope and emperor, and a general corruption within the church—are explicitly noted and deplored. Such a commentary, both hermeneutically and in its contents, was ripe for exploitation, application, and modernization by any who saw him as a prophet and his works as inspired.

In the thirteenth century, there was no shortage of men who so saw him, especially among members of the Franciscan Order. Among such men as Hugh of Digne and the group of learned judges, doctors, notaries, and others, Joachim's books—Salimbene tells us, we recall, that Hugh owned *all* the books of Abbot Joachim—were quite popular. Men like Hugh, John of Parma, and Bonaventure all showed no reluctance in identifying their own order with one of the new orders of spiritual men prophesied by Joachim. Bonaventure was happy to identify Francis as the Angel of Apocalypse 7:2. At the same time, like Joachim, he identifies some major negative apocalyptic developments, and he is notably pessimistic about the powers of the elect to resist temptation. Nonetheless, Bonaventure did not allow his enthusiasm for Joachim or his thought to affect the way in which he interpreted the gospels. Writing under the influence of Hugh of St. Cher, it is often difficult to tell, even with Bonaventure, that a friar is writing. There are signs of great enthusiasm for poverty and for other central Franciscan values, but, at least in his Luke commentary, he never declares that his order or its founder have apocalyptic significance, nor does he regard the abuses he laments as indications of the imminence of the Antichrist. Never does Bonaventure give the impression that Luke should be regarded as a prophetic book or a book replete with apocalyptic content, meaning, and portent.

It is only in Olivi's Matthew commentary (and in his other gospel commentaries) that we see Joachite apocalyptic hermeneutics and thought fully exploited. For Olivi, Matthew was, on the literal and historical level, about the life, teachings, and death of Christ. But on the non-literal plane, the gospel was fraught with signs of apocalyptic developments in his own age. Olivi interprets many literal references to Christ as apocalyptic references to Francis. In many texts, he perceives prophecies of the rise of a new evangelical order—his—and the renewal in it of evangelical poverty and perfection. At the same time, he finds voluminously predicted in Matthew the persecution of this new order. Here Olivi is without doubt thinking of the attacks by the secular masters, the Dominican criticism of the Franciscan claim to absolute poverty, and the debate in his own order over *usus pauper*. He does not hesitate to elevate these events to the apocalyptic plane, nor to identify his adversaries with the Antichrist. Unlike the commentaries written by his Franciscan confreres at the beginning of the thirteenth century, Olivi's, coming as it did after fifty years of intra- and extramural sniping, fully mirrors the conflictual atmosphere of his day, not to mention his own personal vicissitudes. Speaking of the pseudo-Joachite commentary on Jeremiah, David Burr once observed that it relied "so heavily on symbolism from the book of Revelation that it could almost be considered an honorary Apocalypse commentary."[1] The same might be said of Olivi's Matthew commentary. In fact, one helpful way of understanding it is to perceive that the literal sense of Olivi's Apocalypse commentary is more or less identical to, if more detailed than, the spiritual sense of his Matthew commentary.

Olivi's way of interpreting the gospels was to have as little influence as Joachim's. Indeed, it might easily be said, as it can be said of few products of scholastic culture in the thirteenth and fourteenth centuries, that Olivi's gospel commentaries are *sui generis*. By the thirteenth century, most if not all commentaries on the gospels had acquired the characteristics that qualify them to be called "scholastic." A much smaller percentage reflect the distinctive concerns of the writer's order. Before Olivi, none incorporates the hermeneutics or thought of Joachim in their gospel commentaries. By the end of the thirteenth century, then, we have three coexisting currents of style and thought: scholastic structure and rhetoric, Franciscan myth, and Joachite hermeneutics. Some commentators merge those first two currents in their gospel commentaries, but it is only in Olivi that we see the integration of all three elements. In this respect, he has no predecessors.

He would have few, if any successors. If it is fair to say that Olivi's commentaries seem, in retrospect, to be the ones *toward which* thirteenth-century exegetical developments had been leading, and in the fourteenth century, Olivi's gospel commentaries are the kind from which exegesis leads *away*. Exegetes in the fourteenth century tend not to allow current disputes to shape their commentaries, which become less and less particularistic. Of Franciscan commentaries in the early fourteenth century we can say, again, what Beryl Smalley said of Franciscan commentaries written in the early thirteenth century: that it becomes impossible to tell if they were written by a friar at all. The biblical commentary ceases to be the battlefield on which skirmishes between orders, clergy, and pope can be carried out.

It is hard not to observe that this exegetical development occurred after the near-continuous harassment of the Spirituals, the examination and condemnation of Olivi's works, the radicalization of certain wings of the Franciscan Order, and, finally, the upheaval caused to Franciscan identity in general by John XXII's announcement that the central tenet of Franciscan self-understanding was heretical. Franciscan exegetes no longer look at Matthew and find perfectly mirrored back to them the distinctive values of their order. Nor do they tend to see their order and its vicissitudes in terms of the apocalyptic views of Joachim, or of any other apocalypticist for that matter. If the thirteenth century is essentially a history of the gradual Franciscanizing of the gospel, the fourteenth century is the history of its swift and complete de-Franciscanizing. Of the three exegetical currents that flowed into Olivi's commentary—scholastic, Joachite, Franciscan—only one, the first, continues. In the long view, then, the mode of exegesis that triumphed in the fourteenth century is the one that had its origins with *B* and other early scholastic commentaries written in the Laon-Paris milieu. In southern France, exegesis had become louder and more tense as thirteenth-century ecclesiastical politics became more fierce and as Olivi himself came under personal attack. In the fourteenth century, soft-footed exegetes stop shouting and again begin to whisper.

To observe that these intellectual developments occur *after* punishment by the papacy, first, of the Spirituals and, then, of all the order is not, however, to say that they were *caused* by that persecution. The present state of evidence simply does not allow us to say whether there was a causal connection or not. Nicholas of Lyra shows no notable appreciation for Joachite thought. He is never tempted to give his order the sort of apocalyptic significance with which Olivi (or Bonaventure for that matter) endowed it. We know that he was well aware of the condemnation of Olivi's works in 1319 and of the papal condemnation in 1326, and he was certainly (perhaps more importantly) aware of the atmosphere of persecution that preceded these censures. What we cannot say with any confidence is that these denunciations changed the way he and his Franciscan confreres interpreted the gospels.

What is not in doubt is that the mode of exegesis that triumphed in the fourteenth century is the one that had its origins with *B* and with other early scholastic commentaries written in the Laon-Paris milieu. If exegesis took a detour through Provence in the late thirteenth century, and thus became increasingly particularistic, polemical, and apocalyptic, it returned in the following century to its Parisian roots. Once resettled, it took on the characteristics it originally had there. Exegesis becomes, again, expository, brief, universally applicable—relevant equally to Augustinian, Benedictine, secular clergyman, or friar. The distinctively Franciscan notes are much muted and the Joachite completely silenced. That perhaps made exegesis of the gospels more useful to the church at large. It may also have made it less interesting.

Notes

Introduction

1. Bernard Gui, *Flores chronicarum*, in S. Baluze, *Vitae paparum avenionensium*, ed. and emended by G. Mollat (Paris, 1914–27), 1:142 and 1:166.

2. See M.-T. d'Alverny, "Un adversaire de Saint Thomas: Petrus Ioannis Olivi," in *St. Thomas Aquinas, 1274–1974*, 2 vols. (Toronto, 1974), 2:197.

3. For a recent treatment of Olivi's use of the *Catena Aurea*, see L-J. Bataillon, "Olivi utilisateur de la *Catena Aurea* de Thomas d'Aquin," in *Pierre de Jean Olivi (1248–1298)*, ed. A. Boureau and Sylvain Piron (Paris, 1999).

4. *OFP*, 158.

5. *OFP*, 134.

6. See David Burr, *The Persecution of Peter Olivi* (Philadelphia, 1976), 75–76.

7. It is very difficult to define the "Spirituals" in any satisfactory way, in part because there were both French and Italian Spirituals and they did not share the same agenda. However, by 1270, they were known as the rigorist party within the Franciscan Order, particularly with regard to the issue of poverty. Olivi was often seen as their leader and the poisonous source from whom they derived their heretical doctrine. This is so, even though Olivi would certainly have abominated some of the things done and said in his name, particularly in the fourteenth century.

8. Burr, *Persecution*, 82.

9. Beryl Smalley, *The Study of the Bible in the Middle Ages*, 3rd ed. (Oxford, 1983), vii.

10. Beryl Smalley, *The Gospels in the Schools c. 1100–c. 1280* (London, 1985).

11. See Smalley's comment in *Study of the Bible:* "I was surprised to find how conservative they were in substance. They cling to the tradition of the biblical moral school" (xiii); and "One could hardly guess from reading them that Hugh was a Dominican and John a Franciscan" (xiii).

12. Many of Hugh's commentaries, as Smalley points out, "represent the fruit of team work." See Smalley, *The Gospels,* 125. It is still unclear which and how many of Alexander's gospel commentaries were produced *postquam esset frater,* though it is almost certain that his Matthew commentary was. See ibid., 124.

13. Ibid., 126.

14. Ibid., 166.

15. Ibid., 171.

16. Ibid., 192.

17. Ibid.

18. Ibid., 211–12.

19. D. Monti, "Bonaventure's Interpretation of Scripture in His Exegetical Works," doctoral dissertation, University of Chicago, 1979, 170. The dating of Bonaventure's Luke commentary will be considered more fully below. It was, however, probably written when the author was a *bachelarius biblicus* at Paris ca. 1248 and delivered again during Bonaventure's Parisian regency (1254–57).

20. That is unless one were to argue that heresiology was a peculiar concern of Dominicans. Smalley rightly points out that one of the distinctive features of Thomas's exegesis of the gospels is "his relentless pursuit of heretics." See Smalley, *The Gospels,* 262. However, Thomas differs from his mendicant colleagues only in degree here, not in kind.

21. Ibid., 276.

22. Ibid., 225, 240.

23. The dispute is analyzed in K. Madigan, "Aquinas and Olivi on Evangelical Poverty: A Medieval Debate and Its Modern Significance," *The Thomist* 61 (October 1997): 567–86.

24. "Erat quidam Petrus Iohannis hereticus, unus complicibus Ioachimi abbatis heresiarche, cum ergo non constat cuius Petri Iohannis hoc opus sit, non alienum putavi ab officio meo imprudentem letorem admonere" (Olivi, *Mtt.* 159vb).

25. Decima Douie, "Olivi's 'Postilla super Matthaeum' (MS. New College B. 49)," *FS* (1975): 79.

26. *Tractatus super Quatuor Evangelia di Gioacchino da Fiore,* ed. E. Buonaiuti (Rome, 1930). The *Tractatus* has been analyzed by H. Mottu, *La manifestation de l'Esprit selon Joachim de Fiore* (Neuchâtel and Paris, 1977). Mottu quite significantly changed his views about the heterodoxy of Joachim. See "La mémoire du futur: Signification de l'ancien testament dans la pensée de Joachim de Fiore," in *L'età dello Spirito e la fine dei tempi in Gioacchino da Fiore e nel gioachimismo medievale.* Atti del II congresso internazionale di studi gioachimiti, ed. A. Crocco (San Giovanni in Fiore, 1986), 13–28.

27. See the preface to the third edition of Smalley's *Study of the Bible* (1983), xiii: "I must change [my position] and say that the spiritual exposition in its old age produced a thriving child, though not one I should care to adopt." Whether the spiritual exposition was in "its old age" or not is another question.

28. Indeed, one of the comments Smalley made at the end of her life had to do with the neglect of Olivi: "Thirty years' work has opened up new perspectives on medieval Bible study and provided new material. It has left some areas almost as blank as they were. The late thirteenth century includes the challenging figure of Peter John Olivi, whose numerous postills are still for the most part waiting to be read" (*Study of the Bible*, xxv–xvi).

29. For two standard bibliographical surveys, see M. Bloomfield, "Joachim of Flora: A Critical Survey of His Canon, Teachings, Sources, Biography, and Influence," *Traditio* 13 (1957): 249–311; *idem*, "Recent Scholarship on Joachim of Fiore and His Influence," in *Prophecy and Millenarianism: Essays in Honor of Marjorie Reeves*, ed. Ann Williams (Essex, 1980), 21–52. Fundamental studies include H. Grundmann, *Ausgewählte Aufsätze*, in *Schriften der Monumenta Germaniae Historica* (Stuttgart, 1977), 25.2; M. Reeves, *The Influence of Prophecy in the Later Middle Ages: A Study in Joachimism* (Oxford: 1969; repr. Notre Dame, Ind., 1993), which contains a valuable bibliography of work published since 1968; *idem*, "The Originality and Influence of Joachim of Fiore," *Traditio* 36 (1980): 269–316; B. McGinn, *The Calabrian Abbot: Joachim of Fiore in the History of Western Thought* (New York, 1985); R. E. Lerner, "Refreshment of the Saints: The Time after Antichrist as a Station for Earthly Progress in Medieval Thought," *Traditio* 32 (1976): 97–144; Delno C. West, ed., *Joachim of Fiore in Christian Thought: Essays on the Influence of the Calabrian Prophet*, 2 vols. (New York, 1975).

30. Of which, see especially E. R. Daniel, ed., *Abbot Joachim of Fiore. Liber de Concordia Novi ac Veteris Testamenti* (Philadelphia, 1983). The Centro Internazionale di Studi Gioachimiti S. Giovanni in Fiore, in cooperation with the Istituto Storico Italiano per Il Medio Evo and the Monumenta Germaniae Historica, is planning an *opera omnia* of Joachim, of which several editions have already appeared. See G.-L. Potestà, ed., *Dialogi de prescientia Dei et predestinatione electorum*, Fonti per la storia dell'Italia medievale, Antiquitates 4 (Rome, 1995); and K.-V. Selge, ed., and G.-L. Potestà, trans., *Introduzione all'Apocalisse* (Rome, 1995).

31. See M. Reeves and B. Hirsch-Reich, *The Figurae of Joachim of Fiore* (Oxford, 1972).

32. In addition to Reeves, *Influence of Prophecy*, Part II, chap. 2, see Bernhard Töpfer, *Das kommende Reich des Friedens* (Berlin, 1964), 108–15; R. Moynihan, "Development of the 'Pseudo-Joachim' Commentary 'super Hieremiam,'" *Mélanges de l'école française de Rome, Moyen Âge, Temps Modernes* 98 (1986): 109–42; F. Simoni, "Il *Super Hieremiam* et il gioachimismo francescano," *Bullettino dell'Istituto Storico Italiano per il Medio Evo* 82 (1970): 13–46; and Stephen Wessley, *Joachim of Fiore and Monastic Reform* (New York, 1990), 116–24.

33. See, e.g., Reeves, *Influence of Prophecy,* Part II, chap. 4; *idem,* "The Abbot Joachim's Disciples and the Cistercian Order," *Sophia* 19 (1951): 355–71; M. Bloomfield and M. Reeves, "The Penetration of Joachism into Northern Europe," *Speculum* 29 (1954): 772–93; and E. R. Daniel, "A Re-Examination of the Origins of Franciscan Joachitism," *Speculum* 43 (1968): 671–76.

34. J. Ratzinger, *Die Geschichtstheologie des heiligen Bonaventura* (Munich, 1959) [Eng. trans. by Z. Hayes, *The Theology of History in St. Bonaventure* (Chicago, 1971)]; E. R. Daniel, "Saint Bonaventure: Defender of Franciscan Eschatology," in *S. Bonaventura, 1274–1974,* 4 vols. (Grottaferrata, 1974), 4:793–806; *idem,* "St. Bonaventure's Debt to Joachim," *Medievalia et Humanistica,* n.s. 2 (1982): 61–75; *idem,* "Apocalyptic Conversion: The Joachite Alternative to the Crusade," *Traditio* 25 (1969): 127–54; *idem, The Franciscan Concept of Mission in the High Middle Ages* (Lexington, Ky., 1975; rev. ed., Franciscan Institute, 1992); B. McGinn, "The Significance of Bonaventure's Theology of History," *Journal of Religion* 58 Supplement (1978): s64–81; G.–L. Potestà, *Angelo Clareno* (Rome, 1990). For an earlier but still useful treatment, see D. Douie, *The Nature and Effect of the Heresy of the Fraticelli* (Manchester, 1932). The most comprehensive recent treatment, which will remain authoritative for many decades to come, is David Burr, *The Spiritual Franciscans* (University Park, Penn., 2001). I regret this book was published too late to incorporate into this study.

35. See, most recently, *OPK.*

CHAPTER ONE   The Scholastic Gospel

1. There is, of course, an enormous literature on this problem. For a good treatment in English, see W. R. Farmer, *The Synoptic Problem,* 2nd ed (Macon, Ga., 1985).

2. "Isti igitur quattuor euangelistae universo terrarum orbe notissimi, et ob hoc fortasse quattuor, quoniam quattuor sunt partes orbis terrae, per cuius uniuersitatem Christi ecclesiam dilatari ipso sui numeri sacramento quodammodo declararunt, hoc ordine scripsisse perhibentur: primus Mattheus, deinde Marcus, tertio Lucas, ultimo Iohannes" (Augustine, *De Consensu Evangelistarum* 1.2.3. ed. F. Weihrich, *CSEL* 43 [Vienna: F. Tempsky, 1904], p. 3). Augustine wrote *De Consensu* around the year 400 to answer critics who charged that the evangelists had contradicted one another. See *De Consensu* 1.7.10, p. 10, where he explains his motivations for writing.

3. "Marcus eum subsecutus tamquam pedisequus et breviator eius uidetur. cum solo quippe Iohanne nihil dixit, solus ipse perpauca, cum solo Luca pauciora, cum Mattheo vero plurima et multa paene totidem adque ipsis uerbis siue cum solo siue cum ceteris consonante" (*De Consensu* 1.2.4, p. 4).

4. Eusebius, *Historia Ecclesiastica,* ed. G. Bardy, *SC* 31 (Paris: 1986) 3.39.16, p. 157.

5. *Historia Ecclesiastica* 3.39.15, p. 156.

6. See the judgment of D. Harrington: "That Mark wrote in Rome is suggested not only by Papias but also by Latin loanwords in the text and by the atmosphere of impending persecution that pervades the Gospel. Since Mark 13 does not presuppose the destruction of the Jerusalem Temple, the Gospel was most likely composed before 70 AD. A setting in the 60s at Rome seems best" ("The Gospel According to Mark," in *The New Jerome Biblical Commentary,* ed. R. E. Brown, J. A. Fitzmyer, and R. E. Murphy [Englewood Cliffs, N.J. 1990], 596).

7. "Primus omnium Matheus est, publicanus cognomine Levi, qui evangelium in Iudaea hebreo sermone edidit ob eorum uel maxime causam qui in Iesum crediderant ex Iudaeis et nequaquam legis umbram succedente evangelii veritate seruabant; secundus Marcus, interpres apostoli Petri, et Alexandrinae ecclesiae primus episcopus, qui Dominum quidem Salvatorem ipse non vidit sed ea quae magistrum audierat praedicantem iuxta fidem magis gestorum narrauit quam ordinem; tertius Lucas medicus natione Syrus Antiochenensis, cuius laus in evangelio, qui et ipse discipulus apostoli Pauli in Achaiae Boetiaeque partibus volumen condidit quaedam altius repetens et, ut ipse in proemio confitetur, audita magis quam visa describens; ultimus Iohannes apostolus et euangelista" (Jerome, *Mtt.* 1:62). Many commentators added that John was written in Ephesus under Nerva.

8. Augustine, *De Consensu* 1.6.9, p. 9; Jerome, *Mtt.* 1:3; Gregory, *Homiliae in Hiezechielem Prophetam,* ed. M. Adriaen, *CC* 142 (Turnhout: 1971), 47–53.

9. *De Consensu* 1.6, pp. 9–10.

10. *Homilia 4 in Hiezechielem,* 47.

11. The literature on the origins and authorship of the *Gloss* is quite extensive. For a clear, short introduction to the issues, see Smalley, *Study of the Bible,* 55–66; and *idem,* "Glossa Ordinaria," in *Theologische Realenzyklopädie* 13 (1984): 452–57, which has an excellent bibliography. See also the fine summary in the Introduction by Margaret Gibson to *Biblia Latina cum glossa ordinaria: facsimile reprint of the editio princeps Adolph Rusch of Strassburg 1480–81,* ed. Karlfried Froehlich and Margaret T. Gibson, 4 vols. (Turnhout, 1992), 1: vii–xi; and E. Ann Matter, "The Church Fathers and the *Glossa Ordinaria,*" in *The Reception of the Church Fathers in the West,* 2 vols. (Leiden, 1993), 2: 83–112.

12. "Sed quoniam sacras litteras in nouem codicibus . . . collegimus," in *Institutiones* 1.9.3, ed. R. A. B. Mynors (Oxford, 1937), p. 36. The nine books were: (1) Genesis to Ruth; (2) the six books of Kings; (3) the four major and twelve minor prophets; (4) the psalter; (5) Wisdom literature; (6) Job, Tobit, Esther, Judith, Maccabees, Ezra-Nehemiah; (7) the four gospels; (8) Paul and Canonical Epistles; (9) the Acts of the Apostles and the Apocalypse.

13. The first to attribute the marginal glosses to Strabo was Johannes Trithemius (ca. 1490). See the Introduction by Margaret Gibson to *Biblia Latina cum glossa ordinaria,* p. viii n. 19.

14. See J. de Ghellinck, *Le mouvement théologique du XIIe siècle* (Bruges, 1948), 104–12.

15. See J. de Blic, "L'oeuvre exégétique de Walafrid Strabon et la Glossa Ordinaria," *RTAM* 16 (1949): 5–28.

16. On the first century of the school, see J. J. Contreni, *The Cathedral School of Laon from 850 to 930: Its Manuscripts and Masters* (Munich, 1978). See also L. Hödl, R. Peppermüller, and H. J. F. Reinhardt, "Anselm von Laon und seine Schule," in *Theologische Realenzyklopädie* 3: 1–5; and R. W. Southern, *St. Anselm and His Biographer* (Cambridge, 1963), 357–61.

17. *Historia Calamitatum: Studio critico e traduzione italiana di Antonio Crocco* (n.p.: Empireo, 1968), 3.

18. Smalley, *Study of the Bible,* 62.

19. Gibson, "Introduction" to *Biblia Latina cum glossa ordinaria,* p. viii.

20. See Margaret T. Gibson, "The Twelfth-century Glossed Bible," in *Studia Patristica* 23, ed. E. A. Livingstone (Louvain, 1990), 244; and Guy Lobrichon, "Une nouveauté: Les gloses de la Bible," in *Le Moyen Age et la Bible* (*Bible de tous les temps 4*), ed. G. Lobrichon and P. Riché (Paris, 1984), 95–114.

21. See Smalley, *The Gospels,* 62–65, 107–8; and G. Lacombe and B. Smalley, "Studies in the Commentaries of Cardinal Stephen Langton," in *Archives d'Histoire Doctrinale et Littéraire du Moyen Age* (1930): 1–182.

22. *PL* 162: 1228–1500.

23. See Smalley, *The Gospels,* 19, 21.

24. See *PL* 162:1396, where the commentator refers to "principalem vicarium Christi." On the use and evolution of the term "vicar of Christ" in the High Middle Ages, see M. Maccarrone, *Vicarius Christi: Storia del titolo papale* (Rome, 1953), 92–100.

25. J. P. Bonnes, "Un des plus grands prédicateurs du XIIe siècle, Geoffroy du Loroux, dit Geoffroy Babion," in *Revue bénédictine* 51 (1945–46): 190–99.

26. D. Van den Eynde, "Autour des 'Enarrationes in Evangelium S. Matthaei,'" in *RTAM* 26 (1959): 50–84.

27. See ibid., 67–69. Van den Eynde also points out that Peter Cantor used "Babion."

28. Friedrich Stegmüller, *Repertorium biblicum medii aevi,* 11 vols. (Madrid, 1950–80), 2: no. 2604, pp. 359–60. Smalley has augmented the number of manuscripts as a result of her researches in Oxford, Cambridge, and Paris. See Smalley, *The Gospels,* 21.

29. Ibid., 29.

30. See Van den Eynde, "Autour," 50–52.

31. One of Smalley's principal accomplishments was to piece together this very complex chain of influence. See the summary of her research on this question in *The Gospels,* 269.

32. Ibid., 30. See also Smalley's remark on p. 2: "Custom changed during the twelfth and thirteenth centuries. The gospels took a more central place in the syllabus."

33. See Van den Eynde, "Autour," 50: "Early Scholasticism, so rich in glosses and commentaries on the Psalms and the Epistles of St. Paul, knows only very few on the Gospel of St. Matthew."

34. Smalley, *The Gospels*, 29.

35. The one element that it does not have, which will become conventional in the thirteenth century, is the intricate, almost atomistic division of biblical chapters at the beginning of each commentary chapter.

36. Smalley, *The Gospels*, 29.

37. For biographical details, see A. Paravicini Bagliani, *Cardinali di curia et 'familiae' cardinalizie dal 1227 ad 1254*, 2 vols. (Padua, 1972): 1:256–65. For Hugh's writings, see T. Kaeppeli, *Scriptores Ordinis Praedicatorum Medii Aevi*, 4 vols. (Rome, 1970–1993), 2:61–70.

38. I have used the edition of Hugh's Matthew commentary found in *Postilla super IV evangelia fratris Hugonis Cardinalis* (Basel, 1482).

39. For this and other details on the circumstances surrounding Hugh's exegesis of the gospels, see Smalley, *The Gospels*, 125–43.

40. See H.-F Dondaine, "L'Objet et le medium de la vision béatifique chez les théologiens du XIIIe siècle," *RTAM* 19 (1952): 60–130, 82–83.; Smalley, *The Gospels*, 120–26; Robert E. Lerner, "Poverty, Preaching and Eschatology in the Revelation Commentaries of 'Hugh of St Cher,'" in *The Bible in the Medieval World: Essays in Memory of Beryl Smalley*, ed. K. Walsh and D. Wood (Oxford, 1985), 157–89.

41. Lerner, "Poverty, Preaching and Eschatology," 181.

42. Smalley, *The Gospels*, 126.

43. Ibid.

44. "Ioseph figura praedicatorum, qui Christum cum matre, id est fidem Christi et ecclesiae tulerunt ad gentes, relicto Herode, id est, Iudaeorum infidelitate." (*Glossa* at *Qui consurgens*).

45. "Quam cito Christus apparuit mundo, incoepit in eum persecutio, quae figurauit persecutionem sanctorum, et dum infans quaeritur, infantes occiduntur: in quibus form martirii nascitur, ubi infantia ecclesiae dedicatur. Figurat mors paruulorum passionem omnium martyrum, qui parvii, id est, humiles et innocentes occisi sunt" (*Glossa* at *Occidit omnes pueros*).

46. *PL* 162: 1257.

47. "Gerit etiam Herodes personam persecutorum qui tempore apostolorum in Judaea fuerunt, quando scilicet Christus in membris suis, id est in apostolis suis fugit ad gentes. . . . Plorat ergo Ecclesia per compassionem martyres interfectos, et vox illa auditur in Rama, id est in excelso, id est in coelo" (*PL* 162: 1260–61).

48. See, e.g., these two on the Herod story: "Sed quaeritur juxta litteram: Quomodo Rachel ploraverit filios suos, cum tribus Juda, quae Bethlehem tenebat, non de Rachel, sed de sorore ejus Lia fuerit orta? Quod facile solvitur. . . .

Quaeritur: Quare Joseph non timuit ire in Galilaeam sicut in Judaeam, cum ibi regnaret Archelaeus tam bene?" (*PL* 162: 1260).

49. Hugh, *Mtt.* p. 9.

50. "Significat Dyabolus qui turbatur quando Iesus, id est salvus, nascitur in corde hominis et diligenter inquirit tempus et locum ut occidat adhuc ipsum in infantia" (Hugh, *Mtt.* p. 9).

51. "De studio enim debet exire qui eligitur ad prelaturum vel ad predicandum debet exire de studio, non semper ibi manere" (Hugh, *Mtt.* p. 10).

52. "In illo deserto quod est inter Ierusalem et Iericho Christus diabolum vicit, ubi figuraliter dixerat Adam incidisse in latrones et eum vicisse" (*Glossa* at *Tunc Iesus ductus est*).

53. "Post baptismum, quia nulla est mora a tentatione: Ut mox doceat in desertum pugnare, docet baptizatos de mundo exire, in quiete Deo vacare. . . . Hic est ordo recte conversationis, ut post acceptam Spiritus Sancti gratiam contra Diabolum artius accingamur" (*Glossa* at *Tunc Iesus ductus est*).

54. "Baptizatus autem Christus vadit statim in desertum, ductu Spiritus: quia omnis fidelis post baptismum debet postponere mundum, et aut petat corporaliter eremum, aut vacans a tumultu saeculi, faciat in mente desertum et ductu Spiritus accingatur contra diabolum" (*PL* 162: 1270).

55. *PL* 162: 1272.

56. *PL* 162: 1274.

57. The text was popular among interpreters in the second and third centuries. See M. Steiner, *La tentation de Jésus dans l'interprétation patristique de Saint Justin a Origène* (Paris, 1962).

58. "Queritur quomodo hae tentationes factae sunt, quum Marcus dicat, quod quadraginta diebus in deserto fuit, et tentabatur a Satana? Videtur enim velle quod omnes tentationes in deserto essent. Dicunt igitur quidam quod animo factae sunt hae tentationes a diabolo, non visibiliter apparente. Suggerebat enim ei diabolus, ut de lapidibus faceret panes, et ascenderet supra pinnam, et inde se praecipitaret, ut diabolum adoraret, propter regna mundi. Alii dicunt, quod visibiliter ei apparuit, ut homo, quod verius est, et locutus est cum eo" (*PL* 162: 1273).

59. "Iterum quaeritur quomodo assumpsit? Alii dicunt, quod eum transportavit, et statuit supra pinnam: quod non est mirum, si permisit se transportari a diabolo, qui permisit se levari in cruce a membris diaboli. Alii dicunt quia duxit eum per viam usque in Jerusalem, quod videtur velle Lucas, qui dicit: *Et duxit eum in sanctam civitatem,* et ascenderunt supra pinnam, sicut et alii homines" (*PL* 162: 1274).

60. "*In desertum.* Ad litteram in illud quod est inter Iherusalem et Iericho, ubi ille incidit in latrones" (Hugh, *Mtt.* p. 20).

61. "Hic est ordo recte conversationis ut post acceptam Spiritus Sancti gratiam seculum deferentes in desertum claustri veniamus. Quia quamvis dicat desertum a mundo, tamen in veritate est paradisus, et ortus deliciarum" (Hugh, *Mtt.* p. 20).

62. "Item ut ostenderet convenientiam legis, prophetarum et evangelii. Hoc est contra Manicheos, qui dicunt Vetus Testamentum a dyabolo" (Hugh, *Mtt.* p. 21).

63. Smalley, *The Gospels,* 262. As Smalley points out, Thomas often identifies the Cathars, his contemporaries, as "Manichees." So does Hugh. Still a desideratum in scholarship is a study that would demonstrate the influence of Catharism, if such there was, on "orthodox" high medieval theology and exegesis.

64. Ibid., 143. The 'biblical moral' school is a term Smalley introduced in her earlier study, *Study of the Bible,* particularly in connection with the glosses of Stephen Langton (d. 1228), who, in his commentaries in the form of lectures at Paris given 1175–90, had "perfected the technique of moralizing Scripture as an aid to preaching" (p. 267). Langton is, of course, credited with dividing the books of the Bible into the chapters which are, more or less, still in use today.

65. "Dyabolus persuadet praedicatori ut doceat lapides, id est comminationes, emollire propter temporale emolumentum" (Hugh, *Mtt.* p. 21).

66. "Vel lapides sunt austeritas penitentiae, Dyabolus dicens ad religiosum, Satis fuisti in conventu. Si filius Dei es, vade infirmariam ad recreandum" (Hugh, *Mtt.* p. 21).

67. Smalley, *The Gospels,* 141.

68. Ibid., 143.

69. Ibid., 126.

70. Ibid., 138.

71. Ibid., 126.

72. Ibid., 138.

CHAPTER TWO   The Joachite Gospel

1. On this tradition, see McGinn, *The Calabrian Abbot,* 74–88.

2. Mottu, *La manifestation de l'ésprit,* 41, my translation.

3. While manuscript evidence has to be used with caution, this seems to have been the least widely produced and circulated of Joachim's major works. Interestingly, however, it was known by Salimbene and Hugh of Digne, as we shall see in the following chapter.

4. For the history of the *Tractatus,* see Buonaiuti's introduction to his edition, pp. xi–lxxi; Mottu, *La manifestation de l'ésprit,* 48–57; and McGinn, *The Calabrian Abbot,* 33.

5. Joachim preferred Luke to the other synoptics because of its greater fidelity to the historical order of Christ's life and because, more than any other canonical gospel, it reflects the future of the church. See *Tractatus,* 172 and 143; and McGinn, *The Calabrian Abbot,* 33 and 46 n. 121.

6. Joachim, *Expositio in Apocalypsim* (Venice, 1527; facs. ed., Frankfort, 1964), 64va. All subsequent references are to this facsimile edition.

7. See McGinn, *The Calabrian Abbot,* 124–25.

8. The typological method has been widely discussed. For two brief accounts in English, see R. M. Grant and D. Tracy, *A Short History of the Interpretation of the Bible* (Philadelphia, 1985), 28–33; and K. Froehlich, *Biblical Interpretation in the Early Church* (Philadelphia, 1984), 9–10.

9. On Origen's exegesis, see Karen Jo Torjesen's fine study, *Hermeneutical Procedure and Theological Method in Origen's Exegesis* (New York, 1986).

10. Obviously, there is one important difference between reading the Old Testament typologically and reading the New Testament typologically. Typological exegesis of the Old Testament requires reference to the New Testament, while typological reading of the New Testament does not involve a third set of sacred scriptures in the light of which the New Testament takes its prophetic meaning. The notion that the New Testament *did* need a third set of scriptures to clarify its meaning would, however, have a real future. In the thirteenth century, the Franciscan Gerardo of Borgo San Donnino would suggest that Joachim's three principal writings were those scriptures in the light of which the previous two testaments had to be read. Gerardo's case will be considered more fully in the following chapter.

11. Tyconius, *Liber Regularum,* ed. F. C. Burkitt (Cambridge, 1894), 108; Augustine, *De doctrina Christiana* 3:31 in *CC* 32 (Turnhout, 1962), 95–96.

12. As Joachim himself puts it in the *Tractatus:* "immo una est dicentium sanctorum patrum sententia, eorum que mistice dicenda occurrunt, alia referenda esse ad caput, alia ad ipsius capitis membra" (85–86). See this remark in Joachim's *Liber Concordie Novi ac Veteris Testamenti* (Venice, 1519): "Generalis denique regula est mysteriorum: ut quod non potest referri ad caput referatur ad membra." The first four books of the *Liber Concordie* have been edited by E. R. Daniel (Philadelphia, 1973). References to the first four books of this work will be to Daniel's edition and to the sixteenth-century Venice edition, while references to the fifth book will be to the Venice edition.

13. "Plura scripta sunt de Domino Ihesu Christo, que numquam sane possunt intelligi, nisi ad eius corpus" (*Liber Concordie* 3.1.10).

14. For a history of the term, see R. Grant, *The Spirit and the Letter* (New York, 1957).

15. *Liber Concordie* II.1.3 (Daniel, p. 65). I use the translation provided by Daniel in *Apocalyptic Spirituality: Treatises and Letters of Lactantius, Adso of Montier-en-Der, Joachim of Fiore, the Franciscan Spirituals, Savonarola,* trans. and introduced by Bernard McGinn (New York, 1979), 122.

16. See, e.g., Olivi, *Mtt.* 8vb: "In senario enim designatur perfectio laboris et operis. In septenario vero, perfectio quietis et ultimi finis. Etiam senarius et septenarius sunt numeri universitatis et temporum huius vite."

17. For an outstanding survey of the history of this as well as of other historical patterns in exegesis, see R. E. Lerner, "Refreshment of the Saints."

18. By this term, I mean that view of the end of history which sees the time and nature of the last things as at least partially predictable from an interpretation of the biblical text in correlation with an interpretation of the "signs of the times." The classical apocalypticist sees the end-time as an imminent period of crisis, of growing evil, and of the persecution of the righteous. He believes that the end-time will be brought to a close by decisive divine intervention in history resulting in the judgment of the wicked and vindication of the just. This "apocalyptic eschatology" was a product of intertestamental Judaism and has been much discussed in recent biblical scholarship. See, e.g., John J. Collins, *Between Athens and Jerusalem: Jewish Identity in the Hellenistic Diaspora* (New York, 1983). The question of how far Jesus of Nazareth was influenced by this form of eschatology has generated an enormous literature, of which A. Schweitzer's *The Quest of the Historical Jesus* (New York, 1964) is among the most influential and enduring contributions. For a discussion of apocalyptic eschatology in ancient and medieval Christianity before Joachim, see McGinn, *The Calabrian Abbot*, chap. 1.

19. Chiliasm may here be defined as that reading of Apocalypse 20:4–6 which sees in the description of the thousand-year reign of the saints a literal prophecy of a millennial kingdom to be enjoyed by Christ and the saints on earth. Chiliasm came increasingly to be regarded as suspect over the first four centuries of church history, in large part because of traditions that associated with it perpetual banqueting and sexual bliss.

20. On the tradition of the spiritual interpretation of the Apocalypse (often called the "Tyconian" or "Augustinian" tradition), see Wilhelm Kamlah, *Apokalypse und Geschichtstheologie: Die mittelalteriche Auslegung der Apokalypse vor Joachim von Fiore* (Berlin, 1935); and McGinn, *The Calabrian Abbot*, chap. 2.

21. See Kamlah, *Apokalypse*, 76, 100–101; John van Engen, *Rupert of Deutz* (Berkeley, 1983), 275–82; and McGinn, *The Calabrian Abbot*, 88–89. This twelfth-century historicizing tendency is also evident in Book One of the Premonstratensian canon Anselm of Havelberg's *Dialogi, SC* 118 (Paris, 1966), 68–114.

22. Joachim, *Expositio*, ff. 39r–39v.

23. The notion that the Apocalypse could be read as a continuous prophecy was to have a real future among masters of the Franciscan Order such as Alexander Bremen, Nicholas of Lyra, and Peter Auriol. See Alexander Minorita, *Expositio in Apocalypsim* (Weimar, 1955); Petrus Auriol, *Compendium sensus literalis totius divinae scripturae* (Quaracchi, 1896); and Nicholas de Lyra, *Biblia Sacra cum glossis* (Venice, 1588). On the Franciscan interpretation of Apocalypse exegesis, see *OPK*, chaps. 1–2. For an analysis of Nicholas of Lyra's Apocalypse commentary, see Philip D. Krey, "Nicholas of Lyra: Apocalypse Commentary as Historiography," doctoral dissertation, University of Chicago, 1989. This is not, however, how Olivi or many other Franciscans interpreted the book. Olivi saw the book more as a *recapitulative* prophecy, with *each* of the seven parts of the book prophesying part or all of the history of the church. The contrast should not be drawn

too sharply, however, as Joachim also concedes that "all of the times belong to all of the parts." Thus, Joachim sees the seven bowls given to the angels in the fifth part of the Apocalypse as a recapitulative treatment of all of the church's persecutions. See *Expositio*, 186va; and McGinn, *The Calabrian Abbot*, 147.

24. The notion that church history was to unfold in seven successive periods was not original to Joachim. For a discussion of this historical pattern, see R. Lerner, "Refreshment of the Saints," 116–17. Here the author points out that the pattern was evident no later than Bede's Apocalypse commentary. Note that Bede, unlike Joachim, did not see the Apocalypse as a continuous prophecy of the course of church history.

25. There are several editions of Joachim's *Liber Introductorius* which summarizes the argument and exegetical principles of the commentary, perhaps the best being edited by K.-V. Selge, Gioacchino da Fiore, *Introduzione all'Apocalisse* (Rome, 1995). For Joachim's analysis of the structure of the Apocalypse, see *Expositio*, ff. 11ra–12rb.

26. See *Expositio*, 76r, 116r–v, and 130r.

27. See *Liber Concordie* II. 1. 2, p. 62 for a definition of concordia: "Concordiam proprie esse dicimus similitudinem eque proportionis novi ac veteris testamenti." For the notion that this harmony or similarity is given in the literal sense, see ibid., V. 1, f. 60va.

28. See *Expositio*, 3va. The concord of seven persecutions is elaborated in Books III and IV of the *Liber Concordie* and in the abbot's *figurae*. Joachim's *figurae* were designed to illustrate in pictorial form intricate aspects of his apocalyptic thought. Except for certain later details, they were almost certainly produced by the abbot himself. For these, see L. Tondelli, M. Reeves, and B. Hirsch-Reich, eds., *Il libro delle figure dell'abate Gioacchino da Fiore* (Turin, 1953). Figures XVIIIa and XVIIIb are particularly pertinent to the *concordia* of two Testaments. See also M. Reeves and B. Hirsch-Reich, "The Seven Seals in the Writings of Joachim of Fiore," in *RTAM* 21 (1954): 239–47, in which Joachim's *De Septem Sigillis* is edited. The authors also discuss some of the ways in which Joachim's concords vary in his writings.

29. *Expositio*, 6vb. See also 39vb, 57vb, 86va, and 133ra.

30. For this threefold historical pattern, see *Liber Concordie*, II. 1.5–15, pp. 68–85, *Expositio*, 5r–6r; and *Tractatus*, 21–25 and 154–55. For how the three *ordines* correspond with the three *status*, see, e.g., *Tractatus*, 91, 155, and 157; and *Expositio*, 5r–v and 18vb.

31. See *Expositio*, 39vb and 57vb.

32. McGinn, *The Calabrian Abbot*, 125.

33. This is a recurrent theme in the *Expositio*. See, e.g., 3va, 95va, 99v, 110ra, 139rb, 153vb.

34. See *Tractatus*, 73.

35. See *Liber Concordie*, p. 232: "Ita, etsi multa scripta sunt a patribus in expositione novi testamenti, perfecta tamen eius apertio in tertio statu seculi facienda

servatur." See also *Tractatus,* 21, where Joachim states that the spiritual under-standing was given to the church "secundum partem, tempore apostolorum" and "danda est plenius circa finem."

36. *Expositio,* 145vb. See also 134ra, which alludes to an event in Joachim's life in which he heard at Messina of the future alliance of the Muslims and the heretics.

37. *Expositio,* 133r.

38. *Expositio,* 133r, 168r, 196v, 197r, and 207r–v. Note that on 10r, however, the fifth head is identified as one of the kings of Babylon. The first four kings are Herod, Nero, Constantius, and Mohammed. For a pictorial representation, see Joachim's *figura* in *Il Libro delle Figure,* Vol II, Tavola XIV.

39. *Expositio,* 195v, 196vb, 198r.

40. See Joachim's *Expositio de prophetia ignota,* which is edited in B. McGinn, "Joachim and the Sibyl," *Cîteaux* 24 (1973): 136, ll. 263–88. There is also a new edi-tion: M. Kaup, ed., *De prophetia ignota,* MGH Studien und Texte 19 (Hannover, 1998). This text is not altogether flattering to the coming holy pope, as it suggests that the Antichrist will succeed in confusing the pope. For a more complimen-tary text, see *Liber Concordie* V, f. 121v. On the development of this important leg-end, see H. Grundmann, "Die Papstprophetien des Mittelalters," in *Archiv für Kulturgeschichte* 19 (1929): 77–138; and Reeves, *Influence of Prophecy,* 395–504.

41. See *Expositio,* 112ra for a text regarding the Antichrist's distortion of scripture.

42. See *Expositio,* 175v–176r.

43. The classic treatment of this is in Reeves, *Influence of Prophecy,* 175–241 and 251–90. See also B. McGinn, "Apocalyptic Traditions and Spiritual Identity in Thirteenth-Century Religious Life," in *The Roots of the Modern Christian Tra-dition,* ed. E. R. Elder (Kalamazoo, 1984), 1–26.

44. Mottu, *La Manifestation,* 50.

45. "Matheus, Lucas et Marcus, qui precesserunt in scribendo Iohannem" (*Tractatus,* 4).

46. "Ut autem hoc ita esse intelligamus, inipsis evangeliorum principiis insis-tendum est: ut notato in eis quodam viventi ordine, quo velut per quedam ascen-sionum incrementa, ac humilibus ascenditur ad sublimia, intelligamus in eis non humanum ingenium set spiritum Omnipotentis, ut promiserat Filius, esse lo-quutum" (*Tractatus,* 4).

47. "si tamen quod sinistrum ibi dicitur, locamus inter hominem et leonem, passionem scilicet inter nativitatem Domini et eius felicem resurrectionem, in-venitur primus locus datus Matheo, cui nativitas; secundus Luce, cui passio; tertius Marco, cui resurrectio; quartus Iohanni, cui ascensio data est" (*Trac-tatus,* 5).

48. "qui videlicet ordo et annotatio evangeliorum qualiter ab imo incipiens in summo perficiat fidem nostram, in ipsis ut iam dixi evangeliorum principiis, ipsa ordinata elevatio docet" (*Tractatus,* 5).

49. "etenim quia scribe et pharisei Christum, quem sciebant esse secundum carnem filium David, nesciebant filium Dei secundum deitatem, non oportebat primum evangelistam qui scripsit evangelium apud Iudeos divina Christi scribere sacramenta" (*Tractatus*, 5).

50. "ait ergo primus evangelista Matheus: 'liber generationis Ihesu Christi filii David filii Abraam.' Quod tale est ac si diceretur: loquuturus de ortu Christi vobis, qui carnales estis et secundum carnem ambulatis . . . ipse est enim Ihesus filius Marie, quem ego quidem predico vobis filium Abrahe et David, quia adhuc estis carnales" (*Tractatus*, 5).

51. "secundum vero spiritalem intellectum possumus ipsa quattuor evangelia .IIII. temporibus assignare" (*Tractatus*, 6).

52. "quatinus in evangelio Mathei, quod incepit ab Abraam, accipiamus totam divinam paginam prioris Testamenti, que annuntiabat Salvatorem mundi nasciturm ex semine David et Abrahe, secundum carnem. in evangelio Luce, quod agit de pueritia et profectu Christi usque ad annos duodecim, doctrinam lactentis Ecclesie, que incipiens a Iohanne Baptista, velut per intervalla temporum pervenit ad incrementum usque ad hec tempora nostra: iuxta illud Danielis: 'pertransibunt plurimi et multiplex erit scientia.' in evangelio Marci, in quo agitur de perfecta Christi etate, hoc est de tempore predicationis sue, doctrinam spiritalem de qua dicit apostolus: 'sapientiam loquimur inter perfectos.' que videlicet doctrina spiritalis incipiens a tempore in quo venturus est Helias perseveratura est usque in finem seculi. in evangelio Iohannis sapientiam illam ineffabilem que erit in futuro, quando videbimus eum sicuti est dicente Paulo: 'videmus nunc per speculum in enigmate: tunc autem facie ad faciem'" (*Tractatus*, 6–7).

53. For example: "et quoniam caro iuxta apostolum concupiscit adversus spiritum et spiritus adversus carnem, ita nos oportet intelligere oppositos ex adverso Christum et Antichristum, ac si carnem et spiritum, nimirum quia, ille, idest Antichristus, carnales amplexatur et largitur divitias" (*Tractatus*, 67).

54. "verum quia nec Christus qui est veritas, nec diabolus qui est auctor mendatii, visibiliter apparent, sicut in Ecclesia humilium creditur esse Christus; ita in synagoga superborum regnare creditur Antichristus" (*Tractatus*, 68).

55. On the early patristic interpretation of this pericope, see M. Steiner, *La tentation de Jésus*.

56. *Tractatus*, 156.

57. "igitur in .xxxx. diebus sicut et in .xxxx. annis quibus filii Israel manserunt in deserto, .xxxx. generationes designantur annorum, post quarum consummationem, graviores et amariores pre solito, pater mendacii temptationes immittet" (*Tractatus*, 156). Notice that this text contains a *concordia* between the Israelites' wandering in the desert and Christ's fasting in the desert. Joachim's own distinctive understanding of *allegoria* is illustrated in the way in which he interprets the forty days in the desert as representative of the forty generations of church history.

58. "quod autem post ieiunium xxxx dierum et xxxx noctium esuriit Ihesus, designat christianum populum, fidei viribus infirmatum, esurire miracula . . . sequitur: 'tunc assumpsit eum diabolus' . . . quasi in sanctam civitatem assumet diabolus populum fidelem et statuet eum supra pinnaculum templi, cum, commotis undique gentibus adversus Ecclesiam, statuet illum velud in lubricum, omnibus auxiliis atque propugnaculis destitutum. et quia non erit in pedibus eius stabilitas, loquens per ora ministrorum suorum, quasi consulens eis, persuadebit illis, ob requiem obtinendam, ruinam, dicens eis: si secundum quod scriptum est, electi Dei perire non possunt . . . hec in suggestione ipsius quocienscumque est monachus in gravi temptatione, et suggeritur ei ab eodem diabolo proprium dimittere monasterium . . . 'iterum assumpsit eum diabolus in montem' . . . set et nunc servos Dei gravissimis primo temptationibus affligit ac deinde cum se videt talibus eos machinis superare non posse, incipit pulsare eos aura elationis, rapiens eos in quoddam sanctitatis fastigium et suggerens eis existimare se ceteris sanctiores et ad ultimum pulsans eos spiritu ambitionis . . . superatis his duabus temptationibus, putant aliquid esse et querunt suo studio ad prelationem conscendere . . . in fine quadraginta generationum, querant filii diaboli subvertere fidem nostram" (*Tractatus*, 156–64).

59. He normally introduced his typological readings by stating "*nota pro mysteriis*" or by announcing that he is now reading the text *mistice* or *allegorice*.

60. In the first chapter of the Matthew commentary, for example, Olivi makes the following remark: ". . . Deus sub certo ordine et numero tempora et status populi Dei distinguit, et sic ergo omnia referuntur in Christum tanquam in finem suum. Unde sicut infra patebit sub diversarum parabolarum misterio Christus diversimode distinguit tempora ecclesie seu populi Dei. Ex quo patet quod non sunt usquequa contempnendi *illi qui tempora ecclesie sub certis statibus et generationibus distinxerunt* (*Mtt.* 8vb–9ra; my emphasis). In the second chapter of the commentary, Olivi says: "Et ut perpendamus hec misteria non frustra precessisse invenies post duodecim tridenarios annorum, *quos quidam vocant generationes ecclesie*" (*Mtt.* 17ra; my emphasis). Both references seem to be to Joachim.

CHAPTER THREE   Franciscan Apocalyptic, 1240–1300

1. "In isto castro specialiter et plus habitabat frater Hugo. Et erant ibi multi notarii et iudices atque medici et alii litterati, qui diebus sollemnibus ad cameram fratris Hugonis conveniebant, ut de doctrina abbatis Ioachim audirent ipsum loquentem atque docentem et exponentem sacre Scripture misteria et predicentem futura. Erat enim magnus Ioachita et omnes libros abbatis Ioachim de grossa littera habebat" (Salimbene, *Cronica* [Bari, 1966], 337).

2. Reeves, *Influence of Prophecy*, 184.

3. Ibid.

4. See *OPK*, 5.

5. E. R. Daniel, "A Re-examination of the Origins of Franciscan Joachitism," *Speculum* 43 (1968): 671–76.

6. Reeves, *Influence of Prophecy*, 186.

7. On this theme, see S. Bihel, "S. Franciscus fuitne Angelus sexti sigilli?" *Antonianum* 2 (1927): 29–70; and Stanislao da Campagnola, *L'angelo del sesto sigillo e l'"alter Christus"* (Rome, 1971).

8. Angelo da Clareno, *Historia septem tribulationum ordinis minorum*, in *Archiv* 2 (1886): 282.

9. Two cherubim, two olives of Zechariah, two witnesses of Christ, the two shining stars of the Sibylline prophecy, and so forth. See Luke Wadding, *Annales Minorum* (Rome, 1732) 3: 380–83.

10. *OPK*, 9.

11. On Gerard, see H. Denifle, "Das Evangelium aeternum und die Commission zu Anagni," *Archiv* 1 (1885): 49–142; and Reeves, *Influence of Prophecy*, 187–90.

12. Ibid., 76.

13. Ibid., 518.

14. For a more recent defense of this view, see Simoni, "Il *Super Hieremiam* et il gioachimismo francescano," 13–46.

15. Reeves, *The Influence of Prophecy*, 145–60; and "The Abbot Joachim's Disciples in the Cistercian Order," *Sophia* 19 (1951): 355–71.

16. See B. Töpfer, *Das kommende Reich des Friedens*, 108–15. Reeves has replied to the critique in *Influence of Prophecy*, 156–58 n. 2.

17. Wessley, *Joachim of Fiore and Monastic Reform* , 116–24; and Moynihan, "Development of the 'Pseudo-Joachim' Commentary,'" 109–42.

18. See Reeves, *Influence of Prophecy*, 148 n. 1 for a list of references to biblical pairs.

19. See *Collationes in hexaemeron* in Bonaventure, *Opera* 5 (Quaracchi, 1882–1902); and *Collationes in hexaemeron et bonaventuriana quaedam selecta* (Quaracchi, 1934).

20. Reeves, *Influence of Prophecy*, 181.

21. *Collatio* 16, pp. 403–8.

22. "Secundum comparationem arboris vel seminis ad semen tempora sibi mutuo succedunt; secundum comparationem germinis ad germinans, mutuo sibi correspondent" (*Collatio* 16, p. 403).

23. *Collatio* 16, pp. 405–6, 408.

24. "Et necesse fuit, ut in hoc tempore veniret unus ordo, scilicet habitus propheticus, similis ordini Iesu Christi, cuius caput esset Angelus, ascendens ab ortu solis habens signum Dei vivi et conformis Christo" (*Collatio* 16, p. 405). See also *Collatio* 16, p. 408.

25. Bonaventure himself says: "Quis autem ordo iste futurus sit, vel iam sit, non est facile scire" (*Collatio* 22, p. 441). On the scholarly debate, see Ratzinger, *The Theology of History in Saint Bonaventure*, 46–71 and 155–63; and *OPK*, 41–44.

26. See *Collationes* 4, 6, 7, and 19.

27. "Quando pugna erit inter Christum et antichristum, inter doctrinam veritatis et falsitatis; tunc sol fiet sicut saccus cilicinus, et aliquis doctor veritatis vel praelatus secundum veritatem obscurabitur per errores" (*Collatio* 13, p. 392).

28. "Alii autem stabunt fortissimi, etsi videantur obscurari quantum ad reputationem" (*Collatio* 13, p. 392).

29. "Unde necesse est, ut prius ruant, et fiat ruina et postea restauratio; tanta erit tribulatio, ut in errorem inducantur, si fieri potest, etiam electi" (*Collatio* 15, p. 402). The scriptural reference here is to Mt. 21:24.

30. Though Bonaventure does speak in terms of a threefold pattern of Nature, Sin, and Grace. See, e.g., *Collatio* 21, p. 432.

31. See, e.g., *Collatio* 13, p. 389: "Et hoc potissime refertur ad tempus novi testamenti, quando Scriptura manifestata est, et maxime in fine, quando Scripturae intelligentur, quae modo non intelliguntur." See also *Collatio* 20, p. 428: "Et ideo figurae nondum explanatae sunt, sed quando luna erit plena, tunc erit apertio Scripturarum, et liber aperietur."

32. See, e.g., *Collatio* 2, pp. 341–42.

33. "Tunc implebitur prophetia Ezechielis, quando civitas descendet de celo . . . quando erit conformis triumphanti, seundum quod possibile est in via" (See *Collatio* 16, p. 408).

34. *OPK,* 44.

35. See *OPK,* 53.

36. For example, in the Matthew commentary there is, so far as I can see, no *highly developed* notion of a "double" Antichrist, i.e., one mystical and one great— that is, of an idea which would become central to Olivi's mature apocalyptic scenario. Nevertheless, I shall argue in chapter 7 that the basic idea is there *in nuce* in the Matthew commentary and that it is an idea that appears in the Luke commentary in much greater detail.

37. "[L]'Olivi avesse, in tutta la sua attività di teologo e di esegeta, sempre ben chiaro il giudizio sul suo tempo e sulla connessione con tutto lo svolgimento della storia della Chiesa e che già fossero presenti alla sua meditazione storica seppure ancora in maniera occasionale quei concetti che, come vedremo, in più organico e sistematico rapporto, svilupperà nella *Lectura super Apocalipsim*" (Manselli, *La "Lectura super Apocalypsim" di Pietro di Giovanni Olivi* [Rome, 1959], 159).

38. Manselli has taken up the question of Joachim's influence on the Apocalypse commentary at length in *La "Lectura,"* 185 ff. This analysis, as we shall see, has been quite controversial.

39. *Lectura super Apocalypsim,* MS Bibl. Angelica 382, ɪva. The Apocalypse commentary will subsequently be abbreviated as *Apoc.* All subsequent references are to this manuscript of the commentary. As Manselli notes, Olivi does not introduce an eighth vision, as does Joachim. See Manselli, *La "Lectura,"* 179, n. 3.

40. E.g., Olivi asserts that "sexta et septima visio principaliter describunt solum statum finalem ecclesie" (*Apoc.,* 2ra). This is not to say that recapitulation

is not important for Joachim. See *Expositio,* f. 15vb: "Sane liber iste quantum ad sex partes suas infra limitem secundi status extendit et retinet passus suos ita ut incipiens a resurrectione domini perveniat usque ad finem eius et iterum atque iterum redeat ad principium sui. In singulis denique quinque partium recapitulatio fit." I would like to thank David Burr for drawing my attention to this passage. Joachim notes that there is recapitulation in the later parts of the Apocalypse as well, though he insists that it is less pronounced there.

41. "Primo visio literaliter et aperte tangit septem ecclesias Asye sibi contemporaneas, allegorice vero describit septem status generales ecclesie" (*Apoc.,* 1va).

42. A number of Olivi's Franciscan contemporaries also divided the Apocalypse into seven visions and saw at least some of them as furnishing a tour of church history. William of Meliton, John of Wales, John of Russel, and Vital du Four all see in the first four visions a prophecy of all of church history in seven periods, while the last three are said to deal with the end times. See D. Burr, "Olivi, the *Lectura super Apocalypsim* and Franciscan Exegetical Tradition," in *Francescanesimo e Cultura Universitaria* (Perugia, 1990), 118–19; *idem,* "Franciscan Exegesis and Francis as Apocalyptic Figure," in *Monks, Nuns, and Friars in Mediaeval Society,* ed. E. B. King, J. T. Schaefer, and W. B. Wadley (Sewanee, 1989), 51–62; and *OPK,* 82–84.

43. Manselli has argued that Olivi borrowed his first five ages "directly and explicitly" from Richard of St. Victor and the sixth and seventh from Joachim and has asserted that it is in Olivi's use of these last two ages that "Joachim's influence is most evident." See *La "Lectura,"* 179. In the Apocalypse commentary, Olivi uses the word *status* to refer both to the sevenfold pattern of church history and to the Joachimist threefold pattern of salvation history. See, e.g., *Apoc.,* 1va, where Olivi refers to the "septem status ecclesie" and 2ra, where he talks about "septem tempora." See also *OPK,* 45–46, for a discussion of the Parisian use of the sevenfold pattern.

44. *Apoc.,* 26ra.

45. *Apoc.* 27va.

46. *Apoc.* 48vb–49ra, 63ra–va.

47. *Apoc.,* 9rb–10va; 49vb–50ra.

48. See Burr, *Persecution,* 21.

49. "initium quarte visionis non sic expresse distinguitur a fine tertie nec initium sexte a fine quinte sicut distinguitur in ceteris visionibus" (*Apoc.,* 2ra).

50. *Apoc.* 7rb.

51. *Apoc.* 46va–vb.

52. *Apoc.* 60vb, 73rb. Sometimes this new understanding of the Bible is conceived in terms of improved perception of the course of history as seen in the Bible and especially the Apocalypse. See, e.g., *Apoc.,* 8ra, 43ra, 83rb. Olivi occasionally sees these seven periods of church history as reflective of and in concordance with seven periods of Old Testament history. See, e.g., *Apoc,* 2ra–va.

53. Of Joachim's influence on Olivi with regard to the sevenfold scheme of church history, Manselli has said: "Sette dunque le età della Chiesa, come pensa l'Olivi, ispirandosi senza dubbio, sia pure con modificazioni personali, alla analoga divisione di Gioacchino da Fiore." See *La "Lectura,"* 150.

54. Ibid., 186. For other respects in which Manselli believes Olivi to differ from Joachim, see pp. 165–67, where he asserts that Olivi has no interest in the parallelism and *concordie* between the *status* and *tempora* in Joachim. See Manselli's conclusion on p. 190: "il gioachimismo dell'Olivi va ricondotto in quest'ultima opera a proporzioni abbastanza modeste."

55. Ibid., 165. See also p. 187: "l'Olivi si mantiene, relativamente alla questione trinitaria, del tutto libero da influenze gioachimitiche: la teoria dell *appropriatio* quindi delle tre età alle tre Persone Trinitarie e nella sua ultima opera praticamente scomparsa."

56. Burr, *Persecution,* 19.

57. David Burr, "Bonaventure, Olivi and Franciscan Eschatology," *CF* 53 (1983): 27 n. 22. Marjorie Reeves has also pointed out that Olivi's interpretation of the key of David given to the Philadelphian church correlates the three-*status* scheme with each of the three persons of the Trinity. See Reeves, *Influence of Prophecy,* 196.

58. See, e.g., *Apoc.* 8ra, 43ra, 55rb, 60vb, 73rb, 83rb, 119ra, 120rb.

59. *Apoc.,* 52va–vb. Olivi attributes Joachim's errors to the fact that he stood at the very dawn of the third *status*. See *Apoc.* 84ra.

60. Burr, *Persecution,* 19.

61. *Apoc.,* 52rb–va, 55rb, 72vb, and 76ra. Olivi sees these two texts as literal references to St. Francis.

62. For the stigmata parallel, see *Apoc.,* 13rb, 52va; for the suggestion that Francis may rise from the dead, see *Apoc.* 55va. Even the unimpeachably orthodox Bonaventure could suggest that the parallel might extend to a resurrection on Francis's part. See *Sermones de S. patre nostro Francisco,* in *Opera* 9, pp. 382–85; and chapter 15 of the *Legenda maior,* in *Opera* 8, p. 347. However, as Burr has pointed out, "Bonaventure gives the term 'resurrection' a highly metaphorical sense when applying it to Francis and does not refer it to any future occurrence." See Burr, *Persecution,* 20 n. 30. Olivi's earliest suggestion of this idea occurs, as we shall see in the following chapter, in the Matthew commentary.

63. Burr, *Persecution,* 10.

64. For an analysis of the nature of the carnal church in Olivi's thought, see ibid., 20–24; and Burr, "The Apocalyptic Element in Olivi's Critique of Aristotle," *Church History* 40 (1971): 26.

65. "Unde et sicut primus Herodes necavit infantes ut occideret Christum infantem, sic circa primordialem infantiam huius ordinis, regibus mundi devote adorantibus Christi paupertatem in ipso, novus Herodes doctorum carnalium dampnavit statum evangelicum mendicitatis" (*Apoc.* 54ra–rb). It is clear that Olivi

is thinking of the secular masters here. However, as David Burr has pointed out, "it is not clear whether Olivi has one person in mind (e.g., William of St. Amour) or is using the name 'Herod' to designate the whole group." See Burr, *Persecution*, 21, n. 34.

66. See chapter 4.

67. "ita quod multi, qui magisteriis et prelatione videbantur quasi sol, sic facti sunt nigri, ut usque hodie sentiant et doceant statum evangelicum mendicitatis non esse statum perfectionis, vel esse statum evangelice mendicitatis esse statum dampnationis, aut saltem minime perfectionis, et quod habere aliquid in communi est perfectius et magis evangelicum quam non habere" (*Apoc.*, 53ra).

68. See, e.g., *Apoc.* 67rb: "Quidam eorum dicunt paupertatem altissimam non esse de substantia perfectionis eius, et quod eius est habere sufficientia aut saltem necessaria in communi; quidam vero quod usus pauper, id est altissime paupertatis secundum debitas circumstantias proportionatus non est de substantia eius."

69. "Acceperunt enim ingenium et clavem ad aperiendam et exponendam doctrinam Aristotelis et Averrois, commentatoris eius, et ad excogitandum profunda et voraginosa dogmata obscurantia solem christiane sapientie et evangelice vite et purum aerem religiosi status ipsius. . . . Quidam etiam talia dogmata philosophica sine paganica suis theologicis tractantibus inseruerunt ut ex eis multi clerici Parisius philosophantes omnes articulos fidei rejecerint praeter virtutem dei et solam philosophiam mundanam dixerint esse veram et humano regimini sufficientem. Dixeruntque mundum ab eterno fuisse . . . ponuntque unum solum intellectum in omnibus hominibus, et fere negant arbitrii libertatem" (*Apoc.*, 67rb–va).

70. *Apoc.*, 66rb.

71. *Apoc.*, 67ra–rb. See also 50va, 56vb, 83vb, and 101ra. See Burr, *Persecution*, 28 ff., for an excellent analysis of Olivi's attitude toward Aristotle. Olivi was in part following Bonaventure in regarding the triumph of Aristotelian philosophy as a negative apocalyptic sign. See Bonaventure's interpretation of the number 666 (Rev. 13:18) in *Collationes de septem donis spiritus sancti*, in *Opera* 5, p. 497.

72. See *Apoc.* 91ra–rb, 93ra–rb, and 101ra–rb. At one point, Olivi suggests without explicit approval the possibility that a descendant of Frederick the Second would function as one of the evil secular leaders and succeed in attracting several kings to his side, as well as install a pseudopope who would use his power to attack evangelical poverty. See *Apoc.* 93ra.

73. *Apoc.* 91rb.

74. *Apoc.* 9va, 55va, 92vb–93ra.

CHAPTER FOUR   The Franciscan Order under Attack, 1250–1325

1. For details of the controversy, see M.-M. Dufeil, *Guillaume de Saint-Amour et la polémique universitaire parisienne, 1250–59* (Paris, 1972), or the now somewhat dated account in English, D. Douie, *The Conflict between the Seculars*

and the Mendicants at the University of Paris in the Thirteenth Century (London, 1954). On the ecclesiological dimensions of the controversy, the classic piece is Y. Congar, "Aspects ecclésiologiques de la querelle entre mendiants et séculiers," *Archives d'histoire doctrinale et littéraire du moyen âge* 28 (1961): 35–151.

2. The bull may be found in H. Denifle, *Chartularium Universitatis Parisiensis*, 4 vols. (Paris, 1889), 1: 237–43, pp. 265–70.

3. Found in *Chartularium* 1:244, 247, pp. 276–87.

4. Bonaventure's *quaestiones* may be found in *Opera Omnia* 5 (Quaracchi, 1891), 117–95. William's are in Magistri Guillelmi de Sancto Amore, *Opera Omnia* (Constance, 1632), 73–87.

5. The *De Periculis* is found in William's *Opera Omnia*, 17–72. There have been several other editions of the tract, e.g., in E. Brown, ed., *Appendix ad Fasciculum rerum expetendarum* II (London 1690; repr. Tucson, Ariz. 1967), 18–41; and a partial edition in M. Bierbaum, *Bettelorden und Weltgeistlichkeit an der Universität Paris* (Münster 1920), 1–36.

6. Thomas's *Contra impugnantes* has been edited in *Opuscula Theologica* II (Turin and Rome, 1954), 5–110.

7. The text has been edited by M. Bierbaum in *Franziskanische Studien*, Beiheft 2 (Münster in Westfalen, 1920), 37 ff. See F. Pelster, "Thomas von York als Verfasser des Tractates 'Manus quae contra Omnipotentem tenditur,'" in *AFH* 25 (1922): 3–22.

8. See *Chartularium* 1:288, pp. 331–33.

9. Gerard of Abbeville, *Contra adversarium perfectionis Christiana*, ed. S. Clasen, *AFH* 31 (1938): 276–329; 32 (1939): 89–200.

10. *Contra adversarium*, Bk. II, part I., pp. 89–100.

11. Malcolm Lambert, *Franciscan Poverty: The Doctrine of the Absolute Poverty of Christ and the Apostles in the Franciscan Order, 1210–1323* (London, 1961), 133.

12. Bonaventure's *Apologia* may be found in *Opera Omnia* 8 (1898), 233–330.

13. Thomas's *De perfectione spiritualis vitae* is edited in *Opuscula* II, pp. 115–53. His *Contra pestiferam doctrinam* is edited in *Opuscula* II, pp. 159–90. John Pecham's *Tractatus pauperis* may be found in many partial editions. Chapters 1–6 are in *Tractatus pauperis* (Paris, 1925); chaps. 7–9 in *SF* 29 (1932): 47–62, 164–93; chaps. 10 and 16 are in *Tractatus tres de paupertate* (Aberdeen, 1910), 21–87; chaps. 11–14 are in *CF* 14 (1944): 84–120; and ch. 15 is in *Fratris Ricardi de Mediavilla quaestio disputata* (Quaracchi, 1925), 79–88.

14. The erroneous statements drawn up by Gerard may be found in Bierbaum, ed., *Franziskanische Studien*, 169–207.

15. The bull is edited in C. Eubel, ed., *Bullarii Franciscani Epitome* (Ad Claras Aquas, 1908), 290–300. Lambert calls this bull "nothing more than a compressed version of the *Apologia Pauperum*" (*Franciscan Poverty*, 144).

16. For the joint letter, see Wadding, *Annales minorum* 3:380–83. For analyses of the dispute, see W. A. Hinnebusch, *History of the Dominican Order* (Staten

Island, 1965), 161, 296, and 322; *OFP,* 149–51; and Burr, "The *Correctorium* Controversy and the Origins of the *Usus Pauper* Controversy," *Speculum* 60 (1985): 331–42.

17. Bonaventure's *Epistola de tribus quaestionibus,* probably written by February 1257, was intended to answer an anonymous Dominican's charge that the order is hypocritical in claiming not to receive money when in fact it does. It also addresses other charges involving Franciscan practice. See *Opera* 8, p. 331 ff. for the text of the letter.

18. An anonymous Oxford Dominican provides this information in a text documenting his brothers' attempts to stop the Dominican criticism and punish the critics. The chronicle is edited in A. G. Little, *The Grey Friars of Oxford* (Oxford, 1892), 320–35.

19. See Pecham's *Contra Kilwardby* in *Tractatus de paupertate* (Aberdeen, 1910), 129–49. It is not absolutely clear that Kilwardby had made these arguments, though it is safe to assume that they came from the larger Dominican camp.

20. *OFP,* 153.

21. The letter has been published in Benedictus Reichert, "Litterae encyclicae magistrorum generalium," in *Monumenta Ordinis Fratrum Praedicatorum Historica* 5 (Rome, 1900), 100–104.

22. The two condemnations were made by Stephen Tempier, bishop of Paris. A parallel condemnation occurred in 1277 by the Dominican archbishop of Canterbury, Robert Kilwardby. See *Chartularium* 1: 486–87 and 543–58. Despite this Dominican opposition, the Dominican Order soon moved toward establishing Thomism as the only permissible position. In 1278, the General Chapter sent two friars to England to investigate those criticizing Thomas's writings. See *Chartularium* 1:566 ff.

23. See M. Bihl, "Statuta generalia ordinis edita in capitulis generalibus celebratis Narbonae an. 1260, Assisii an. 1279 atque Parisiis an. 1292," *AFH* 34 (1941): 40; and *OFP,* 148.

24. *Summa Theologiae,* 60 vols. (Blackfriars, 1972), 2a2ae, 186. 9; *Quaestiones quodlibetales,* quod. 1, a. 20; *OFP,* 148–49; and Burr, "The *Usus Pauper* Controversy," in *Speculum* 60, no. 2 (April 1985): 337–38.

25. For William's response, see P. Glorieux, *Le correctorium corruptorii "Quare"* (Le Saulchoir, 1927), 302–8 and 405–7.

26. For *Exiit,* see Emil Friedberg, *Corpus Iuris Canonici* (Leipzig, 1879–81, repr. Graz, 1959), 2:1110–12. Nicholas was not the first pope, nor was William the first Franciscan, to argue in this way. Popes Gregory IX and Innocent IV had said similar things. See Gregory's *Quo Elongati* in J. Sbaralea, ed. *Bullarium Franciscanum* (Rome, 1759–1904), 1:68 and Innocent's *Ordinem vestrum* 1:400. The idea was present in some early rule commentaries. See, e.g., D. Flood, *Hugh of Digne's Rule Commentary* (Grottaferrata, 1979), 95.

27. *Summa,* 1a2ae, 108. 1–2. I have generally relied on the editors' translation of the *Summa.* Rather than transcribe the Latin for every passage, I have ex-

cerpted in the text only those Latin phrases I deemed very significant to an understanding of Thomas's meaning, or, where appropriate, I have put the entire Latin text in a note.

28. "Sic igitur lex nova nulla alia exteriora opera determinare debuit praecipiendo vel prohibendo nisi sacramenta, et moralia praecepta quae de se pertinent ad rationem virtutis, puta non esse occidendum, non esse furandum, et alia hujusmodi" (*Summa*, 1a2ae. 108. 2, sed contra).

29. *Summa*, 108. 1. resp. 2.

30. *Summa*, 108. 2. 3.

31. "Ad tertium dicendum quod illa praecepta Dominus dedit Apostolis, non tanquam caeremoniales observantias, sed tanquam moralia instituta. Et possunt intelligi dupliciter. Uno modo, secundum Augustinum in libro *De Consensu Evangelist.*, ut non sint praecepta, sed concessiones. Concessit enim eis ut possent pergere ad praedicationis officium sine pera et baculo et aliis huiusmodi, tanquam habentes potestatem necessaria vitae accipiendi ab illis quibus praedicabant: unde subdit, *Dignus enim est operarius cibo suo.* Non autem peccat, sed supererogat, qui sua portat, ex quibus vivat in praedicationis officio, non accipiens sumptum ab his quibus Evangelium praedicat, sicut Paulus fecit" (*Summa* 1a2ae, 108.2. resp. ad 3um).

32. See Augustine, *De Consensu*, 173–82.

33. "Alio modo possunt intelligi, secundum aliorum Sanctorum expositionem, ut sint quaedam statuta temporalia Apostolis data pro illo tempore quo mittebantur ad praedicandum in Iudaea ante Christi passionem. Indigebant enim discipuli, quasi adhuc parvuli sub Christi cura existentes, accipere aliqua specialia instituta a Christo, sicut et quilibet subditi a suis praelatis, et praecipue quia erant paulatim exercitandi, ut temporalium sollicitudinem abdicarent, per quod reddebantur idonei ad hoc quod Evangelium per universum orbem praedicarent. Nec est mirum si, adhuc durante statu veteris legis, et nondum perfectam libertatem Spiritus consecutis, quosdam determinatos modos vivendi instituit. Quae quidem statuta, imminente passione, removit, tamquam discipulis iam per ea sufficienter exercitatis. Unde Luc. XXII dixit, Quando misi vos sine sacculo, et pera et calceamentis, numquid aliquid defuit vobis? At illi dixerunt: Nihil. Dixit ergo eis: Sed nunc qui habet sacculum, tollat; similiter et peram. Iam enim imminebat tempus perfectae libertatis, ut totaliter suo dimitterentur arbitrio in his quae secundum se non pertinent ad necessitatem virtutis" (*Summa* 1a2ae, 108. resp. ad 3um).

34. This section is heavily indebted to *OFP.*

35. One third of these were in Italy. This probably meant that one in every thousand Italians was a Franciscan in 1250. As David Burr has said of this development, "One out of every thousand people cannot be expected to emulate Saint Francis, even in Italy." See *OFP,* 4. For these figures, see L. Pellegrini, *Insediamenti Francesccani nell'Italia del duecento* (Rome, 1984), 185 n. 58.

36. See *OFP,* 1–16 for a discussion of these and other factors in the loss of rigor over the first few decades of Franciscan history.

37. There *is* evidence from Italy of a debate over the degree of restricted use suitable to a Franciscan, but no evidence of a debate before 1279 concerning the theoretical issue of the relationship of the vow and *usus pauper*. The problem seems to have centered in the March of Ancona and occurred in the wake of a rumor, spread during the Council of Lyons in 1274, that the pope was prepared to force the Franciscan Order to accept property. There really is no evidence of a similar problem in other provinces in Italy. See Angelo da Clareno, *Historia*, 302–5; and *OFP*, 27–29.

38. Burr, "The *Usus Pauper* Controversy," 333.

39. As already noted in the first chapter, the *Letter to R.* does not indicate that poverty was an important element in the conflict with Brother Ar. However, as also noted, the *Attack* does begin by announcing that Olivi had already shown his opponents' view of poverty to be erroneous. Koch has argued that the work Olivi is referring to here is the *Tractatus de usu paupere* ("Die Verurteilung"). If so, then Brother Ar. and his friends were also Olivi's opponents on the issue of poor use, as David Burr thinks is likely. See his "The *Usus Pauper* Controversy," 341.

40. See *Littera septem sigillarum*, 52; and Burr, *Persecution*, 61–62 ; and *OFP*, 90.

41. *OFP*, 141.

42. See chap. 6 of *OFP*.

CHAPTER FIVE   Olivi's Gospel Commentaries in Context

1. Olivi is sometimes referred to in contemporary writings as "Petrus Iohannes." However, "Petrus Iohannis" is more common and probably correct. His name, therefore, is "Peter, son of John," not "Peter John." The name "Olivi" may be a Latinized form of "Olieu." See A. Thomas, "Le vrai nom du frère mineur Petrus Johannis Olivi," *Annales du Midi* 25 (1913): 68–69; and Burr, *Persecution*, 6. I would like to note the special debt I have in this chapter to Burr, *Persecution*. It led me to virtually all of the primary sources I have used in this chapter, and Burr's own narrative of Olivi's life and vicissitudes is one whose influence I cannot, nor would not want to, escape.

2. This information is furnished to us by the Dominican inquisitor Bernard Gui, *Pratica inquisitionis*, ed. C. Douais (Paris, 1886), 287. Bernard got this information from a book produced by some of Olivi's followers after the latter's death. This passage is quoted in Burr, *Persecution*, 5; and in C. Partee, "Peter John Olivi: Historical and Doctrinal Study," *FS* 20 (1960): 215.

3. Burr, *Persecution*, 5.

4. A possibility suggested by Partee, "Peter John Olivi," 216. Partee seems to be relying on a suggestion made in H. Felder, *Geschichte des wissenschaftlichen Studien im Franziskanerorden bis um Mitte des 13. Jahrhunderts* (Freiburg im B., 1904), pp. 211, 358 et seq., and 539. It was expected that each custody would provide a school in one of its convents where those destined for advanced study

would be sent. See J. Moorman, *A History of The Franciscan Order* (Oxford, 1968), 123. The constitutions produced at the General Chapter of Narbonne (at about the time Olivi entered the order), however, specify that the period of study at such schools be at least three to four years. See Bihl, "Statuta generalia," 72–73.

5. Olivi mentions having heard Bonaventure's exegesis of the apocalyptic number 666 at Paris. This exegesis occurs in the eighth of Bonaventure's *Collationes de Donis Sancti Spiritus,* which was delivered in Paris on April 1, 1268. The text in question may be found in Bonaventure's *Opera Omnia* 5 (Quaracchi, 1891), 497. See Burr, *Persecution,* 6, and Partee, "Petrus Iohannis Olivi," 216, for further references in Olivi's own works to his years in Paris.

6. The Narbonne Constitutions edited in Bihl, "Statuta generalia," 72–73 state that the friars were expected to remain at university schools for at least four years.

7. In a letter written around 1281 or 1282, Olivi declares that he feared "Parisian ambitions." He goes on to express delight in Christ's decision to frustrate the world in its desire to elevate him to a merely "human *magisterium*." This letter may be found in *Quodlibeta Petri Ioannis Provenzalis,* ed. L. Soardus (Venice, 1509), f. 51v. Because it is not certain who was the recipient of this letter, scholars have referred to this epistle as the *Letter to R.* See Burr, *Persecution,* 32. Even if we assume (as Olivi does) that he was destined to become a master, there are reasons to doubt that it was modesty which nudged him from his destiny. As David Burr has pointed out, "Olivi's writings reveal no serious doubts concerning the compatibility of either study or the *magisterium* with Franciscan vows" (*Persecution,* 31). Moreover, by the time this letter was written, Olivi had already earned a reputation for doctrinal heterodoxy. In fact, Olivi himself gives evidence in the same letter that his failure to proceed to the *magisterium* may have been connected to doubts about his orthodoxy. See *Letter to R.,* p. 51v. If he was indeed destined for the *magisterium,* it was probably his heterodoxy (real or supposed), not his humility, which kept him from getting there.

8. In 1385 Bartholomew of Pisa described Olivi as *a bachalarius formatus Parisius.* See Ehrle, "Petrus Johannis Olivi, sein Leben und seine Schriften," in *Archiv* 3 (1887): 409–552, at p. 412, where the passage from Barholomew is quoted. The passage is taken from Bartholomew's *Liber de Conformitate Vitae S. Francisci ad vitam Domini Iesu;* it may be found in *AF* 4 (1906): 339. Some modern scholars have assumed the accuracy of Bartholomew's witness. There are, however, reasons to doubt this source. Writing almost a century after Olivi's death, Bartholomew may have assumed that Olivi was a formed bachelor from the existence of his *Quaestiones in Libros Sententiarum Magistri Petri Lombardi.* However, this *Sentence* commentary was not produced by Olivi until 1287–88, when he was serving as lector in the order's *studium* in Florence, and there is no evidence that he produced an earlier commentary. See V. Heynck, "Zur Datierung der Sentenzenkommentare des Petrus Johannis Olivi und des Petrus de Trabibus," *FS* 38 (1956): 371–98. Some of the individual *quaestiones* later included

in Olivi's *Sentence* commentary were written early in his career but only later incorporated into the complete commentary written in Florence.

9. Olivi is placed in Montpellier by the *Letter to R.*, 51v and 52r. A later reminiscence in Olivi's *Sentence* commentary places him at Narbonne during this period. See *In Secundum Librum* 1: 633. See also Burr, *Persecution*, 6; and Partee, "Peter John Olivi," 217 n. 13.

10. During this period, Olivi also commented on Isaiah and Job and probably on other biblical books as well. These were probably also the years in which Olivi was writing some of the questions later incorporated into his *Quaestiones super sententias.* He also completed his *Tractatus de usu paupere* (found in Vat. lat. 4986 with the incipit "Quoniam contra paupertatem evangelicam") between 1279 and 1283, an important work which reflects the burgeoning strife within the order on the issue of *usus pauper*. Before completing this treatise, Olivi had written perhaps sixteen of his seventeen *Quaestiones de perfectione evangelica*, one of the most important sources for his understanding of the Franciscan life.

11. Angelo da Clareno, *Historia*, 288.

12. Angelo's report that Jerome burned Olivi's questions is corroborated by a fourteenth-century list of Olivi's condemnations found in Leo Amorós, "Series condemnationum et processuum contra doctrinam et sequaces Petri Ioannis Olivi," *AFH* 24 (1931): 502. According to this source, Jerome burned the questions at a meeting of the brothers gathered at Montpellier. Corroboration may be found in other fourteenth-century documents which seem to have been directed against the Spirituals by the community. See Raymundus de Fronchiaco, *Sol ortus, Archiv* 3 (1887): 13; and "Notice et extraits d'un manuscrit franciscain," *CF* 15 (1945): 86. These sources are discussed in Burr, *Persecution*, 36.

13. Olivi says that he satisfied Jerome on the question of marriage in a work produced after the 1283 censure, found in D. Laberge, "Fr. Petri Ioannis Olivi, O.F.M., tria scripta sui ipsius apologetica annorum 1283 et 1285," *AFH* 28 (1935–36): 127. Olivi asserts that he said something on the second two subjects in his *Letter to R.*, ff. 51v and 52r. It is sometimes said in the scholarship that he answered Jerome on these questions, though note here he says that these remarks were made "*ante* tempora fratris Hieronymi." These texts are discussed in Burr, *Persecution*, 37 and Olivi's positions on these issues at greater length in chaps. 6 and 7 of the same work.

14. *OFP,* 39.

15. *Letter to R.*, f. 52r.

16. J. H. Sbaralea has suggested Arlotto of Prato, in *Supplementum ad scriptores trium ordinum S. Francisci*, 3 vols. (Rome, 1908–36), 3:597. If Sbaralea is right, it was unfortunate that Olivi feuded with such a man. Before becoming minister general, Arlotto served, as noted above, on the Parisian commission which censured him. Arlotto, however, is probably not the adversary in question, since Olivi's opponent was from his own province, not from Italy. Ehrle has proposed Arnold of Roquefeil, in "Petrus Johannis Olivi," 478. Arnold *was* from Provence.

Later, as its provincial minister, he joined thirty–five brothers from the province in attacking Olivi as a leader of a superstitious sect and a sower of dissension and discord. See Raymundus de Fronchiaco, *Sol Ortus,* 14. Though a better choice than Arlotto of Prato, Arnold is not the man, as proven by Gratien de Paris, who has noted that in the Paris manuscript of his *Letter to R.,* Olivi refers to Brother Ar. as *bone memorie.* Arnold was provincial of Provence as late as 1300, nearly twenty years after this letter was written. See "Une lettre inedité de Pierre de Jean Olivi," in *EF* 29 (1913): 414–22. These theories are discussed in Burr, *Persecution,* 38, and in Partee, "Peter John Olivi," 221.

17. Gratien de Paris, "Une lettre inédite," 419. The text from Raymond may be found in *Sol Ortus,* 16.

18. The most popular theory can be traced back to the fourteenth century and to the leaders of the Spiritual wing of the order. Angelo da Clareno and Ubertino da Casale both assert that the fundamental issue in the dispute was poverty. Olivi's antagonists wished to discredit his views on *usus pauper.* Having failed in this endeavor, they attacked him where he was evidently vulnerable, namely, in his theological and philosophical opinions. See Angelo da Clareno, *Historia,* 291; and Ubertino da Casale, *Sanctitati apostolicae,* in *Archiv* 2 (1886): 388. In essentials, this theory has been advanced in more recent years by Ehrle and, more intricately, by Joseph Koch. See Ehrle, "Petrus Johannis Olivi," 416; and J. Koch, "Die Verurteilung Olivis auf dem Konzil von Vienne und ihre Vorge-schichte," in *Scholastik* 5 (1930): 489–522. There are good reasons to wonder about this explanation. As David Burr has pointed out, one must be suspicious of An-gelo and Ubertino as guides to the reasons for Olivi's difficulties. These two men were writing in a special context where poverty was a particularly important issue; the circumstances in which they were writing may well have skewed their pre-sentation of the process against their champion Olivi. See Burr, *Persecution,* 40. Moreover, the documents written by Olivi himself during this period do not indi-cate that poverty played a pivotal role in the incipient stages of the controversy. Finally, Olivi's theological and philosophical opinions were suspect even before the quarrel with Brother Ar.

19. *Letter to R.,* f. 52v; Burr, *Persecution,* 38.

20. *Attack,* ff. 42r–49v; Burr, *Persecution,* 38.

21. *Letter to R.,* f. 52v; Burr, *Persecution,* 38.

22. The record of Bonagratia's letters exists in Raymond de Fronciacho's *Sol ortus,* 13. This reconstruction of events is based on Koch, "Verurteilung Olivis," 500–502; and Burr, *Persecution,* 38–41. After having been censured by Bonagratia, some of Olivi's friends requested information on his theses in order that they might help him. It was in this context that Olivi produced the *Letter to R.* that we have been discussing.

23. The *Chronica XXIV generalium,* 374–76 implies that Bonagratia decided to form the commission on the basis of a decree agreed upon at the Chapter in Strassburg. This has been questioned. See Burr, *Persecution,* 41, where it is

suggested that the relevant *definitio* may have been "a result rather than a cause of the Olivi process."

24. The terminology is used in the *Chronica XXIV generalium*, 374. Bonagratia probably gave the commission entire works, rather than pre-selected excerpts, from which the commission itself could select offensive passages. See Burr, *Persecution*, 41.

25. In a letter written to the Paris commission in 1285, Olivi says that some were judged false, some ignorant, and some presumptuous. See Damasus Laberge, "Fr. Petri Ioannis Olivi, O.F.M., tria scripta sui ipsius apologetica annorum 1283 et 1285," *AFH* 28 (1935–36): 132.

26. Since this letter was sent with the seals of the seven theologians on the commission, it came to be known as the *Letter of the Seven Seals*. See *Chronica XXIV generalium*, 374–76. The letter is extant and has been edited in G. Fussenegger, "'Littera septem sigillorum' contra doctrinam Petri Ioannis Olivi edita," *AFH* 47 (1954): 45–53. The *rotulus* remains undiscovered.

27. This according to the *Chronica XXIV Generalium*, found in pp. 374–76, corroborated by Olivi in Laberge, "Tria scripta," 132. Olivi's copies of his own writings had, of course, already been confiscated. This latter order refers to copies in the hands of other members of the order. The same passage in the *Chronica* informs us that the Commission of Seven included four masters and three bachelors. The four masters were Arlotto of Prato (later minister general), John of Wales, Simon of Lens, and Brother Droco (provincial minister of France). The three bachelors were Richard of Middleton (later a master), John of Murovalle (also later minister general) and Giles of Bensa. This is confirmed in Olivi, in Laberge, "Tria scripta," 130.

28. *Chronica XXIV Generalium*, 376; Raymundus de Fronciacho, *Sol Ortus*, 14; Burr, *Persecution*, 42.

29. *Contra* the reports of the *Chronicle* and Raymund. Olivi wished neither to imply unconditional acceptance of the commission's judgment on his theses nor to refuse to endorse them, lest he seem to deny the statements of faith they contained. Olivi therefore chose to assent to some of the *Letter*'s statements unconditionally and others conditionally. He offered no defense at all concerning purely philosophical matters. See Olivi's own report in Laberge, "Tria scripta," 134. The Avignon hearing is discussed in Burr, *Persecution*, 42; and Partee, "Peter John Olivi," 225.

30. In Laberge, "Tria scripta," 132–35.

31. I.e., the *Responsio ad litteram magistrorum* found in Laberge, "Tria scripta," 126–30.

32. In Laberge, "Tria scripta," 132–35; Burr, *Persecution*, 43–44; Partee, "Peter John Olivi," 225–26.

33. *Chronica XXIV generalium*, 382.

34. The *Chronica XXIV generalium*, 382 says that the affair remained "undiscussed." Ubertino says Arlotto rescinded the measures against Olivi, strengthen-

ing the case that Arlotto took at least some significant action before his death. See his *Sanctitati apostolicae,* 387. Angelo da Clareno furnishes an elaborate account which reports that Olivi defended his view of the divine presence at Paris before Arlotto and two other members of the commission, Richard of Mediavilla and John of Murrovalle. When he had finished, Arlotto turned to the latter two and said, "Frater Richarde et frater Ioannes, respondete ei." They, of course, could not, having been overwhelmed by the vigor of Olivi's argument and the wisdom and spirit with which he spoke. See Angelo da Clareno, *Historia,* 295 ff. While undoubtedly embellished in many details, Angelo's account may contain a basic truth, namely, that Olivi was given a hearing before some members of the commission in Paris.

35. Ubertino, *Sanctitati apostolicae,* 400 ff; Burr, *Persecution,* 67.

36. Ubertino suggests that it was at the suggestion of Olivi's old minister Jerome of Ascoli, then Pope Nicholas IV. See *Sanctitati apostolicae,* 400. Scholars have disagreed on why Olivi was sent to a convent at Italy rather than kept in southern France. F. Tocco has contended that it represented an effort to weaken the spiritual movement in southern France by sending one of its leaders to Italy. See his *Studi Francescani* (Naples, 1909), 370 ff. As Burr has pointed out, this is a hard view to defend: "If the minister general did not want Olivi to consort with the more radical proponents of Franciscan poverty, Italy was hardly the place to send him." See Burr, *Persecution,* 67–68. Gratien de Paris has suggested, probably more correctly, that the move was intended to separate Olivi not from his supporters but from his enemies. See his *Histoire de la fondation et de l'évolution de l'ordre des frères mineurs au XIIIe siècle* (Paris, 1928), 382.

37. This according to Ubertino, *Sanctitas vestra,* 51–89. Raymond, as we recall, may have been the friend to whom Olivi had addressed his *Letter to R.*

38. Here I follow Burr in *Persecution,* 68; and *OFP,* 107–8.

39. *Chronica XXIV generalium,* 420–22.

40. Raymundus de Fronciacho and Bonaventura de Bergamo, *Infrascripta dant,* in *Archiv* 3 (1887): 141–60 at 157; Raymundus de Fronciacho, *Sol ortus,* 15.

41. The *Chronica XXIV generalium,* 420–22 says that Olivi was not implicated in the charges made by Nicholas IV, which is corroborated by a fourteenth-century conventual source found in Amoros, "Series condemnationum," 504. However, Raymond of Fronsac asserts that one of the pope's letters was aimed at Olivi personally and that Olivi was compelled to recant his position on *usus pauper.* See *Sol ortus,* 14 ff. Another fourteenth-century conventual source says that the pope punished Olivi "for his excesses." See Raymondus de Fronciacho and Bonagratia de Bergamo, *Infrascripta dant,* p. 157. This latter claim is uncorroborated by other sources, likely motivated by partisan concerns and openly disputed by Ubertino, *Declaratio, Archiv* 3 (1887): 192. These sources are discussed in Burr, *Persecution,* 68; and *OFP,* 129 n. 16.

42. The *Chronica XXIV generalium,* p. 421 reports that Olivi affirmed in his explanation that Franciscans are bound only to that way of life understood by the

professors of the community of the order, thus raising the question of whether Olivi's position on *usus pauper* had changed. As Burr has pointed out, "the concession was probably more apparent than real, since Olivi had previously argued that his view of *usus pauper* was implied in the accepted practices of the order." See Burr, *Persecution*, 69.

43. One of the most important themes of Burr's *OFP* is that Olivi's view of *usus pauper* was, in many ways, remarkably moderate and flexible. See, e.g., pp. 68–71 and 137–38. The evidence just considered makes it clear that the zealous had by no later than 1290 produced their own radical wing in Provence. Clearly, leaders of the Franciscan Order were able to distinguish between Olivi and this more fanatical "group." Evidence considered in a moment will demonstrate how alarmed Olivi himself could be with the radical wing of the order in Italy.

44. Ubertino, *Sanctitati apostolicae*, 386; *Declaratio*, 144.

45. In 1295 Olivi penned a letter to his friend Conrad of Offida, a leader of the rigorists in Italy. As is well known, the Italian Spirituals of the late thirteenth century were vigorously opposed to Boniface VIII. Boniface had succeeded their hero Celestine V, once the holy hermit Peter Morrone. Using imagery taken directly out of the Apocalypse, some Italian Spirituals were calling for separation from the carnal church of Boniface. Olivi was positively appalled. He wrote to Conrad in the hopes that his friend might be able to deter the Spirituals from this course of action. See *Epistola ad Conradum de Offida*, in L. Oliger, "Petri Iohannis Olivi de renuntiatione papae Coelestine V quaestio et epistola," *AFH* 11 (1918): 309–77 and discussion in Burr, *Persecution*, 69–72; and *OFP*, 112–24. Several months earlier, Olivi had written a letter to the three sons of King Charles of Naples, who were being held as hostages in Catalonia. The letter is witness to the importance that Olivi had achieved as a leader even outside the order. See *Epistola ad regis Sicilie filios*, in *Archiv* 3 (1887): 534–40.

46. Bernard Gui, *Pratica inquisitionis*, 287.

47. Olivi, *Jn.* Vat. Ottob. lat. 3302, f. 140v, 143v, 176v, 185r, 223r, 226r, 230v, 249r, 257r, 259v, 262r.

48. Olivi, *Lk.* Vat. Ottob. lat 3302, f. 10v, 24r, 27v, 38r, 42v, 44v, 53r, 56v, 57v, 65r, 68v, 69r, 71r, 73v, 75r, 91v, 94r, 98v, 99r, 100r, 102v, 106v, 108r, 108v, 120v.

49. Olivi, *Lk.* 18v, 65r, 99r, 109v, 110v, and 120v.

50. Olivi's intentions are expressed at the beginning of his commentary on Mark-Luke: "Quoniam pauca extra Matthaeum differit, breviter proponamus ac deinde consimilem in Luca tangendo aliqua que ultra ceteros addit aliqualiter pertractemus" (1r).

51. "Intendo autem fere ubique omittere quae super Mattheum et Iohannem diffusius scripsi" (*Lk.*, 38r). This comment is made as Olivi begins to gloss the Lucan genealogy.

52. The Luke commentary refers to the Mark commentary at f. 100r.

53. See *OFP*, 54–55, nn. 28 and 36. The argument here is a slight modification of that presented in Burr, "The Date of Petrus Iohannis Olivi's Commen-

tary on Matthew," *CF* 46 (1976): 131–38, where Burr concluded that the Matthew commentary was probably written in 1280–81.

54. See H. V. Schooner, "La *Lectura in Matthaeum* de S. Thomas," *Angelicum* 33 (1956): 121–42.

55. Thomas, *Mtt.*, 3.

56. The *Opus Imperfectum* was an unfinished commentary on Matthew which, because it was supposedly authored by Chrysostom, exerted a significant influence on many medieval gospel commentaries. In the preface to the first volume of his critical edition of the *Opus Imperfectum*, J. van Banning has argued that the commentary may have been written by a fifth-century Arian bishop or priest whose mother tongue was Latin, perhaps in a Roman province south of the Danube. See his *Opus Imperfectum in Matthaeum*, CCL 87B (Turnholt, 1988), v. The *Opus Imperfectum* was attributed to Chrysostom in virtually all of the extant medieval manuscripts. Erasmus was the first to doubt that the work was written by Chrysostom.

57. *Mtt.*, 5va–vb. Olivi often remarks that Christ's miracles are a "confirmation of doctrine." Indeed, he regards most of the eighth chapter of Matthew as miraculous confirmation of teachings given in the Sermon on the Mount. See Olivi, *Mtt.*, 68vb.

58. Note Olivi's warning about this division: "Predicta autem divisio per quandam antonomasiam est dicta. Non enim sic sunt omnino ab invicem distincte quod nichil unius comprehendatur sub altera sicut in scientiis philosoficis et earum partibus ut plurimum invenitur. Talis enim divisio non posset bono modo his dari quia scriptura sacra non debuit nec decuit tali modo tradi sed alio longe capatiori et altiori sicut in generalibus principiis et in questione de subiecto theologie est aliqualiter ostensum" (*Mtt.* 33vb–34ra). The general principles alluded to refer to Olivi's six *Principia generalia in sacram scripturam* found in BN Lat. 15588 before the Matthew commentary and printed in an early modern edition of Bonaventure's minor works (B. Bonelli, *Supplementum operum omnium S. Bonaventurae* [Trent, 1772]). A superior, modern critical edition is now available in *Peter of John Olivi on the Bible*, ed. David Flood and Gedeon Gál (St. Bonaventure, N.Y., 1997).

59. Bonaventure's John commentary is of the "magisterial" variety, since it includes many theological *quaestiones*. However, his Luke commentary does not include such questions.

60. The practice of introducing such questions into gospel commentaries seems to have started, as we saw in chapter 1, with the author of the *Enarrationes in Evangelium S. Matthaei*. Many manuscripts of Olivi's commentary contain a *tabula quaestionum* at the end of the commentary. There is an extraordinary number of *quaestiones* found in the Prologue and in chapters 1–5 of the *Lectura*. The rate at which Olivi stops to ponder theological questions then begins to drop significantly. This, too, was standard thirteenth-century practice. For a sample of the kind of theological questions commonly asked in thirteenth-century commentaries, consider this list of Olivi's twelve questions on the Genealogy (1:2–16):

1. Why does it put lateral pairs of brothers in only three places? (*Mtt.*, 6va–6vb)
2. Why does it include only four women? (6vb–7ra)
3. How is it true that Boaz is the son of Salmon? (7ra–7rb)
4. How was Ruth accepted into the people of God? (7rb–7va)
5. Why does Matthew call David King and his father Jesse? (7va)
6. Why does Matthew omit three kings between Joram and Uzziah? (7va–8va)
7. How is it true that Josiah became a father at the time of the deportation to Babylon? (8va)
8. How is it true that Salathiel fathered Zorobabel? (8va)
9. How is it true that Josiah fathered Jeconiah? (8ra–8va)
10. Why does Matthew record the genealogy of Joseph and not of Mary when it does not pertain to the genealogy of Christ? (8va–8rb)
11. Why is the genealogy distinguished into three groups of fourteen? (8vb–9vb)
12. Why is there diversity between Matthew and Luke on genealogy? (9vb–10va)

61. For an exception, see Olivi's interpretation of Mt. 16:21 ("From that time on, Jesus began to show his disciples that he must go to Jerusalem and undergo great suffering . . . and be killed, and on the third day be raised"), where Olivi offers a literal, allegorical, moral, and anagogical interpretation for why Christ was raised on the third day. See *Mtt.*, 107vb.

62. Note that Olivi would hardly have considered these as unimportant, secondary senses. Like Joachim and other Franciscan followers of Joachim, Olivi was convinced that his age was one in which "spiritual men" would be able better to understand the meaning of the Bible, especially its spiritual meaning (*intelligentia spiritualis*). Much as he depends upon the Latin Fathers, he was convinced, as was Joachim, that those exegetes of the third and final *status* of history would, with the help of the Holy Spirit, be able to understand the New Testament far more profoundly than their patristic predecessors. In this context, the spiritual readings of the gospels he offers take on special meaning. This context also renders more interesting the question of how Olivi saw himself as an exegete of the Bible.

63. It was, of course, a large part of Olivi's job to transmit to his pupils the inherited wisdom of the fathers on the text in question. He would have been derelict in his responsibility had he written a commentary consisting solely of his own original insights into the gospel (assuming such an enterprise is even possible).

64. Olivi quotes Jerome's commentary on Matthew, Chrysostom's homilies on Matthew, Pseudo-Chrysostom's *Opus Imperfectum,* and Augustine's *De Consensu* most frequently. He quotes from the Matthew commentaries of the other exegetes.

65. The *Catena* was intended to provide a more thorough compilation of authorities than had until then been available. Thomas produced this massive work with the help of an unnamed Greek scholar during the years 1263–67. See Weisheipl, *Friar Thomas* (New York, 1974), 171–73, 370–71. I use the Marietti edition of the *Catena*, 2 vols. (Turin and Rome, 1953). Olivi's use of this text would provide evidence for Smalley's comment in *The Gospels*, 257 that, "It seems certain that [Thomas's] *Catena* underlies many later medieval Gospel commentaries." Fr. Thomas Murtaugh and I both came to the discovery of Olivi's dependence on the *Catena* independently. However, I would like to acknowledge that Fr. Murtaugh seems to have come to the discovery first and that he was able to prove Olivi's use of the *Catena* with a certainty that I had not achieved when he reported the results of his research to me on 24 January 1992.

66. This text has been edited in *PL* 198: 1557–1644.

67. E.g., on the identity of the Essenes, *Mtt.* 22rb; or on the derivation of the word "Jordan," f. 106ra.

CHAPTER SIX   The New Evangelical Order and Olivi's Matthew Commentary

1. See *Tractatus*, 69–73.

2. "itaque in oriente viderunt magi stellam, quia in ipso ortu Ecclesie tradiderunt nobis apostoli intelligentiam spiritalem" (*Tractatus*, 73).

3. *Tractatus*, 73.

4. "Ego autem puto quod sicut Christus apparuit magis post duodecim dies, ita post duodecim centenas annorum consumanda est in spiritu hec revelatio veritatis" (*Tractatus*, 73).

5. "Et ut perpendamus hec misteria non frustra precessisse invenies post duodecim tricenarios annorum, quos quidam vocant generationes ecclesie, magnam plenitudinem illuminationis datam universo orbi, converso iam Constantino, et facto viceno consilio et Arreo condemnato, apparentibusque iam tam in Grecis, quam in Latinis, illis magnis doctoribus, ex quorum fontibus manant usque hodie multa librorum volumina" (Olivi, *Mtt.*, 17ra). As argued in the second chapter, the *quidam* referred to here might well include Joachim.

6. "Et iterum post duodecim centenarum annorum, scilicet in initio tercidecimi, apparuit regula evangelica et eius renovator Christi stigmatibus insignitus, in cuius fine apostolisque creditur magnum aliquid suboriri spectans ad iteratam conversionem gentium et etiam Iudeorum" (Olivi, *Mtt.*, 18ra).

7. "per Christum natum designatur ortus contemplativi et evangelici status in fine temporum suscitandi" (Olivi, *Lk.*, 24v).

8. Olivi, *Lk.*, 10r.

9. Hilary, *Mtt.*, 349.

10. Thomas, *Mtt.*, 123–25.

11. Olivi, *Mtt.*, 74vb.

12. Olivi, *Mtt.* 74vb.

13. "ut nulla inter nobiles et ignobiles, inter divites et egenos in praedicatione distantia sit. Haec magistri rigorem, haec praeceptoris comprobant veritatem, quando omnis apud eum qui salvari potest aequalis est" (Jerome, *Mtt.*, 1:216).

14. "Et nota, quod magis dicit, *Pauperes evangelizantur,* quam virgines vel obedientes, quia paupertas fundamentum est evangelicae perfectionis" (Bonaventure, *Lk.,* 175).

15. See Hugh, *Mtt.,* 42vb; Thomas, *Mtt.,* p. 142; and John of LaRochelle, *Mtt.,* 104ra–106ra.

16. "Unde sub apostolis cepit illuminatio mundi. In martiribus autem claudicatio, contra affectum vite corporalis nimis insignitus, per mortis desiderium et amplexum, fuit perfect rectificata. In Constantino vero leproso leprae ydolatrie et immundiciarum gentilium expurgatur. In anachoritis autem et in consiliis patrum generalibus, tarditas cordium ad auditum divini fuit stimulata et excitata" (Olivi, *Mtt.,* 86rb).

17. "In quinto vero tempore multiplicatis lapsibus mortalium peccatorum, vita sanctorum fuit necessaria, et institutiones divinarum religionum ad extrahendum submergendos de aquis lascivie secularis. In sexto vero tempore paupertas evangelica predicatur" (Olivi, *Mtt.,* 86rb).

18. Thomas, *Mtt.,* 171: "Hic ponitur parabolica doctrina. Et intendit tria. Primo ponit impedimentum evangelicae doctrinae; secundo profectum; tertio dignitatem." For a similar interpretation, see Hugh, *Mtt,* 48vb.

19. Nota quod licet omnes parabole designent cursum fidei et ecclesie seu novi testamenti. Nichilominus prime due respiciunt initium seminationis fidei et ecclesie. Due vero sequentes, scilicet de grano sinapis et de fermento, respiciunt eius dilatationem. Tres vero ultime respiciunt finem, ita quod due priores respiciunt renovationem evangelice paupertatis et perfectionis, ultima vero finalem conversionem mundi (Olivi, *Mtt.,* 95vb).

20. "Reiectio autem omnium propter regnum celorum facta et ordinatio omnium in ipsum venditio et emptio vocatur, quamvis etiam per evangelice paupertatis consilium ad litteram istud fiat. . . . Unde Luc. 12 dicit *Vendite que possidetis et date elemosynam*" (Olivi, *Mtt.,* 98va); "Nota etiam quod utraque parabola in fine conveniat, scilicet in venditione et emptione" (ibid.).

21. "Thesaurus autem dicitur absconditus in agro quia valde est segregatus a noticia et experientia hominum carnalium" (Olivi, *Mtt,* 98va).

22. ". . . Deus sub certo ordine et numero tempora et status populi Dei distinguit, et sic ergo omnia referuntur in Christum tanquam in finem suum. Unde sicut infra patebit sub diversarum parabolarum misterio Christus diversimode distinguit tempora ecclesie seu populi Dei." Did Olivi intend to refer to the Joachimist *status* here? It seems so. Otherwise, his use of both *tempora* and *status* would have been superfluous. Olivi seems to distinguish the two terms here. However, the fact that he uses the term *status* here in a way distinct from *tempus* should not be taken to imply that he uses the term in this way throughout the commentary. At the end of this comment, Olivi also adds: "Ex quo patet quod

non sunt usquequa contempnendi illi qui tempora ecclesie sub certis statibus et generationibus distinxerunt" (*Mtt.* 8vb–9ra). As suggested in the first chapter the anonymous *illi* may refer to, or at least include, Joachim of Fiore. See also this comment on the parables from the thirteenth chapter of the commentary: "Christus in suis parabolis et sermonibus enigmaticis totum ordinem seculi et precipue quo ad gubernationem et cursum humani generis et secreta divine predestinationis et prescientie preferabatur" (*Mtt.*, 98va).

23. Hilary, *Mtt.*, 294.

24. Jerome, *Mtt*, 1:270; Chrysostom, *Mtt.*, Homily 45, pp. 463–71.

25. See Hugh, *Mtt.*, 49r; Thomas, *Mtt.*, 172; Alexander, *Mtt.*, 37rb; John of LaRochelle, *Mtt.* 134v–135v; and Bonaventure, *Lk.* 189–93. Note that in Luke, the Sower is not part of a sequence of seven, so that even if Bonaventure were inclined to see the parable as part of a prophecy of the church in seven ages, its place in Luke would not have allowed him to do so. Even more importantly, Bonaventure is almost nowhere inclined to historicize Lukan pericopes unless his exegetical predecessors had done so, and he almost never historicizes them in terms of his own distinctive theology of history.

26. Olivi, *Mtt*, 96vb–97ra.

27. "Nota quod in hac parabola mistice potest ostendi decursus mundi ab Adam usque ad Christum; et iterum a Christo usque ad finem ecclesie. In primo enim tempore fuit effrenata vagatio pervia demonibus et ideo finaliter ruerunt in ydolatriam, que est cultus demonorum. In secundo fuit superficialis plebs iudeorum qui faciles fuerunt ad promittendum omnia: *Quecumque dixerit Dominus faciemus.* Sed tamen fuerunt semper dure cervicis, in cuius signum legem in tabulis lapideis receperunt; ad tempus quidem credentes, sed in tempore cuiuscumque temptationis a Deo recedentes; sicut patet in omnibus temptationibus ab exitu de Egypto et ultra. In tertio multitudo diviciarum eos scidit in duo regna. Fuitque in eis fallacia pseudoprophetarum promittentium pacem et etiam bona mundi. Affueruntque multa maleficia ad exterminandum veros prophetas et tandem caput prophetarum Christum. In creatione autem primi hominis, exierat Deus seminare seminem suum et cum sic fuisset deperditum tandem in virgine et in ecclesia apostolorum fecit abundantem fructum. . . . Post Christum etiam in ecclesia de gentibus primo fuit vagatio paganorum subiecta demonibus, secundo pertinatia lapidea hereticorum, cito intrantium ad fidem et citius discedentium, tertio opulentatio ecclesiarum et negotiatio diviciarum et symoniarum et litigiorum. Exierat autem Christus ad seminandum seminem evangelice vite, quod in Francisco et eius regula cepit fructum reddere pleniorem et in fine temporum consummandum" (Olivi, *Mtt.*, 97rb).

28. There are no double-seven *concordie* found in the entire Matthew commentary, though, as we shall see in a moment, Olivi did develop slightly more detailed concords in other parables than he found in the Sower.

29. "Allegorice autem post sex dies et post sex quinquagenas annorum a Spiritu Sancto dato apostolis, in quibus per varia martyria archana ecclesia ducta

est in montem excelsum seorsum a synagoga, tunc universum Europe, Africe et Asie, quasi Petrum Iacobum et Iohannem, Christus sub Constantino assumpsit, ostendens se esse solem mundi et dominum Romani Imperii. Et tunc sancti qui per martiria Christo iuncta erant apparuerunt albi sicut nix, quia tunc patuit quid sibi et ecclesie meruerunt. Et tunc cum Christo apparuerunt lex ecclesiasticorum consiliorum et statutorum manans a sacris episcopis quasi a Moyse et zelus ana-choritarum similis Helie. Post hoc autem nubilositas fidei propter excessum sue lucis obumbravit ecclesiam, expellens ab electis Arrianos et ceteros hereticos male sentientes de altitudine Christi. Ita ut electi intrantes in hanc nubem timerent et tunc per doctores audita est vox patris: *Hic est filius meus, etc.*, quia tunc singu-lariter claruit archanum generationis verbi, ita ut solus Iesus apparuit summus Deus et Patri equalis. Sed tandem Orientali ecclesia recedente a Latina, descen-dit Christus et ecclesia ad inferiorem statum et ideo dictum est quod donec Chris-tus in corpore mistico iterum paciatur et resurgat, visio predicta sileatur" (Olivi, *Mtt.*, 110rb).

30. "Tunc enim longe clarius apparebit universo orbi solaris claritas Christi et tunc scietur quod Helias duplex erat venturus, unus scilicet, qui preiret et intro-misit in mundo vitam Christi sicut Johannes preivit previam Christi. In cuius signum coram fratribus suis vectus est in curru igneo ut Helias. Alter vero ad lit-teram qui restituat et reducat ad Christum tribus Iacob" (Olivi, *Mtt.*, 110rb). On Christ's words "Elijah does come, and he is to restore all things" (17:11), Olivi says: "This saying is of great significance, as appears to those who contemplate more diligently the profound secrets of scripture. . . . Many things ought to be said about this, but they will be reserved for another time" ("Nota quod hoc verbum est magni ponderis sicut patet diligentius intuenti et prescrutanti profunda scrip-turarum. . . . Multa autem essent super hoc verbo dicenda, sed alteri tempori reservantur" [*Mtt.*, 110va]).

31. "Sed nichilominus verbum Petri non vacat a misterio. Nam trina debe-bat esse mansio in monte ecclesie in misterium beatissime Trinitatis, scilicet coni-ugatorum significatorum in Moyse, qui uxorem habuit; clericorum significatorum in Christo, que est verbum et sapientia Patris; et religiosorum quorum est vacare ardori Spiritus Sancti et sancte solicitudini designatis in Helia (Olivi, *Mtt.*, 109vb).

32. "Nam in presenti tempore similia cernes si oculos habes" (Olivi, *Jn.* 152v).

33. "Quia etiam tempus plenitudinis gentium in quo et omnis Israel salvus fiet et singulare tempus vitae Christi seu perfectionis evangelice et vitae contem-plative quod tempus proprie Spiritui Sancto appropriatur" (Olivi, *Jn.*, 152v).

34. Olivi, *Jn.*, 152v.

CHAPTER SEVEN   Franciscan Persecution and Olivi's Matthew Commentary

1. "Per Herodem . . . significatur diabolus, qui turbatur, quando Jesus, id est, salus nascitur in corde hominis" (Hugh, *Mtt.*, 7rb). See also Thomas: "Hero-

dem, id est diabolum . . . Item, cum ab Herode, id est diabolo, recedimus, stellam, idest Christi gratiam, invenimus" (*Mtt.*, 30).

2. "Unde et hic initiata est prima persecutio Christi et ecclesie seu capitis et membrorum et ideo in semine omnes in ea representamur" (Olivi, *Mtt.*, 20ra).

3. "Nota quod Herodes significat diabolum regnantem in mundo et omnes principes ypocritas et carnales qui fuerunt, sunt et erunt in populo Dei a tempore suo usque in finem mundi" (Olivi, *Mtt*, 20ra). Some of the manuscripts of the Matthew commentary (e.g., BN Lat. 15588 and Vat. lat. 10900) furnish a significantly different reading by deleting "sunt" from this text. This was an effort on the part of at least one scribe, then followed by others, to moderate the force of the criticism implied in Olivi's interpretation. With this emendation, the text reads more benignly as a critique of past and future carnal leaders and remains innocuously silent about the present.

4. "Nota de misteriis quedam breve. Post xl enim generationes quibus ecclesia a Deo pascitur in deserto, prout habetur Apoc. xii, solvetur Sathanas ad temptandum Christum acerrime in suis membris" (Olivi, *Mtt.*, 33va).

5. Olivi, *Mtt.*, 33vb.

6. On this particular verse, Olivi remarks, "sicut hodie multi similes phariseis consimiliter iudicant homines excessive viventes" (*Mtt.*, 87va). Was Olivi here thinking of those secular clergy criticizing the Friars Minor for excessive living?

7. "Nota pro misterio huius partis quod Iohannes significat intelligentiam veritatis incarcerata sub figuris legis et prophetarum. Hic tamen intellectus in fine legis propter emulationem discipulorum legis ad Christum apparuit dubius. Et ideo misit ad Christum scribas et phariseos. Christus vero per opera ostendit se esse veritatem intelligentie legalis et prophetalis. Expulsisque iudeis a societate Christi et suorum commendatur populis intelligentia legis de summa soliditate et de virtuosa rigiditate et de perspicatia divine sapientie. Et quod fuit quasi nuntius angelicus a patre missus, ut dirigeret viam Christo. Et ex quo intellectus ille in Christo apparuit, ex tunc cessat figura legis et prophetarum" (Olivi, *Mtt.*, 87vb).

8. "Consimilem autem allegoriam potes accipere pro fine temporis ecclesiastici, in quo apparuit alter Iohannes, in quo intelligentia enigmatum evangelii clare refulsit, ut introducatur spiritus Christi, seu Christus in spiritu, seu perfecta vita Christi. Hec autem intelligentia in temporibus ecclesie et quarundam religionum precedentium fuit velata, et propter emulationem quorundam Iudaizantium, hec intelligentia in fine dubia apparebit" (Olivi, *Mtt.*, 87vb); emphasis added. This is one of the several times in the commentary when Olivi refers uncautiously to the "end of the ecclesiastical age" or the "end" of the church.

9. "Mittentur eis duo ex discipulis, scilicet, imbuti magistrali scientia et religione ypocritali et superstitiosa. Videbunturque missi a zelo fidei et intelligentie veritatis" (Olivi, *Mtt.* 87vb).

10. "Intellectus evangelicus et precursor eius Christi passione insignitus ostendetur esse talis ut dicatur in populo quod inter natos mulierum non surrexit maior" (Olivi, *Mtt.*, 87vb).

11. Joachim, of course, never got to the eleventh chapter of Matthew in the *Tractatus.*

12. Olivi cites Origen at *Mtt.,* 106rb.

13. "Nota pro misteriis huius finalis temporis quod sicut in primo adventu Christi, qui fuit in carnem, fuerunt in plebe varie opiniones de Christi persona, discipulis tamen vere et solide confitentibus veritatem propter quam Christi ecclesia fundata est in eis, sic in secundo adventu, qui est in spiritu, sunt et erunt varie opiniones de vita Christi. Sed in discipulis solide confitentibus altitudinem eius fundabitur ecclesia spiritualis, contra quam porte inferi, idest secte infernales Antichristi, non prevalebunt. . . . Nota tamen quod ex quo erunt solidi in prefata confessione, ex tunc vita Christi seu Christus in spiritu vite sue aperte dicet eis, quod tam ipsum quam ipsos oportet ire in Ierusolimam et reprobari a scribis et senioribus ecclesie carnalis" (Olivi, *Mtt.,* 107rb–va).

14. *OFP,* 176. On 16:21 ("he must go to Jerusalem and undergo great suffering at the hands of the elders and chief priests and scribes"), Olivi remarks that: "To condemn a man as if he is guilty is more ignominious when it is done by those who seem more mature and discreet and experienced in the divine law and superior in authority, especially since from the contempt of such men, it easily follows that the accused man is despised by everyone else" ("condemnare tanquam reus est ignominiosius quando fit ab hiis qui videntur maturiores et discretiores et divine legis peritiores et auctoritate superiores et precipue quia ad contemptum talium facile sequitur hominem contemni ab omnibus aliis" [*Mtt.,* 107vb]). Was Olivi thinking of his own condemnations for doctrinal heterodoxy when he made this remark?

15. Thomas's Matthew commentary, as already discussed, was probably written during his first Paris regency. However, others have argued that it was written during his second Paris regency (1269–72), which coincided with the second phase of the controversy. See J. P. Renard, "La *Lectura super Matthaeum* V, 20–28 de Thomas d'Aquin," *RTAM* 50 (1983): 145–90. Notice that if Thomas's Matthew commentary was delivered during the period of his second Paris regency, Olivi probably would have been in Paris at the time. Bonaventure's Luke commentary was delivered between 1254 and 1257, or just during the period when William launched his first attack on the mendicants. Note that his lectures on Luke were first given when Bonaventure was a *bachelarius biblicus* in 1248 and revised to their present form while he was teaching as a master. See Smalley, *The Gospels,* 205. Dominic Monti has argued that some parts of the commentary may have been edited in the 1260s. See his "Bonaventure's Interpretation of Scripture," 170–85.

16. Chrysostom, *Mtt.,* Homily 27, cols. 343–46.

17. Anselm, *Lk.,* 126–27; Bede, *Lk.,* 111–12.

18. Thomas, *Mtt.,* 111.

19. Hugh, *Mtt.,* 33ra; Alexander, *Mtt.,* 25vb.

20. "Per curationem socrus Simonis a febre significatur curatio synagoge ab aestu carnalis concupiscentiae, quo inardescit ille populus carnalis" (Bonaventure,

Lk., p. 109). For Bonaventure's dependence on Hugh in the Luke commentary, see Monti, "The Interpretation of Scripture," 163; and Smalley, *The Gospels,* 206–7.

21. "Et omnes tres vocant domum ubi erat socrus domum Symonis" (Olivi, *Mtt.,* 70rb).

22. "Constat autem quod post ultimam vocationem omnia perfecte reliquit etiam retia" (Olivi, *Mtt.,* 70rb).

23. "Sed quomodo hec domus erat Symonis cum esset in Capharnaum; Petrus vero erat de Bethsayda, sicut habetur Johannis 1. Ad hoc dicitur quod domus ista erat Symonis ex parte uxoris" (Olivi, *Mtt.,* 70rb).

24. Monti, "Bonaventure's Interpretation of Scripture," 170.

25. Ibid.

26. See, e.g., *Tractatus,* pp. 49, 123, 126–28, 204, and 270.

27. For example, in discussing the passage in Mt. 3:1–12, where John is described as wearing camel hair with a leather belt, Olivi argues that John here simply designates the law and exterior, ceremonial religion and contrasts the belt John wears with the belt Christ wears in the Apocalypse (*Mtt.* 24va).

28. This historicizing reading would be influential on Joachim in his *Tractatus.* See pp. 21, 25, 49, 62, 92, 270, and 275.

29. Thomas provides Chrysostom's interpretation, though without attribution, *Mtt.,* 56; John of LaRochelle, *Mtt.,* 31vb–32ra also quotes Chrysostom. Hugh says that Christ did not want to condemn an inferior *sermo, Mtt.,* 13va. Bonaventure does not address the question, probably because the parallel passage in Luke (4:14 ff.) edits out the reference to John's arrest.

30. "est ad pleniorem clarificationem Christi et status eius, quia clarius positum iuxta minus clarum e ipso evidentius illucescit et sensibilius patet eius preeminentia quam habet super statum vel doctorem priorem . . . est ad tollerandum deordinationem et perturbationem repententinarum mutationum et ideo utilis est priorem statum paulative tolli et obscurari" (Olivi, *Mtt.,* 34va).

31. "Quarta est ad ostendendum quod aliquando utile est esse simul in ecclesia plures status et plures doctores quamvis sint longe dispares in perfectionem. Quinta ut daretur exemplum quod tenentes aliquem statum priorem et imperfectiorem debuerant suo statu preferre sequentem et discipulos suos seu venientes ad se destinare ad illum tanquam ad meliorem, sicut fecit Johannes mittens suos ad Christum. Sesta est ut exemplo notabili addisceremus transferre nos a prioribus statibus imperfectis ad novos perfectiores ipsis statibus prioribus in sua celebritate adhuc manentibus sicut quidam ex discipulis Johannis transierunt ad Christi discipulatum, Johannis statu adhuc in sua celebritate manente" (*Mtt.,* 34vb).

32. Origen, *Mtt.,* 1:433–60. This scheme is also represented in the sixteenth of Bonaventure's *Collationes in Hexaemeron,* in *Opera* 5, p. 403.

33. Jerome, *Mtt.,* 2: 85–91; Hilary, *Mtt.,* 106–10.

34. Hugh, *Mtt.,* 65v; Thomas, *Mtt.,* 250, though with slightly different details; Alexander, 53va–vb; and John of LaRochelle, *Mtt.,* 202r–203r.

35. Olivi, *Mtt.*, 121ra.

36. "Prima vocatio facta fuit per Christum et apostolos. Secunda vero quasi circa tertiam facta fuit a tempore generalium consiliorum, que facta sunt post Constantinum. Sicut enim a tempore Moysi manavit lex sic ab illo tempore manaverunt decreta et ecclesiastica statuta regularia. Tertia vero circa sextam fuerunt tempora Augustini et Gregorii Magni quando primo in Grecia et postmodum in Latina ecclesia manaverunt flumina de ore doctorum quasi ex ore Salomonis. Quarta vero vocatio quasi circa nonam fuit post scisma Grecorum a Romana ecclesia et post discipationem ecclesiarum multarum factam per Saracenos, quando et monastica vita in partibus occidentis cepit multiplicari. Et tandem multe species religionum tam militantium quam monachalium oriri. Quinta vero vocatio quasi circa horam undecimam inchoata est per minimum omnium minorum Christi stigmatibus ante omnes primos prehoneratum et insigniis evangelice regule . . . predotatum, quam oportet a collegio et multitudine murmurantium comprimi donec detur sentencia per illum qui dixit *Volo autem et huic novissimo dare sicut et tibi*. Et tunc iterum patebit quod erunt primi novissimi et novissimi primi" (Olivi, *Mtt.*, 122va).

37. Olivi, *Mtt.*, 121rb. Olivi actually says that the historical reading can be given "secundum varios modos allegorizandi."

38. See Olivi, *Mtt.*, 105vb and 112rb. See also this remark on 132ra: "Iudei fuerunt semper cultores preteritorum sanctorum et contemptores ymmo et presecutores presentium et idem fuit et est de carnalibus Christianis."

39. Origen, *Mtt.* 1:628–52; Jerome, *Mtt.*, 138–44; Hilary, 2: 144–50; Chrysostom, Homily 69, coll. 647–51.

40. See Hugh, *Mtt.*, 69va; Alexander, *Mtt.*, 58va; Thomas, *Mtt.*, 271; and John of LaRochelle, *Mtt.*, 219rb–221rb. John calls the servants "predicatores ad fidem incarnationis" (219rb). Olivi identifies the servants as preachers as well, and this is an important element in his interpretation of the parable. Whether he took this idea directly from John seems very doubtful.

41. Olivi, *Mtt.*, 126vb–127ra.

42. "altissima paupertas est fervidus amor et singularis ianua et dispositio ad intrandum et eius oppositum ad contemnendum, et ideo predicta ad cupiditatem ei contraria reducuntur . . . prima invitatio potius vocat ad perfectionem evangelicam . . . tale convivium invitantur inducuntur omnino relinquere et abnegare sibi dilectissima, scilicet carnalia et terrena et suas viciosas ac proprias voluntates" (Olivi, *Mtt.* 127rb–va).

43. "solus contemptus talis convivii et talis invitationis est ex se crimen mortiferum, ita quod aliquis qui in inferiori statu plerumque salvaretur, sit eo ipso damnandus, quo ad maiora ex spirituali gratia invitatus, est invitationis contemptor et gratie sibi facte ingratus . . . frequentem causam huius contemptus, que est presumptio securitatis et salvationis sufficientie sui status prioris" (Olivi, *Mtt.*, 127rb). This is the piece of evidence that leads me to question Decima

Douie's argument ("Olivi's 'Postilla super Matthaeum'," 75) that Olivi had in mind here those who were opposing *usus pauper*. The issue here is possession, not use, and the reference to prior and inferior religious states would seem to rule the Franciscans out altogether.

44. "hic subinnuitur servos apparuisse superiores hiis qui vocabantur per eos. Cum quia dicebant se missos a rege. Cum quia assumebant sibi officium mediatorum et predicatorum" (Olivi, *Mtt.* 127va).

45. "Sicut videmus quod multi iudeorum zelantes carnalem legem estimaverunt Christi et apostolorum doctrinare esse erroneam et perversam et ideo ipsos tanquam erroneos et blasphemos sunt totis viribus persequti" (Olivi, *Mtt.*, 127va).

46. Olivi's response has been partially edited and briefly introduced in M.-T. d'Alverny, "Un adversaire de Saint Thomas: Petrus Ioannis Olivi." Even before the publication of this partial edition, several extracts were published in Franz Ehrle's seminal article on Olivi, "Petrus Johannis Olivi." Yet Olivi's argument and his differences with Thomas have never been analyzed in detail. In this essay, I will use MS Oxford New College 49, as I have throughout, when referring to Olivi's Matthew commentary, since d'Alverny did not edit some of the parts of Olivi's argument under consideration here.

47. See chapter 4.

48. Olivi, *Mtt.*, 77vb.

49. "Primum igitur est erroneum; primo quia est contra expressa verba Scripture" (Olivi, *Mtt.*, 78ra).

50. Olivi, *Mtt.*, 78ra.

51. "Quod autem pro se Augustinum inducit, miror prudentem virum pauca verba unius sancti velle reducere contra expressissima verba Scripture sacre" (Olivi, *Mtt.*, 78rb). As David Burr has pointed out, Olivi would return to this insistence on *precepta* in the *usus pauper* controversy. Burr notes that in his *Tractatus de usu paupere* Olivi had argued that "the form of poverty by which one possesses nothing and lives in the greatest want of things was prescribed (*precepta*) to the apostles and observed by them." He also notes that, as the controversy progressed, it was a word which Olivi's opposition preferred to avoid. See *OFP*, 59.

52. See Gerard of Abbeville, *Contra adversarium perfectionis Christianae.*

53. The diabolical inspiration of the secular and Dominican attack was to be suggested throughout the Matthew commentary. It was also explicitly stated in Olivi's *Tractatus de usu paupere*. See *OFP*, 49 and 55 n. 39.

54. Note that Olivi does not think that the commands are binding on the imperfect or on the secular clergy. For support he alludes to the *Apologia Pauperum*, where Bonaventure argues that Augustine's "concessions" argument applies only to these groups. See *Apologia* 7.20 in *S. Bonaventurae Opera Omnia*, 5: 279. For both Bonaventure and Olivi, the commands are eternally binding on Dominicans

who vow to observe highest poverty. Augustine's "concessions" argument did not apply to them. See Olivi, *Mtt.*, 78rb: "sunt eis precepta tanquam professoribus altissime paupertatis ad quam non astringuntur hii qui non voverunt eam . . . [and then, Olivi's usual sarcasm] sicut patet etiam cecis et surdis." Note that Olivi in the fifth of his *Quaestiones de perfectione evangelica* argues that when Christ commanded the observance of evangelical perfection, he presumed the disciples would take a vow. See Burr, *Persecution,* 12.

55. "Quod autem pro se Augustinum inducit, miror prudentem virum pauca verba unius sancti velle reducere contra expressissima verba Scripture sacre et omnium aliorum sanctorum, et contra expressa dicta Romanorum pontificum, et contra sententiam, vitam et regulam tanti viri quantus fuit sanctus Franciscus, Christi plagis insignitus, et contra alia verba ipsiusmet Augustini et contra lumen irrefragabilium rationum" (Olivi, *Mtt.* 78rb).

56. "Nemo sane mentis debet dicere hanc in passione evacuatam esse tanquam imperfectam, aut tanquam perfectioni virtutis non multam accomodam, et precipue cum non solum innumera verba sanctorum, sed etiam omnes antique imagines Apostolorum oculata fide nos docent eos sic per orbem universum semper incessisse" (Olivi, *Mtt.,* 79va).

57. "falsoque ascribitur hoc sanctis, quia non solum hoc non dicunt, immo expressimum contrarium docent, omnium enim auctoritates expresse dicunt eos ista semper observasse et observare debuisse" (Olivi, *Mtt.,* 78va).

58. The interpretation is indeed Bede's. See Bede, *In Lucae Evangelium Expositio,* ed. D. Hurst, *CCL* 120 (Turnhout, 1960), 383–84. Olivi discusses Bede's reading at *Mtt.,* 78vb.

59. Olivi, *Mtt.,* 79ra–va.

60. Olivi, *Mtt.,* 80rb.

61. "Sextum autem sic est erroneum, quod est Christo et apostolis nimis contumeliosum et non est aliud quam scripturam repugnantem violenter intorquere ad suum affectum et ad operculum imperfectionum nostrarum" (Olivi, *Mtt.,* 80ra).

62. *Summa* 2a2ae, 188.

63. *Summa* 2a2ae, 188.7.

64. "Respondeo dicendum quod, sicut supra dictum est, perfectio non consistit essentialiter in paupertate, sed in Christi sequela" (*Summa* 2a2ae, 188.7. resp.).

65. *Summa* 2a2ae, 188.7. resp.

66. "Nam illis religionibus quae ordinantur ad corporales actiones activae vitae, competit habere abundantiam divitiarum communium" (*Summa* 2a2ae, 188.7. resp.).

67. "Illis autem religionibus quae sunt ordinatae ad contemplandum, magis competit habere possessiones moderatas" (*Summa* 2a2ae, 188.7, resp.).

68. "Sic igitur non oportet quod religio tanto sit perfectior quanto maiorem habet paupertatem: sed quanto eius paupertas est magis proportionata communi fini et speciali" (*Summa* 2a2ae, 188, 7. resp. ad 1um).

69. "Ad primum ergo dicendum quod, sicut dictum est, ex illo verbo Domini non intelligitur quod ipsa paupertas sit perfectio, sed perfectionis instrumentum: et . . . minimum inter tria principalia instrumenta perfectionis" (*Summa* 2a2ae, 188. 7. resp. ad 1um).

70. "Dilectio enim Dei et proximi et spiritualis salus anime sue ac deinde aliorum est principalis finis religionis" (Olivi, *Mtt.*, 80ra).

71. "Temporalis vero et corporalis impugnatio infidelium et corporalis defensio ac redemptio vel nutritio fidelium non est proprie finis religionis" (Olivi, *Mtt.*, 80ra).

72. "Preterea in statu et actu militie religiose principaliter debet intendi spiritualis salus eorum qui sunt in statu illo et spiritualis cultus Dei" (Olivi, *Mtt.*, 79va). Olivi even denies that the military orders fight better with an abundance of riches, which make them more avaricious and proud and less prompt in the obedience of superiors and God.

73. Olivi, *Mtt.*, 80vb.

74. "Quero autem an, dato quod aliqui milites pro cultu Dei sic exponant se religiose militie quod penitus nichil querant nisi sumptus sibi gratis a Christianis dandos, an isti sint in cultu et religione Dei imperfectiores quam si sibi ad hoc coaceruent castra et regna et certe nullus sane mentis dicet quin illud sit maioris virtutis" (Olivi, *Mtt.*, 79va).

75. "Quis enim usque nunc audivit in nova lege sic divicias commendari ut dicatur aliqua religio esse imperfecta, non solum si non habeat divicias, sed etiam nisi habeat divicias habundantes?" (Olivi, *Mtt.*, 79va).

76. "Estne hec doctrina Christi vel Pauli? Dixit hoc unquam aliquis sanctus? Absit!" (Olivi, *Mtt.*, 79v).

77. "Mira res! Christus verbo et facto paupertatem quasi super omnia extollit; iste vero quasi sub omnibus eam deiecit. Scio quod hoc non fecisset beatus Dominicus, qui maledixit omnibus suis quandocumque possessiones reciperent" (Olivi, *Mtt.*, 81ra).

78. As has been pointed out by Jan G. J. van den Eijnden, *Poverty on the Way to God: Thomas Aquinas on Evangelical Poverty* (Leuven, 1994), 198.

79. This is pointed out in *OFP*, 157.

80. On Olivi's views toward Aristotle, see O. Bettini, "Olivi di fronte ad Aristotele," *SF* 55 (1958): 176–97; Burr, *Persecution*, 27–31; *idem*, "The Apocalyptic Element in Olivi's Critique of Aristotle"; and *idem*, "Petrus Ioannis Olivi and the Philosophers," *FS* 31 (1971): 41–71.

81. *Summa* 1a2ae, 108.1. resp.

82. *Summa* 1a2ae, 108.1. resp.

83. "nam lex vetus multa determinabat, et pauca relinquebat hominum libertati determinanda" (*Summa* 1a2ae, 108.1, resp.).

84. "Alia vero sunt opera quae non habent necessariam contrarietatem vel convenientiam ad fidem per dilectionem operantem. Et talia opera non sunt in nova lege praecepta vel prohibita ex ipsa prima legis institutione; sed relicta sunt

a legislatore, scilicet Christo, unicuique, secundum quod aliquis curam gerere debet. Et sic unicuique liberum est circa talia determinare quid sibi expediat facere vel vitare; et cuicumque praesidenti, circa talia ordinare suis subditis, quid sit in talibus faciendum vel vitandum" (*Summa* 1a2ae, 108.1. resp.).

85. "Sic igitur lex nova dicitur lex libertatis dupliciter. Uno modo, quia non arctat nos ad facienda vel vitanda aliqua, nisi quae de se sunt vel necessaria vel repugnantia saluti, quae cadunt sub praecepto vel prohibitione legis. Secundo, quia huiusmodi etiam praecepta vel prohibitiones facit nos libere implere, inquantum ex interiori instinctu gratiae ea implemus" (*Summa* 1a2ae, 108. resp. ad 2um).

86. "Nullam aliam rationem haberemus nisi Christi consilium et exemplum" (Olivi, *Mtt.*, 81ra).

87. Olivi, *Mtt.*, 94va.

88. Ibid.

89. "Et quia accidiosi et amatores carnalis otii, multi sibi estimant necessaria . . . que vir fervidus iudicaret sibi superflua" (Olivi, *Mtt.*, 94vb).

90. "Cum quia non sunt apti ad profunda simul et ardua considerandum pericula spiritualium dignitatum, cum quia ex eo quod presumptuose contemnunt alios indigne" (Olivi, *Mtt.*, 94vb).

91. "Electi etiam quanto spiritualiores et illuminatiores, tanto contra tales fortius invehuntur" (Olivi, *Mtt*, 95ra).

92. See, e.g., Jerome, *Mtt.* 1:62–64; and Chrysostom, Homily 61, cols. 587–94.

93. Rabanus Maurus, *Mtt.*, col. 1013.

94. "Nota quod allegorice in hac parabola ostenditur decursus mundi. Primo quantum ad opus conditionis, quod innuitur in donatione decem milium talentorum facta servis propter quam ille fuit debitor eorum. Secundo quantum ad casum humane prevaricationis et destitutionis. Tertio quantum ad desiderium patrum petentium misericordiam fieri in Christi adventu. Quarto eius exhibitio in Christi adventu" (Olivi, *Mtt.*, 116vb).

95. "Quinto depravatio rectorum in finali ecclesie statu, qui tam ex impietate, quam ex iniusticia crudeli et presumptuosa sunt crudeles in simplices oves et indelicta eorum. Sexto pietas et caritas spiritualium virorum in sexto tempore ecclesie suscitandorum dolentium de perditione simplicium et de impietate regentium et ad deum dirigentium vota sua. Septimo exterminatio crudelium designata in Apocalipsi, per fundamentum Babilonis in mare" (Olivi, *Mtt.*, 116vb).

96. "quo tempore Hierusalem destruenda, quo uenturus Christus, quo consummatio saeculi sit futura" (Jerome, *Mtt.*, 2:186).

97. "In hac parte querunt primo discipuli tria secundum Ieronimum. Primo scilicet quo tempore scilicet Ierusalem esset destruenda, dicentes, *Dic nobis quando hec erunt*. Secundo quo tempore Christus esset venturus, scilicet, in gloria sua, vel potius sub quibus signis, aut que signa preirent eius adventum, ex quibus posset presciri vel dignosci eius adventus. Unde dicunt *quod signum adventus tui?* Tertio quo tempore consummatio seculi sit ventura" (Olivi, *Mtt.*, 133ra).

98. "In hac responsione Christus mixtim tangit plura tempora et precipue tria, scilicet, tempus captivitatis Iudaice per Romanos facte, sive demones, quando scilicet occidendo Christum sunt a vero Dei cultu reicti; et tempus Antichristi et tempus ultimi iudicii" (Olivi, *Mtt.*, 133ra).

99. "Ad intelligentiam autem huius partis sciendum quod sicut prophete sub captivitate Babilonica tres alias captivitates includunt ad tempus Christi spectantes et consimiliter sub liberatione populi Dei de captivitate babilonica tres liberationes electorum includunt complendas in tempore gratie et tandem glorie ecclesie, sic Christus in captivitate Romanorum circa suum tempus fienda duas alias sequentes more prophetico comprehendit. Quod quidem sicut in prophetis monstratum est fieri potuit, quia sic Deus providit eos impleri debere conformiter; quod una potuit per alteram et sub altera designari. Ut autem omnes quodammodo innotescerent et quodammodo se invicem occultarent; sic in ceteris locis ponuntur aliqua magis proprie spectantia ad unam et alibi magis spectantia ad aliam; quod cum sermo contexitur continuatur ac si de una sola ageretur" (Olivi, *Mtt.*, 133va).

100. While the texts concerning the darkening of the sun and moon have to do with the coming of Christ in majesty and the gathering of the elect to him in the last judgment. For that matter, the texts having to do with the destruction of Jerusalem and the persecution of the apostles and the preaching of the gospel throughout the whole universe more properly respect the first time (Olivi, *Mtt.*, 133va).

101. "Ut verbigratia illa que hic dicuntur de multitudine pseudochristianorum et pseudoprophetarum et de prodigiis eorum et de periculo erroris in electos et de refrigerentia caritatis, magis proprie respiciunt tempora Antichristi. Quia vero de obscuratione solis et lune et de adventu Christi in maiestate et de congregatione electorum ad eum per angelos fienda tanguntur magis proprie respiciunt tempus extremi iudicii. Que vero de destructione Ierusalem et de persequtione apostolorum et de predicatione evangelii per orbem universum dicuntur; magis proprie respiciunt tempus primum. Quedam vero sunt ibi que satis communiter predictis temporibus aptari possunt" (Olivi, *Mtt.*, 133va).

102. "Nota tamen quod sicut verba Luce directius respiciunt temporalem captivitaem Iudeorum factam a Romanis; sic verba Mathei, Marci directius respiciunt mala in fine temporum ventura. Et puto quod sicut Christus scienter separavit verba sua ad utrumque tempus quod Spiritus Sanctus fecit; quo unus evangelista directius ferat verba sua ad unum tempus et alii ad aliud, omnis tamen ad utrumque" (Olivi, *Mtt.*, 134vb).

103. "Si autem queratur quare Christus non facit expressivam mentionem de finali temptatione ecclesie precedente temptationem Christi et disponente ad illam, quia non posset ille facere se adorari ab ecclesia nisi prius multipliciter esset prostrata ac seducta et excetata. Dicendum quod prima temptatio erit potius ad excecandum carnales Christianos sub specie veritatis et vere fidei Christi, quasi

ad illuminandum. Illa vero que est proprie Antichristi erit ad punitionem sic exce-catorum et ad finalem illuminationem omnium convertendorum post eius mortem et ad perfectam coronationem omnium martirizandorum sub ipso. Ista igitur fuit aperte predicanda; illa vero non nisi mistice et occulte. Qui autem vult non errare in secunda caveat sibi a prima ut, scilicet, intelligat quid est *abominatio sedens in templo dei* ad damnandum vitam Christi, sicut Cayphas condemnavit personam Christi. Est etiam alia ratio huius; quia per Antichristum et suos fient multa que videbuntur miraculosa et supernaturalia; et ideo ne talibus tanqaum veris crede-retur, oportebat de eis expressam fieri mentionem" (Olivi, *Mtt.,* 135va). It is worth noting incidentally here that this first remark is quoted almost verbatim, and with attribution, in the fourteenth-century *Breviloquium,* an anonymous apocalyptic work of Catalonian provenance recently edited by Harold Lee and others. While we still do not know everything about the community that produced or read this interesting document, except that they included "beguines," it is curious to note that its author obviously knew Olivi's Matthew commentary in some form and striking to realize that this is—unless I'm mistaken—the only comment he cites explicitly and verbally from it. That this is the comment he cites becomes more understandable, I think, once we read through the *Breviloquium* and per-ceive how generally receptive (perhaps under the indirect influence of John of Rupescissa) the author was to the expectation of disasters precursory to what it calls the *tribulatio secunda sub magno Antichristo.* See Harold Lee, Marjorie Reeves, and Giulio Silano, *Western Mediterranean Prophecy: The School of Joachim of Fiore and the Fourteenth-Century "Breviloquium"* (Toronto: 1989), 228–29.

104. "Ad tempus autem secundum, scilicet Antichristi, magis proprie cur-runt verba propter illud de destructione Ierusalem et de die iudicii, quamvis et ista tunc temporis credam implenda dupliciter et sub dupplici sensu. Primo vide-licet mistice et quasi per quandam conformitatem ad tempus mortis Christi et pseudoscribas et per pseudopontifices condemnati. Secundo autem litteraliter et aperte iuxta typum in Symone Mago, qui dixit se filium dei et in Nerone" (Olivi, *Mtt.,* 133vb).

105. Bonaventure, *Lk.,* 523.

106. "Hic agit de multiplici iudicio finali, nam licet illud quod erit in fine mundi simpliciter dicatur finale et ultimum. Nihilominus a tempore Christi et circa dicitur uno modo iudicium esse mundi, iuxta illud Johannis 12, *Nunc iudicium est mundi* [Jn. 12:31]. Spiritualiter tamen vocantur iudicia finalia prima in quibus poni-tur finis alicui solemni statui precedente et hoc modo iudicium destructionis Iero-solimam et synagoge fuit quoddam finale iudicium eius. Sic etiam finalis desolatio ecclesie carnalis circa tempora Antichristi in quo spiritualis ecclesia purgabitur et renascetur, quoddam finale iudicium vocatur. Christus igitur more prophetico tria predicta finalia iudicia hic similiter comprehendit" (Olivi, *Lk.,* 100v).

107. "Sic tamen quod una pars tre magis respicit primum de synagoga et alia magis secundum de ecclesia carnali et alia magis tertium de fine mundi in quo mundi figura preteribit, et alia quasi communiter et pariter omnia tria. Illud tamen

de ecclesia carnalis non sic distinguitur ab aliis et maxime a tertio sicut fit Mtt. 24 aut in dictis aliquibus prophetarum" (Olivi, *Lk.*, 101r).

108. "Nota tamen quod sicut verba Luce directius respiciunt temporalem captivitatem Iudeorum factam a Romanis, sic verba Mathei, Marci directius respiciunt mala in fine temporum ventura" (Olivi, *Mtt.*, 134vb).

109. "Spiritualiter tamen intelligantur per hoc antichristi finalium temporum quorum duo ut docti estimant dicent se finaliter Deum. Primus tamen cum hoc dicit se messiam Iudeorum in lege promissum, ultimus vero se Christum. An tamen ille ultimus qui Ezek. 38 et 39 designatur per Gog . . . non mihi constat" (Olivi, *Lk.*, 101r).

110. "Ante hos autem erit mysticus Antichristus qui cum suis pseudoantichristis, id est, conplicibus contra Christi vitam et spiritum ipsemet supra montem ipsam publice condemnans sicut Cayphas cum toto suo consilio Christi personam eiusque doctrinam solemniter condemnavit. Et quia iste in multa astutia et potentia plures seducent, ideo Christus hortatur electos esse tunc pervigiles et attentos, dicens videte ne seducamini" (Olivi, *Lk.*, 101r).

111. "Intelligendum ergo quod sicut destructionem synagoge factam per Vespasianum et Titum paulo ante preiverunt quaedam proelia Neronis et Vespasiani tunc duces eius per quae Vespasianus inductus est ad Ierosolimam finaliter obsidendam et tandem per Titum filium suum conterendam quod sic circa suum finem . . . prius quidam proelia assimilata cuiuslibet et intestinis proeliis Iulii cum Pompeio et Antonii cum Octaviano, postquam mysticus Antichristus Anne et Caiphe assimilatus persequatur spiritum Christi et eius electos. Quo facto seu potius ante quam totaliter consummetur surgeant proelia magnum Antichristum quasi Neronem et Simonem Magum introducentia et carnalem ecclesiam electorum persecutricem quasi alteram synagogam finaliter subvertentia et electos ad plenum purgantia. Quo facto sequitur destuctio Antichristi et suorum principalium compliciorum" (Olivi, *Lk.*, 101v).

112. "post triduum repperitur in templo, ut esset indicio quia post triduum triumphalis illius passionis in sede caelesti et honore divino fidei nostrae se resurrecturus offerret, qui mortuus credebatur" (Ambrose, *Lk.*, p. 58).

113. "Quarto triduum trienni quod in Apoc. vocatur tempus et tempora et dimidium temporis ut menses 42 in quo Antichristus tam mysticus quam expressus saevient, ita quod verus Christus et Deus videatur absentatus ab ecclesia sua" (Olivi, *Lk.*, 31v).

114. "Nam circa imminentem adventum Elie per Antichristum tam mysticum quam apertum est horribiliter reedificanda" (Olivi, *Lk.*, 61v).

115. "Rursus per Martham ecclesia temporalibus occupata; per Mariam vero ecclesia evangelica paupertatis . . . per litigium vero Marthe litigium mystici Antichristi" (Olivi, *Lk.*, 64v).

116. "Adverte autem quam mirifice in passione nostri capitis passio totius scilicet ecclesie sit allegorice extemplata. Secundum enim septem apertiones septem sigillorum sub septiplicibus spiritualibus preliis septiformiter rotanda erat

ecclesia, sed in sexta et septima instar Christi debet crucifigi sicut et signa crucis in Francisco manifeste protendunt. Secundum hoc autem omnes illusiones et contumelie Christo illate significant diversa genera contumeliarum in toto decursum ecclesie sibi et suis illatarum et inferendarum" (Olivi, *Mtt.*, 154vb).

117. Jerome, *Mtt.*, 2: 300–301.

118. "Unde et a quibusdam non indocte creditur quod ante resurrexionem generalem saltem bis debuerit esse duplex resurrexio partialis et exemplaris. Prima videlicet in Christo et resurgentibus secum, secunda post crucifixionem vite et regule sue factam a principalibus erronee ecclesie seu potius synagoge, que vocatur spiritualiter Sodoma et Egyptus" (Olivi, *Mtt.*, 155rb).

119. "A viro valde spirituali audivi revelatum esse quod in angelo sexti signaculi cum quibusdam consociis suis de illo implebitur istud, ut sicut est conformis Christo in passione, sic sit in resurrexione. Et ut discipuli illius temporis qui fere in errorem ducentur de celis habeant instructorem et comfortatorem sicut apostoli habuerunt Christum resurgentem" (Olivi, *Mtt.*, 155rb–va). Oxford New College 49 has "angulo" for "angelo," but the other mss I have examined have "angelo." David Burr has suggested that Olivi's "very holy man" might be Conrad of Offida. See Burr, *Persecution*, 20 n. 30. See also Burr's analysis of this passage and its analogue in the Apocalypse commentary in "Olivi, Apocalyptic Expectation, and Visionary Experience," *Traditio* 41 (1985): 275–77.

120. "Quid tamen sit de hoc divino iudicio et consilio teneo relinquendum" (Olivi, *Mtt.*, 155rb).

121. The commission's judgment is quoted in Burr, "Olivi, Apocalyptic Expectation, and Visionary Experience," 275. In the same article, p. 277, Burr notes that Olivi was criticized for this opinion in his own lifetime as well.

122. Hilary, *Mtt.*, 2:22. Hilary adds that the two fishes were the Prophets and the preaching of the Baptist.

123. "Nota pro misteriis quod sicut in vespere a Christo fracti et multiplicati sunt quinque panes et duo pisces, sic in fine synagoge quinque libros Moysi, id est, legem et duos pisces, id est, libros prophetales et historiales, qui erant in condimentum legis, Christus apparuit et in sensus misticos multiplicavit et aliquid simile creditur facturus in fine ecclesie, respectu utriusque Testamenti" (Olivi, *Mtt.*, 101va).

124. As does Olivi's interpretation of the scribes in Matthew 16:3 who can interpret the appearance of the sky but not the signs of the times: "Nota etiam quod scribe superficiem celi, id est, corticem scripturarum noverant sed significationes spiritualium sensuum Christi non videbant neque videre volebant, sed simile erit circa finem ecclesie" (*Mtt.*, 105vb).

125. "Mistice autem per triduum significatur triplex tempus, scilicet, nature, scripture et gratie. . . . Vel per triduum significatur tempus dupplicis littere, scilicet veteris et novi testatementi seu iudeorum et gentium. Tertium autem erit tempus spiritualis concordie et intelligentie, in quo dona Spiritus diffundentur" (Olivi, *Mtt.*, 104vb).

126. A more explicitly Joachimist passage occurs when Olivi interprets Christ's prophecy in Matthew 16:21 that the Son of Man would be raised "on the third day:" "Allegorice vero post legem et gratiam pervenitur ad gloriam. Et post legem nature et scripture pervenitur ad legem gratie. Et post litteram veteris et novi testamenti sive post tempus Iudeorum et gentium veniet concordia utrorumque et tunc resurget intelligentia spiritualis" (*Mtt.*, 107vb).

127. "Potest hic queri quare Christus voluit nunc cum tali gloria intrare Ierosolimam plus quam alias. Dicendum quod ante mortem eius fieret aliqua notabilis clarificatio sue persone et sue fidei ac doctrine" (Olivi, *Mtt.*, 123vb).

128. "Semper circa fines est aliqua solemnis clarificatio veritatis. Unde sicut ultimus finis synagoge introduxit claritatem Novi Testamenti et ultimus finis mundi introducit claram visionem Dei et finis ecclesie circa Antichristum introducit claram contemplationem fidei, sic decuit quod fructus doctrine Christi in suo fine clarius radiaret" (Olivi, *Mtt.*, 123vb). Olivi also offers this interpretation of the feast of the Triumphal Entry: "Et nota pro misteriis quod totum festum a Christo exhibitum allegorice designat festum ex conversione omnium gentium Christo quando in spiritu magnifice intrat metropolim cordis quasi rex in suam civitatem et tanquam Deus in suum templum" (*Mtt.*, 124ra). As with Joachim, the eschatological conversion of all nations was a crucial ingredient in Olivi's vision of the end.

129. Indeed, Olivi was constrained by his social role as a *lector* in one of the order's convents to transmit inherited opinion to pupils who were expected to be familiar with patristic commentary on the gospels. A monastic writer rather than a teacher, Joachim was not faced with the same pedagogical requirements, and was free to pursue his apocalyptic interests in a way not available to Olivi.

CHAPTER EIGHT   Papal condemnation and Possible Consequences

1. The story of the process against Olivi's Apocalypse commentary has been well told in Joseph Koch, "Der Prozess gegen die Postille Olivis zur Apokalypse," in *RTAM* 5 (1933): 303–15; in Edith Pásztor, "Le polemiche sulla 'Lectura super Apocalipsim' di Pietro di Giovanni Olivi fino alla sua condanna," in *Bullettino dell'Istituto Storico Italiano per il Medio Evo e Archivio Muratoriano* 70 (1958): 365–424; Burr, *Persecution*, 80–87; and, easily the fullest, most up-to-date, and reliable account, *OPK*, chaps. 9–11. The following account is heavily dependent upon these studies.

2. The document is preserved in Etienne Baluze, *Stephani Baluzii Miscellaneorum* (Paris: F. Muguet, 1678), 213–67.

3. As Burr points out, this is because the first commission had a static view of church history, in which the church does not change in any essential way. See *Persecution*, 84.

4. The full title of the author's work is *Allegationes super articulis tractis per dominum papam de Postilla, quam composuit fr. Petrus Iohannis super Apocalipsim,*

quorum articulorum tenores inferius continentur. The text may be found in MS Paris Bibl. Nat. lat 4190, ff. 40 et seq. The author's brief comments on the *Lectura super Matthaeum* may be found on f. 44v. I wish to thank David Burr for bringing this text to my attention.

5. "Primo igitur premicto quod causa motiva Ordinis Fratrum Minorum, ad condempnandum dictam Postillam et alios libros fr. Petri Iohannis et quare pro parte Ordinis predicti Vestre fuit Sanctitati supplicatum quod dicta Postilla per Sedis Apostolice iuditium dampnaretur, fuit quod in multis questionibus et in multis aliis tractatibus dicti fr. Petri et specialiter in dicta Postilla multa heretica, blasphema, temeraria, fantastica et infamatoria contra Sanctam Romanam Ecclesiam et eius auctoritatem, honorem et reverentiam continentur" (MS Paris lat. 4190, f. 40; text quoted in Pasztor, "Le polemiche," 378).

6. "Idem dominus Ioannes Vigesimussecundus condemnavit de multorum consilio magistrorum in theologia postillam fratris Petri Ioannis ordinis Fratrum Minorum super Apocalypsim. . . . Condemnavit etiam postillam eiusdem fratris Petri Ioannis super Matthaeum, et postillam etiam eiusdem super canonicas, in quibus, ut in postilla super Apocalypsim, continentur haereses aliquae in effectu consimiles" (in Nicolas Eymerich, *Directorium Inquisitionis* [Rome, 1585], 268, col. 2E).

7. *Glossae seu Postillae perpetuae in universa Biblia* (Rome, 1471–72).

8. See K. Madigan, "Nicholas of Lyra," in *Biographical Dictionary of Christian Theologians,* ed. Patrick Carey and Joseph Lienhard (Westport, Conn.: Greenwood, 2000), 382–84. Lyra's works are untranslated. However, see *Nicholas of Lyra, Biblia sacra cum glossis, interlineari, et ordinaria, Nicolai Lyrani Postilla, ac moralitatibus, Burgensis, additionibus, et Thoringi replicis* (Venice, 1588), the edition used here; *Oratio ad Honorem S. Francisci* (Paris, 1641); *Tractatulus contra Quendam Judaeum* (Antwerp, 1634); B. H. Hailperin, *Rashi and the Christian Scholars* (Pittsburgh, 1963); J. Preuss, *From Shadow to Promise* (Cambridge, 1969); and *Nicholas of Lyra: the Senses of Scripture,* ed. P. Krey and L. Smith (Leiden, 2000).

9. See Lyra, *Mtt.,* 2r–2v.

10. "Isto ergo modo ordinantur evangelia: quia primo ponitur evangelium Matthaei, sicut facies hominis primo opponebatur aspectui prophetae, et secundo loco evangelium Marci, qui destera pars prior est quam sinistra et tertio evangelium Lucae, et quarto evangelium Iohannis quia facies aquilae erat in posteriori parte" (Lyra, *Mtt.,* 2v).

11. "Ista animalia sunt quatuor evangelia seu quatuor evangelistae quae aliquando dicuntur quatuor, aliquando unum. Licet enim Matthaeus principaliter versetur circa humanitatem, Iohannes circa divinitatem, Lucas circa sacerdotium: Marcus circa regnum: quilibet tamen ipsorum ista quatuor considerat" (Lyra, *Mtt.,* 2v).

12. See, e.g., Lyra, *Mtt.,* 4v: "Matthaeus in homine intelligitur, quia circa humanitatem Christi principaliter immoratur."

13. "In hac parte Hieronymi ostendit intentionem principalem evangelistae Matthaei seu subiectum sui evangelii, quia genealogiam ordinate ab Abraham usque ad Christum descripsit, ut ostenderet quod ipse Christus est verus homo et verus Deus" (Lyra, *Mtt.* 4r).

14. Lyra, *Mtt.*, 4v.

15. See preceding note and Lyra, *Mtt,* 5r: "Hunc errorem volens Matthaeus excludere in principio evangelii sui ostendit ipsum a David descendentem per ipsius genealogiam."

16. "Per socrum Petri quae mulier erat, sensualitas significatur, quae mulier ab Augustino vocatur, ipsa vero iacet febricitans concupiscentiae calore. Per Christum autem qui est imago patris, ratio, secundum quam homo factus est ad imaginem Dei, significatur. Igitur moraliter socrus Petri sanatur, cum sensualitas per rationem ad debitum ordinem moralis virtutis reuocatur" (Lyra, *Mtt.*, p. 31).

17. "Salvator enim noster cum corpus passibile ad nostram salutem accepisset, aliquando declinabat ad loca familiarium sibi & devotorum ad quietem habendam post labores: & isto modo venit ad domum Petri" (Lyra, *Mtt.*, p. 31).

18. "Hic quarto ostendit evangelista in Christo veritatem deitatis et humanitatis ex demonis tentatione" (Lyra, *Mtt.*, 15r). Lyra makes the same sort of comment when he comes to consider why Christ is represented as having experienced hunger: "per hoc in se et veritatem humanae infirmitatis ostendit" (Lyra, *Mtt.* 15v).

19. Lyra, *Mtt.*, 15v.

20. Lyra, *Mtt.*, 15r–v.

21. "Ut carnem innocentem pro nobis maceraret et exemplum fidelibus daret: et per hoc quod post baptismum talia egit, nobis ostendit, quod qui inchoat novam vitam, debet seipsum Deo offerre per ieiunium et orationem" (Lyra, *Mtt.*, 15rd).

22. "Isti inuitati sunt Iudaei quibus data est lex in qua facta est promissio de incarnatione Christi" (Lyra, *Mtt.*, 68r).

23. "Servi autem qui missi sunt ad vocandum inuitatos istos, fuerunt prophetae, qui clarius denunciaverunt ea de Christo, quae obscurius erant posita in lege. Hortabantur enim populum Iudaicum expectare Christi adventum & tendere in ipsum per fidem & bona opera" (Lyra, *Mtt.*, 68r).

24. "*Et nolebant.* quia nolebant verbis prophetarum obedire" (Lyra, *Mtt.*, 68r).

25. "Isti serui secundo missi fuerunt illi, qui de propinquo denunciaverunt adventum Christi, ut Iohannes Baptista & discipuli Christi missi ab eo in omnem ciuitatem & locum quo ipse erat venturus" (Lyra, *Mtt.*, 68r).

26. "*Ecce prandium meum paraui,* vidilicet sacramenta ecclesie & doctrinam, quibus reficitur anima & potissime sacramento eucharistiae: in quo datur nobis caro Christi in cibum & sanguis eius in potum" (Lyra, *Mtt.* 68r).

27. "quia Iudaei predicationem Christi et apostolorum contemptaverunt" (Lyra, *Mtt.*, 68r).

28. "Causa autem huius fuit cupiditas rerum temporalium. . . . Per laborem vineae intelligitur omnis occupatio corporalis circa terrena impediens divina. Per negociationem vero, occupatio mentalis circa talia" (Lyra, *Mtt.*, 68v).

29. See, e.g., the *Glossa Ordinaria* on Matthew 22:5: *"Alius in villam.* In villam ire, est terreno larori immoderate incumbere. Negociari vero, terrenis lucris inhiare" (*Mtt.*, 68v).

30. "quia Iohannes Baptista ab eis est incarceratus et occisus. Similiter Iacobus frater Iohannis et Stephanus et alli discipuli Christi et similiter prophetae multi in testamento Veteri" (Lyra, *Mtt.*, 68v).

31. "scilicet exercitu Romanorum sub principibus Tito et Vespasiano, qui ex divina ordinatione venerunt contra Ierusalem xlii anno post Christi passionem" (Lyra, *Mtt.*, 68v).

32. "Hic consequenter describitur vocatio gentium benigna: quia Iudaeis repellentibus fidem Christi ab apostolis praedicatam, apostoli de mandato domini transierunt ad praedicandum gentibus per totum mundum" (Lyra, *Mtt.*, 68v).

33. "quia fides catholic diffusa est per orbem universum" (Lyra, *Mtt.*, 68v).

34. Lyra, *Mtt.*, 62v.

35. "Quia ad literam in primitiva ecclesia conversi Iudaei murmuraverunt de hoc, quod consimilis gratia fiebat gentibus sicut et ipsis" (Lyra, *Mtt.*, 62r).

36. "Per tria vera sata significantur tres regulae religiosorum, scilicet, regula B. Augustini, & regula Beati Benedicti & regula Beati Francisci, quae fundantur in perfectione charitatis" (Lyra, *Mtt.*, 46r).

37. *OPK*, 260.

CONCLUSION

1. *OPK*, 21.

Bibliography

In the case of unpublished works, only those manuscripts actually cited in the text or notes are listed.

Works by Olivi

Manuscripts of the Biblical Commentaries

Lectura super Ioannem. MS Vatican, Vat. Ottab. lat. 3302.
Lectura super Lucam. MS Vatican, Vat. Ottab. lat. 3302.
Lectura super Marcum. Vatican, Vat. Ottab. lat. 3302.
Lectura super Matthaeum. MS Oxford, New College 49.
Lectura super Apocalypsim. Rome, Bibl. Angelica 382.
Quaestiones de perfectione evangelica (as numbered in MS. Rome, Vat. lat. 4986).

8. *An status altissime paupertatis sit simpliciter melior omni statu divitiarum.* In *Das Heil der Armen und das Verderben der Reichen,* edited by Johannes Schlageter. Werl/Westfalen: Dietrich-Coelde-Verlag, 1989.

9. *An usus pauper includatur in consilio seu in voto paupertatis evangelice, ita quod sit de eius substantia et integritate.* In David Burr, *De usu paupere: The* Quaestio *and the* Tractatus. Florence: Leo S. Olschki, 1992.

15. *An vivere de prebendis vel quibuscunque redditibus vel vivere de possessionibus absque vendicatione cuiuscunque dominii vel iuris possit esse licitum pauperibus evangelicis.* MS. Florence, Bibl. Laur. 448.

Editions of Other Works by Olivi

Epistola ad Conradum de Offida. In Livarius Oliger, "Petri Iohannis Olivi de renuntiatione papae Coelestini V quaestio et epistola." *AFH* 11 (1918): 309–73.

Epistola ad R. In Petrus Iohannis Olivi, *Quodlibeta Petri Ioannis Provenzalis,* edited by L. Soardus. Ff. 51v–53r. Venice, 1509.

Epistola ad regis Sicilie filios. Archiv 3: 534–40.

Expositio super Regulam. In David Flood, *Olivi's Rule Commentary: Edition and Presentation.* Wiesbaden: Franz Steiner Verlag GMBH, 1972.

Impugnatio XXXVII articulorum. In Petrus Iohannis Olivi, *Quodlibeta Petri Ioannis Provenzalis,* edited by L. Soardus. Ff. 42r–49v. Venice, 1509.

De perlegendis philosophorum libris. In Ferdinand Delorme, "Fr. Petri Joannis Olivi tractatus 'De perlegendis philosophorum libris.'" *Antonianum* 16 (1941): 31–44.

Quaestiones in Secundum Librum Sententiarum. Edited by Bernard Jansen. Bibliotheca Franciscana Scholastica Medi Aevi, 4–6. Quaracchi: Collegium S. Bonaventurae, 1921–1926.

Responsio P. Ioannis ad aliqua dicta per quosdam magistros Parisienses de suis quaestionibus excerpta. In Damasus Laberge, "Fr. Petri Ioannis Olivi, O.F.M., tria scripta sui ipsius apologetica annorum 1283 et 1285." *AFH* 28 (1935–36): 130–55, 374–407.

Responsio quam fecit P. Ioannis ad litteram magistrorum praesentatam sibi in Avionione. In Damasus Laberge, "Fr. Petri Ioannis Olivi, O.F.M., tria scripta sui ipsius apologetica annorum 1283 et 1285." *AFH* 28 (1935–36): 126–30.

WORKS BY OTHERS

Manuscripts of Biblical Commentaries

Alexander of Hales. *Postilla super Matthaeum.* Assisi, Communale 355.
John of LaRochelle. *Postilla super Matthaeum.* Oxford New College 48.
John of Wales. *Collationes super Matthaeum.* Oxford Magdalen College 27.

Editions of Biblical Commentaries

Albertus Magnus. *Commentarium super Matthaeum.* Edited by B. Schmidt. *Alberti Magni Opera Omnia.* 34 vols. Vol. 21.1–2. Münster: Aschendorff, 1987.

Ambrose of Milan. *Expositio Evangelii Secundum Lucam.* Edited by M. Adriaen. *CC* 14. Turnhout: Brepols, 1957.

Bede. *In Lucae evangeliam expositio.* Edited by D. Hurst. *CC* 120. Turnhout: Brepols, 1960.

Biblia Latina cum glossa ordinaria: facsimile reprint of the editio princeps Adolph Rusch of Strassburg 1480–81. Edited by Karlfried Froehlich and Margaret T. Gibson. 4 vols. Turnhout: Brepols, 1992.

Bonaventure. *Commentarius in Evangelium S. Lucae*. Edited by PP. Collegii a S. Bonaventura. 11 vols. Quaracchi: Collegium S. Bonaventure, 1882–1902. Vol. 7.

Gregory the Great. *Homiliae in Hiezechielem Prophetam*. Edited by M. Adriaen. *CC* 142. Turnhout: Brepols, 1971.

Hilary of Poitiers. *Sur Matthieu*. Edited by J. Doignon. *SC* 254, 258. Paris: Éditions du Cerf, 1978–79.

Hugh of St. Cher. *Postilla super Matthaeum. Postilla super IV evangelia fratris Hugonis Cardinalis*. Basel: Bernhard Richel, 1482.

Jerome. *Commentaire sur S. Matthieu*. Edited by E. Bonnard. *SC* 242, 259. Paris: Éditions du Cerf, 1977–79.

Joachim of Fiore. *Expositio in Apocalypsim*. Venice: F. Bindoni and M. Pasini, 1527. Facsimile edition, Frankfurt a.M.: Minerva, 1964.

———. *Liber Concordia Novi ac Veteris Testamenti*. Edited by E. Randolph Daniel. Philadelphia. Transactions of the American Philosophical Society, 1983. Vol. 73, Part 8. For Book V, *Liber Concordie Novi ac Veteris Testamenti*. Venice: Simon de Zuere, 1519.

———. *Psalterium decem chordarum*. Venice: F. Bindoni and M. Pasini, 1527.

———. *Tractatus super Quatuor Evangelia*. Edited by Ernesto Buonaiuti. Rome: Istituto Storico Italiano, Fonti per la Storia d'Italia, 1930.

———. (pseudonymous.) *Super Jeremiam*. Venice: Bernardinus Benalius, 1525.

John Chrysostom. *Homiliae in Matthaeum*. In *PG*, edited by J.-P. Migne. Vols. 57, 58. Paris: Garnier, 1844–62.

Origen. *Origenes Matthäuserklärung*. Edited by E. Klostermann and L. Fruchtel. Vol. 1. Leipzig: J. C. Hinrichs, 1935. Vol. 2. 2d ed. Berlin: Akademie-Verl., 1976. Vol. 3. Berlin, J. C. Hinrichs, 1955.

Petrus Auriol. *Compendium sensus literalis totius divinae scripturae*. Quaracchi: Collegium S. Bonaventurae, 1896.

Rabanus Maurus. *Commentariorum in Matthaeum libri octo*. In *PL*, edited by J.-P. Migne. Vol. 107, cols. 727–1156. Paris: Garnier, 1844–64.

Remigius of Auxerre. *Homiliae in Matthaeum*. In *PL*, edited by J.-P. Migne. Vol. 131, cols. 865–932. Paris: Garnier, 1844–64.

Thomas Aquinas. *Lectura super Matthaeum*. Turin and Rome: Marietti, 1951.

———. *Glossa continua super Evangelia (Catena Aurea)*. 2 vols. Turin and Rome: Marietti, 1953.

Other Primary Works

Adso Dervensis. *De Ortu et Tempore Antichristi*. Edited by D. Verhelst. *CC* 45. Turnhout: Brepols, 1976.

Amorós, Leo. "Aegidii Romani impugnatio doctrinae Petri Ioannis Olivi an. 1311–12, nunc primum in lucem edita." *AFH* 27 (1934): 399–451.

———. "Series condemnationum et processuum contra doctrinam et sequaces Petri Ioannis Olivi." *AFH* 24 (1931): 399–451.

Angelo Clareno. *Historia septem tribulationum ordinis minorum. Archiv* 2 (1886): 108–327.

———. *Liber Chronicarum sive tribulationum ordinis minorum di Frate Angelo Clareno.* SantaMaria degli Angeli: Edizioni Porziuncola, 1999.

Anonymous. *Allegationes super articulis.* MS Paris Bibl. Nat. lat. 4190, ff. 40r–49v.

Anselm of Havelberg. *Dialogi. SC* 118. Paris: Éditions du Cerf, 1966.

Aurelius Augustinus. *De Consensu Evangelistarum.* Edited by F. Weihrich. *CSEL* 43. Vienna: F. Tempsky, 1904.

———. *De Doctrina Christiana.* Edited by J. Martin. *CC* 32. Turnhout: Brepols, 1962.

Baluze, Etienne. *Stephani Baluze Miscellaneorum.* Paris: F. Muguet, 1678.

———. *Vitae paparum avenionensium.* Edited and emended by G. Mollat. Paris: Letouzey et Ané, 1914–27.

Bernardus Guidonis. *Practica inquisitionis heretice pravitatis.* Paris: Alphonse Picard, 1886.

Bihl, Michael. "Statuta generalia ordinis edita in capitulis generalibus celebratis Narbonae an. 1260, Assisii an. 1279 atque Parisiis an. 1292." *AFH* 34 (1941): 13–94, 284–358.

Bonaventure. *Collationes in hexaemeron et bonaventuriana quaedam selecta.* Quaracchi: Collegium S. Bonaventurae, 1934.

———. *Opera Omnia.* 11 vols. Quaracchi: Collegium S. Bonaventurae, 1882–1902.

Chronica XXIV Generalium. AF 3: 1–575. Quaracchi: Collegium S. Bonaventurae, 1897.

Denifle, Heinrich. *Chartularium Universitatis Parisiensis.* 4 vols. Paris: Ex typis fratrum Delalain, 1889–97.

Emmen, Aquilino. "Pierre de Jean Olivi, O.F.M, sa doctrine et son influence." *Cahiers de Joséphologie* 14 (1966): 209–70.

Eusebius of Caesarea. *Historia Ecclesiastica. SC* 31. Paris: Éditions du Cerf, 1986.

Fussenegger, Geroldus. "'Littera septem sigillarum' contra doctrinam Petri Ioannis Olivi edita." *AFH* 47 (1954): 45–53.

Gerard of Abbeville. *Contra adversarium perfectionis Christianae.* Edited by S. Clasen. *AFH* 31 (1938): 276–329; 32 (1939): 89–202.

Guido Terreni. *Concordia Evangelista.* Cologne, 1650.

Lee, Harold, Marjorie Reeves, and Giulio Silano, eds. *Western Mediterranean Prophecy.* Toronto: Pontifical Institute of Medieval Studies, 1989.

Migne, J.-P. *Patrologiae cursus completus, series graeca.* Paris: Garnier, 1844–66.

———. *Patrologiae cursus completus, series latina.* Paris: Garnier, 1844–66.

Nicholaus Eymeric. *Directorium Inquisitionis.* Rome: In Aedibus Populi Romani, 1585.

Raymundus de Fronchiaco. *Sol Ortus. Archiv* 3 (1887): 7–32.

Raymundus de Fronchiacho and Bonagratia de Bergamo. *Infrascripta dant. Archiv* 3 (1887): 141–60.

Salimbene da Parma. *Cronica.* Bari: Laterza, 1966.

Thomas Aquinas. *Summa Theologiae*. Edited by Blackfriars. 61 vols. New York: McGraw Hill, 1964–81.

Tondelli, L., M. Reeves, and B. Hirsch-Reich, eds. *Il Libro delle Figure dell'Abate Gioacchino da Fiore*. Turin, 1953.

Ubertino da Casale. *Sanctitas vestra*. *Archiv* 3 (1887): 51–89.

———. *Sanctitati apostolicae*. *Archiv* 2 (1886): 377–416.

William of Saint Amour. *Opera Omnia Magistri Guillelmi de Sancto Amore*. Constance: Apud Alitophilos, 1632.

Secondary Literature

Alexander, Paul. "Medieval Apocalypses as Historical Sources." *American Historical Review* 73 (1968): 1997–2018.

Alverny, Marie-Thérèse d'. "Un adversaire de Saint Thomas: Petrus Ioannis Olivi." In *St. Thomas Aquinas, 1274–1974*. 2 vols. 2: 179–218. Toronto: Pontifical Institute of Medieval Studies, 1974.

Barone, Giulia. "L'oeuvre eschatologique de Pierre Jean-Olieu et son influence. Un bilan historiographique." In *Fin du monde et signes des temps. Visionnaires et prophètes en France méridionale (Fin XIIe, début XVIe siècle) Cahiers de Fanjeaux* 27. 49–61. Toulouse: Privat, 1992.

Bartoli, Marco. "Olivi e il 'sacramento del potere.'" *Bullettino dell'Istituto Storico Italiano per il Medio Evo* 99 (1993): 91–115.

———. "Celestino V, il caso del papa eretico e i francescani spirituali." In *Aspetti della spiritualità ai tempi di Celestini V. Atti dei convegni: Ferentino, 23 febbraio e 21 maggio 1992*. 57–73. Ferentino: Associazione culturale "Gli Argonauti," 1993.

Bataillon, J. "Olivi utilisateur de La Catena Aurea de Thomas Daquin." In *Pierre de Jean Olivi (1248–1298): Pensée scolastique, dissidence spirituelle et société*, edited by Alain Boureau and Sylvain Piron. 115–20. Paris: Librairie Philosophique J. Vrin, 1999.

Benz, Ernst. *Ecclesia Spiritualis*. Stuttgart: Kohlhammer, 1934.

Bettini, Orazio. "Olivi di fronte ad Aristotele." *SF* 55 (1958): 176–97.

Bettoni, Efrem. *Le dottrine filosofiche di Pier di Giovanni Olivi*. Pubblicazioni dell'Università cattolica del S. Cuore. Nuova Serie, 73. Milan: Società Editrice, 1959.

Biget, Jean Loui. "Culte et rayonnemente Pierre Déjean Olieu en Languedoc au debut du XIVe siècle." In *Pierre de Jean Olivi (1248–1298). Pensée scolastique, dissidence spirituelle et société*, edited by Alain Boureau and Sylvain Piron. 277–308. Paris: Librairie Philosophique J. Vrin, 1999.

de Blic, J. "L'oeuvre exégétique de Walafrid Strabon et la Glossa Ordinaria." *RTAM* 16 (1949): 5–28.

Bloomfield, Morton W. "Joachim of Flora: A Critical Survey of His Canon, Teachings, Sources, Biography, and Influence." *Traditio* 13 (1957): 249–311.

Bonnes, J. P. "Un des plus grands prédicateurs du XIIe siècle, Geoffroy du Loroux, dit Geoffroy Babion." *Revue bénédictine* 51 (1945–46): 190–99.

Bousset, Wilhelm. *Die Offenbarung Johannis.* Göttingen: Vandenhoeck and Ruprecht, 1906.

Brady, Ignatius. "Sacred Scripture in the Early Franciscan School." In *La Sacra Scrittura e i Francescani.* 65–82. Rome: Editiones Antonianum, 1973.

Brooke, Rosalind. *Early Franciscan Government.* Cambridge: Cambridge University Press, 1959.

Burnham, Louisa A. "The Visionary Authority of Na Prous Boneta." In *Pierre de Jean Olivi (1248–1298): Pensée scolastique, dissidence spirituelle et société,* edited by Alain Boureau and Sylvain Piron. 319–40. Paris: Librairie Philosophique J. Vrin, 1999.

Burr, David. "The Apocalyptic Element in Olivi's Critique of Aristotle." *Church History* 40 (1971): 15–29.

———. "Bonaventure, Olivi, and Franciscan Eschatology." *CF* 53 (1983): 23–40.

———. "The *Correctorium* Controversy and the Origins of the *Usus Pauper* Controversy." *Speculum* 60 (1985): 331–42.

———. "The Date of Petrus Iohannis Olivi's Commentary on Matthew." *CF* 46 (1976): 131–38.

———. "Did the Béguins Understand Olivi?" In *Pierre de Jean Olivi (1248–1298): Pensée scolastique, dissidence spirituelle et société,* edited by Alain Boureau and Sylvain Piron. 309–18. Paris: Librairie Philosophique J. Vrin, 1999.

———. "Ecclesiastical Condemnation and Exegetical Theory: The Case of Olivi's Apocalypse Commentary." In *Neue Richtungen in der hoch- und spätmittelalterlichen Bibelexegese,* Schriften des Historischen Kollegs, Kolloquien 32, edited by Robert E. Lerner. 149–62. Munich: Oldenbourg Verlag, 1996.

———. "Franciscan Exegesis and Francis as Apocalyptic Figure." In *Monks, Nuns, and Friars in Mediaeval Society,* edited by Edward B. King, Jacqueline T. Schaefer, and William B. Wadley. 51–62. Sewanee: The Press of the University of the South, 1989.

———. "Islam and Antichrist in Medieval Franciscan Exegesis." In *Medieval Western Views of Islam.* 131–52. New York: Garland Press, 1996.

———. "Mendicant Readings of the Apocalypse." In *The Apocalypse in the Middle Ages,* edited by Richard K. Emmerson and Bernard McGinn. 89–102. Ithaca, N.Y.: Cornell University Press, 1992.

———. "Na Prous Boneta and Olivi." *CF* 67 (1997): 477–500.

———. "Olivi, Apocalyptic Expectation, and Visionary Experience." *Traditio* 41 (1985): 273–88.

———. "Olivi, the *Lectura super Apocalypsim* and Franciscan Exegetical Tradition." In *Francescanesimo e Cultura Universitaria.* 115–35. Perugia: La Società, 1990.

———. "Olivi's Apocalyptic Timetable." *Journal of Medieval and Renaissance Studies* 11 (1981): 237–60.

————. *Olivi and Franciscan Poverty: The Origins of the Usus Pauper Controversy.* Philadelphia: University of Pennsylvania Press, 1989.

————. *Olivi's Peaceable Kingdom: A Reading of the Apocalypse Commentary.* Philadelphia: University of Pennsylvania Press, 1993.

————. "Olivi on Prophecy." *Cristianesimo nella storia* 17 (1996): 369–91.

————. "Olivi, Prous, and the Separation of Apocalypse from Eschatology." In *That Others May Know and Love: Essays in Honor of Zachary Hayes, O.F.M.; Franciscan, Educator, Scholar,* edited by M. Cusato and F. E. Coughlin. St. Bonaventure, N.Y., 1997.

————. *The Persecution of Peter Olivi.* Transactions of the American Philosophical Society. Vol. 66. Part 5. Philadelphia: American Philosophical Society, 1976.

————. "Petrus Ioannis Olivi and the Philosophers." *FS* 31 (1971): 41–71.

————. *The Spiritual Franciscans. From Protest to Persecution in the Century after Saint Francis.* University Park, Pa.: 2001.

da Campagnola, Stanislao. *L'angelo del sesto sigillo e l' "alter Christus."* Rome, 1971.

Cenci Cesare. *Petri Iohannis Olivi, Opera: Censimento dei manoscritti.* Grottaferrata: College of St. Bonaventure, 1999.

Cohn, Norman. *The Pursuit of the Millennium.* Rev. ed. New York: Oxford University Press, 1970.

Collingwood, R. G. *The Idea of History.* New York: Oxford University Press, 1946.

Collins, John J. *The Apocalyptic Imagination: An Introduction to the Jewish Matrix of Christianity.* New York: Crossroad, 1984.

————. *Between Athens and Jerusalem: Jewish Identity in the Hellenistic Diaspora.* New York: Crossroad, 1964.

Congar, Yves. "Aspects ecclésiologiques de la querelle entre mendiants et séculiers." *Archives d'histoire doctrinale et littéraire du moyen âge* 28 (1961): 35–151.

Dahan, Gilbert. "L'exegèse des livres prophetiques chez Pierre de Jean Olieu." In *Pierre de Jean Olivi (1248–1298): Pensée scolastique, dissidence spirituelle et société,* edited by Alain Boureau and Sylvain Piron. 91–114. Paris: Librairie Philosophique J. Vrin, 1999.

————. *Les intellectuels chrétiens et les juifs au moyen age.* Paris: Cerf, 1990.

Daniel, E. Randolph. "Apocalyptic Conversion: The Joachite Alternative to the Crusades." *Traditio* 25 (1969): 127–54.

————. *The Franciscan Concept of Mission in the High Middle Ages.* Lexington: University of Kentucky Press, 1975; rev. ed., Franciscan Institute, 1992.

————. "Joachim of Fiore: Patterns of History in the Apocalypse." In *The Apocalypse in the Middle Ages,* edited by Richard K. Emmerson and Bernard McGinn. 72–88. Ithaca, N.Y.: Cornell University Press, 1992.

————. "A New Understanding of Joachim: The Concords, the Exile, and the Exodus." In *Gioacchino da Fiore tra Bernardo di Clairvaux e Innocenzo III,* edited by R. Rusconi. 209–22. Atti del quinto congresso internazionale di studi gioachimiti, San Giovanni in Fiore, 16–21 settembre 1999. Rome: Viella, 2001.

————. "A Re-examination of the Origins of Franciscan Joachitism." *Speculum* 43 (1968): 671–76.

————. "St. Bonaventure: Defender of Franciscan Eschatology." In *S. Bonaventura, 1274–1974*. 4 vols. 4:793–806. Grottaferrata: College of St. Bonaventure, 1974.

D'Avray, D. L. *The Preaching of the Friars*. Oxford: Oxford University Press, 1985.

Denifle, Heinrich. "Das Evangelium aeternum und die Commission zu Anagni." *Archiv* 1 (1885): 49–142.

Desbonnets, Theophile. *De intuition à l'institution*. Paris: Éditions Franciscaines, 1983.

Döllinger, J. J. Ignaz von. *Beiträge zur Sektengeschichte des Mittelalters*. 2 vols. Munich: Beck, 1890; reprint, New York: Burt Franklin, 1960.

Doucet, Victorinus. "De operibus manuscriptis Fr. Petri Ioannis Olivi in bibliotheca Universitatis Patavinae asservatis." *AFH* 28 (1935): 426–41.

————. "P. J. Olivi et l'Immaculée Conception." *AFH* 26 (1933): 560–63.

Douie, Decima. *The Conflict between the Seculars and the Mendicants at the University of Paris in the Thirteenth Century*. Aquinas Society of London. Aquinas Paper No. 23. London: Blackfriars, 1954.

————. *The Nature and Effect of the Heresy of the Fraticelli*. Manchester: Manchester University Press, 1932.

————. "Olivi's 'Postilla super Matthaeum'" (MS. New College B. 49). *FS* 35 (1975): 66–92.

Dufeil, Michel M. *Guillaume de Saint-Amour et la polémique universitaire parisienne, 1250–59*. Paris: Éditions Picards, 1972.

Ehrle, Franz. "Die Spiritualen, ihr Verhältniss zum Franciscanerorden und zu den Fraticellen." *Archiv* 1 (1885): 509–69; 2 (1886): 106–64, 249–336; 3 (1887): 553–623; 4 (1888): 1–190.

————. "Petrus Johannis Olivi, sein Leben und seine Schriften." *Archiv* 3 (1887): 409–552.

————. "Zur Vorgeschichte des Concils von Vienne." In *Archiv* 2 (1886): 353–416; 3 (1887): 1–195.

Emmerson, Richard K. *Antichrist in the Middle Ages: A Study of Medieval Apocalypticism, Art and Literature*. Seattle: University of Washington Press, 1981.

van Engen, John. *Rupert of Deutz*. Berkeley: University of California Press, 1983.

Esser, Cajetan. *Origins of the Franciscan Order*. Chicago: Franciscan Herald Press, 1970.

Eunden, Jan J. G. (Van Den). *Poverty on the Way to God: Thomas Aquinas on Evangelical Poverty*. Publications of the Thomas Institute of Utrecht ; new ser., v. 2. Leuven: Peeters, 1994.

Farmer, W. R. *The Synoptic Problem*. 3rd ed. Dillsboro, N.C.: Western North Carolina Press, 1976.

Flood, David. "The Franciscan and Spiritual Writings of Peter Olivi." *AFH* 91 (1998): 471–75.

————. "The Order's Masters: Franciscan Institutions from 1226 to 1280." In *Dalla "Sequela Christi" di Francesco D'Assisi all'apologia Della Povertà. Atti Del XVIII Convegno Internazionale, Assisi, 18–20 ottobre 1990,* edited by Roberto Rusconi. Spoleto: Centro Italiano di Studi Sull'alto Medioevo, 1992.

————. *Peter of John Olivi on the Bible.* Edited by Gedeon Gál. St. Bonaventure, N.Y.: Franciscan Institute Publications, 1997.

————. "The Peter Olivi Colloquium in Mönchengladbach." *Franziskanische Studien* 65 (1983): 393–96.

————. *Peter Olivi's Rule Commentary: Edition and Presentation.* Wiesbaden: Franz Steiner Verlag GMBH, 1972.

————. "Poverty as Virtue, Poverty as Warning, and Peter of John Olivi." In *Pierre de Jean Olivi (1248–1298): Pensée scolastique, dissidence spirituelle et société,* edited by Alain Boureau and Sylvain Piron. 157–72. Paris: Librairie Philosophique J. Vrin, 1999.

————. "Recent Study on Petrus Johannis Olivi." *Franziskanische Studien* 73 (1991): 262–69.

————. "The Theology of Peter John Olivi: A Search for a Theology and Anthropology of the Synoptic Gospel." In *The History of Franciscan Theology,* edited by Kenan B. Osborne. 127–84. St. Bonaventure, N.Y.: Franciscan Institute Publications, 1994.

Froehlich, Karlfried. *Biblical Interpretation in the Early Church.* Philadelphia: Fortress, 1984.

Garner, Jeff B. "The Condemnation of Peter John Olivi's *Lectura Super Apocalypsim* as Contained in *Littera Magistrorum:* A Translation and Review." Lawrence: University of Kansas, 1993.

de Ghellinck, J. *Le mouvement théologique du XIIe siècle.* Bruges: Éditions "De Tempel," 1948.

Grant, Robert M., and David Tracy. *A Short History of the Interpretation of the Bible.* Philadelphia: Fortress Press, 1985.

Gratien de Paris. "Une lettre inédite de Pierre de Jean Olivi." *EF* 29 (1913): 414–22.

Grundmann, Herbert. *Ausgewählte Aufsätze.* Vol 2. *Schriften der Monumenta Germaniae Historica.* Vol. 25.2. Stuttgart: Hiersemann, 1977.

————. "Die Papstprophetien des Mittelalters." *Archiv für Kulturgeschichte 19* (1929): 77–138.

————. "Zur Biographie Joachims von Fiore und Rainers von Ponza." *Deutsches Archiv für Erforschung des Mittelalters* 16 (1960): 528–44.

Heynck, Valens. "Zur Datierung der Sentenzkommentare des Petrus Johannis Olivi und des Petrus de Trabibus." *Franziskanische Studien* 38 (1956): 371–98.

Hinnebusch, W. A., *History of the Dominican Order.* Staten Island, N.Y.: Alba House, 1965.

Jarraux, Louis. "Pierre Jean Olivi, sa vie, sa doctrine." *EF* 25 (1933): 129–53, 277–98, 513–29.

Kamlah, Wilhelm. *Apokalypse und Geschichtstheologie: Die mittelalterliche Auslegung der Apokalypse vor Joachim von Fiore*. Historische Studien 285. Berlin: Ebering, 1935.

Kermode, Frank. *The Sense of an Ending: Studies in the Theory of Fiction*. New York: Oxford University Press, 1966.

Koch, Joseph. "Der Prozess gegen die Postille Olivis zur Apokalypse." *RTAM* 5 (1933): 302–15.

————. "Die Verurteilung Olivis auf dem Konzil von Vienne und ihre Vorgeschichte." *Scholastik* 5 (1930): 489–522.

Krey, Philip D. "Nicholas of Lyra: Apocalypse Commentary as Historiography." Doctoral dissertation, University of Chicago, 1989.

Lambert, Malcolm. *Franciscan Poverty: The Doctrine of the Absolute Poverty of Christ and the Apostles in the Franciscan Order, 1210–1323*. London: S.P.C.K., 1961.

Lambertini, Roberto. "La difesa dell'ordine francescano difronte alle critiche dei secolari in Olivi." In *Pierre de Jean Olivi (1248–1298): Pensée scolastique, dissidence spirituelle et société*, edited by Alain Boureau and Sylvain Piron. 193–206. Paris: Librairie Philosophique J. Vrin, 1999.

————. "Usus and Usura: Poverty and Usury in the Franciscans, Responses to John XXII's Quia Vir Reprobus." *Franciscan Studies* 54 (1994–97) : 185–210.

Larguier, Gilbert. "Autour de Pierre De Jean Olivi. Narbonne et Le Narbonnais, fin XIIIe, debut XIVe siècle." In *Pierre de Jean Olivi (1248–1298): Pensée scolastique, dissidence spirituelle et société*, edited by Alain Boureau and Sylvain Piron. 265–276. Paris: Librairie Philosophique J. Vrin, 1999.

Leff, Gordon. *Heresy in the Later Middle Ages*. 2 vols. Manchester: University Press, 1967.

Lerner, Robert E. "An 'Angel of Philadelphia' in the Reign of Philip the Fair." In *Order and Innovation in the Middle Ages*. 343–64. Princeton, N.J.: Princeton University Press, 1976.

————. "Antichrists and Antichrist in Joachim of Fiore." *Speculum* 60 (1985): 553–70.

————. "Ecstatic Dissent." *Speculum* 67 (1992): 33–57.

————. "Joachim and the Scholastics." In *Gioacchino da Fiore tra Bernardo di Clairvaux e Innocenzo III,* edited by R. Rusconi. 251–64. Atti del quinto congresso internazionale di studi gioachimiti, San Giovanni in Fiore, 16–21 settembre 1999. Rome: Viella, 2001.

————. "The Medieval Return to the Thousand-Year Sabbath." In *The Apocalypse in the Middle Ages,* edited by Richard K. Emmerson and Bernard McGinn. 51–71. Ithaca, N.Y.: Cornell University Press, 1992.

————. "Peter Olivi on the Conversion of the Jews." In *Pierre de Jean Olivi (1248–1298): Pensée scolastique, dissidence spirituelle et société,* edited by Alain Boureau and Sylvain Piron. 207–16. Paris: Librairie Philosophique J. Vrin, 1999.

————. "Poverty, Preaching, and Eschatology in the Revelation Commentaries of 'Hugh of St. Cher.'" In *The Bible in the Medieval World: Essays in Memory of Beryl Smalley*, edited by Katherine Walsh and Diana Wood. *Studies in Church History*. Subsidia 4. 157–89. Oxford: Basil Blackwell, 1985.

————. *The Powers of Prophecy: The Cedar of Lebanon Vision from the Mongol Onslaught to the Dawn of the Enlightenment*. Berkeley: University of California Press, 1983.

————. "Recent Work on the Origins of the 'Genus Nequam' Prophecies." *Florensia* 7 (1993): 141–57.

————. "Refreshment of the Saints: The Time after Antichrist as a Station for Earthly Progress in Medieval Thought." *Traditio* 32 (1976): 97–144.

————. *Refrigerio dei Santi: Gioacchino da Fiore e l'escatologia medievale*. Rome: Viella, 1985.

————. "Writing and Resistance among Beguins of Languedoc and Catalonia." In *Heresy and Literacy, 1000–1530*, edited by P. Biller and A. Hudson. 186–204. Cambridge: Cambridge University Press, 1994.

Little, Lester. *Religious Poverty and the Profit Economy in Medieval Europe*. Ithaca, N.Y.: Cornell University Press, 1978.

Lobrichon, Guy, and Pierre Riché. *Le moyen âge et la bible. Bible de tous les temps* 4. Paris: Beauchesene, 1984.

Lowith, Karl. *Meaning in History*. Chicago: University of Chicago Press, 1949.

de Lubac, Henri. *La posterité spirituelle de Joachim de Fiore. I. de Joachim a Schelling. II. de Saint-Simon à nos jours*. Paris: Lethielleux, 1979, 1981.

Maccarrone, M. *Vicarius Christi: Storia del titolo papale*. Rome: Facultas Theologica Pontificii Athenaei Lateranensis, 1953.

Madigan, Kevin. "Aquinas and Olivi on Evangelical Poverty: A Medieval Debate and Its Modern Significance." *The Thomist* 61 (1997): 567–86.

Maier, Annaliese. "Per la storia del processo contro l'Olivi." *Rivista di Storia della Chiesa in Italia* 5 (1951): 326–39.

Manselli, Raoul. "Une grande figure serignanaise: Pierre de Jean Olivi." *EF* 12 (1972): 69–83.

————. *La "Lectura super Apocalypsim" di Pietro di Giovanni Olivi*. Istituto Storico Italiano per il Medio Evo. Studi Storici, nn. 19–21. Rome: Sede dell'Istituto, 1955.

————. *Spirituali e beghini in Provenza*. Istituto Storico Italiano per il Medio Evo. Studi Storici, nn. 31–34. Rome: Sede dell'Istituto, 1959.

————. "La terza età, Babylon e l'Anticristo Mistico." *Bullettino dell'Istituto Storico Italiano per il Medio Evo* 82 (1970): 47–79.

Markus, Robert A. *Saeculum: History and Society in the Theology of St. Augustine*. Cambridge: Cambridge University Press, 1970.

Matter, E. Ann. "The Church Fathers and the *Glossa Ordinaria*." In *The Reception of the Church Fathers in the West*. 2 vols. 2: 83–112. Leiden: Brill, 1993.

McGinn, Bernard. "The Abbot and the Doctors: Scholastic Reactions to the Radical Eschatology of Joachim of Fiore." *Church History* 40 (1971): 30–47.

―――. "Angel Pope and Papal Antichrist." *Church History* 47 (1978): 155–73.

―――. *Apocalyptic Spirituality.* New York: Paulist Press, 1979.

―――. "Apocalyptic Traditions and Spiritual Identity in Thirteenth-Century Religious Life." In *The Roots of the Modern Christian Tradition,* edited by E. R. Elder. 1–26. Kalamazoo: Cistercian Publications, 1984.

―――. "Apocalypticism in the Middle Ages: A Historiographical Sketch." *Mediaeval Studies* 37 (1975): 252–86.

―――. "Awaiting an End: Research in Medieval Apocalypticism 1974–1981." *Medievalia et Humanistica,* n.s. 11 (1982): 263–89.

―――. *The Calabrian Abbot.* New York: Macmillan, 1985.

―――. "Early Apocalypticism: The Ongoing Debate." In *The Apocalypse in English Renaissance Thought and Literature,* edited by C. A. Patrides and Joseph Wittreich. 2–39. Manchester: Manchester University Press, 1984.

―――. "Joachim and the Sibyl." *Citeaux* 24 (1973): 97–138.

―――. "The Significance of Bonaventure's Theology of History." In *Celebrating the Medieval Heritage,* edited by David Tracy. *Journal of Religion* 58 Supplement (1978): s64–s81.

―――. *Visions of the End: Apocalyptic Traditions in the Middle Ages.* Columbia University Records of Civilization: Sources and Studies. No. 96. New York: Columbia University Press, 1979.

Monti, Dominic. "Bonaventure's Interpretation of Scripture in His Exegetical Works." Doctoral dissertation, University of Chicago, 1979.

Moorman, John. *A History of the Franciscan Order.* Oxford: Clarendon Press, 1968.

Mottu, Henri. *La manifestation de l'Esprit selon Joachim de Fiore.* Neuchâtel and Paris: Delachaux and Niestlé, 1977.

―――. "La mémoire du futur: Signification de l'ancien testament dans la pensée de Joachim de Fiore." In *L'età dello spirito e la fine dei tempi in Gioacchino da Fiore e nel gioachimismo medievale,* Atti del II congresso internazionale di studi gioachimiti, edited by A. Crocco. 15–28. San Giovanni in Fiore: Centro Internazione di Studi Gioachimiti, 1986.

Moynihan, Robert. "Development of the 'Pseudo-Joachim' Commentary 'super Hieremiam.'" *Mélanges de l'école française de Rome. Moyen Âge, Temps Modernes* 98 (1986): 109–42.

Pacetti, Dionisio. "L''Expositio super Apocalypsim' di Mattia di Svezia." *AFH* 54 (1961): 273–302.

Partee, Carter. "Peter John Olivi: Historical and Doctrinal Study." *FS* 20 (1960): 215–60.

Pasnau, Robert. "Olivi on the Metaphysics of Soul." *Medieval Philosophy and Theology* 6 (1997): 109–32.

―――. "Petri Iohannis Olivi Tractatus De Verbo." *FS* 53 (1993): 121–53.

————. *Theories of Cognition in the Later Middle Ages.* New York, Cambridge University Press, 1997.

Pásztor, Edith. "L'apport de Raoul Manselli a l'histoire de l'eschatologie médiévale." *Cahiers de Fanjeaux 27, Fin du monde et dignes des temps. Visionnaires et prophètes en France méridionale* (fin XIIe début XVIe siècle). 21–31. Toulouse: Privat, 1992.

————. "L'escatologia gioachimita nel francescanesimo: Pietro di Giovanni Olivi." In *L'attesa della fine dei tempi nel Medioevo,* edited by O. Capitani and J. Miethke. 169–93. Bologna: Il Mulino, 1990.

————. "Giovanni XXII e il gioachimismo di Pietro di Giovanni Olivi." *Bullettino dell'Istituto Storico Italiano per il Medio Evo e Archivio Muratoriano* 82 (1970): 81–111.

————. "Le polemiche sulla 'Lectura super Apocalipsim' di Pietro di Giovanni Olivi fino alla sua condanna." *Bullettino dell'Istituto Storico Italiano per il Medio Evo e Archivio Muratoriano* 61 (1975): 231–41.

Peano, Pierre. "Raymond Geoffroi ministre general et défenseur des spirituels." *Picenum seraphicum* 11 (1974): 190–203.

Piron, Sylvain. "Compléments à l'inventaire des manuscrits d'Olivi." *AFH* 90 (1997): 591–96.

————. "Les oeuvres perdues d'Olivi: Essai de reconstitution." *AFH* 91 (1998): 359–96.

Potestà, Gian-Luca. *Angelo Clareno: Dai poveri eremeti ai fraticelli.* Rome: Istituto Storico Italiano per il Medio Evo, 1990.

————, ed. *Dialogi de prescientia Dei et predestinatione electorum.* Fonti per la storia dell'Italia medievale. Antiquitates 4. Rome: nella sede dell'Istituto, 1995.

————. "I frati minori e lo studio della Bibbia. Da Francisco d'Assisi a Nicolo di Lyra." In *La Bibbia nel Medio Evo,* edited by G. Cremascoli and C. Leonardi. 269–90. Bologna, 1996.

————. "Gli Studi Su Angelo Clareno." *AFH* 81 (1989): 225–53.

————. *Storia ed escatologia in Ubertino da Casale.* Milan: Vita e pensiero, 1980.

Ratzinger, Joseph. *The Theology of History in St. Bonaventure.* Translated by Zachary Hayes. Chicago: Franciscan Herald Press, 1971. English translation of *Die Geschichtstheologie des heiligen Bonaventura.* Munich: Schnell & Steiner, 1959.

Reeves, Marjorie. "The Abbot Joachim's Disciples and the Cistercian Order." *Sophia* 19 (1951): 355–71.

————. *The Influence of Prophecy in the Later Middle Ages: A Study in Joachimism.* Oxford: Clarendon Press, 1969; reprint Notre Dame, Ind.: University of Notre Dame Press, 1993.

————. *Joachim of Fiore and the Prophetic Future.* New York: Harper and Row, 1977.

————. "The Originality and Influence of Joachim of Fiore." *Traditio* 36 (1980): 269–316.

————. "The Seven Seals in the Writings of Joachim of Fiore." *RTAM* 21 (1954): 211–47.

Reeves, Marjorie, and Beatrice Hirsch-Reich. *The Figurae of Joachim of Fiore.* Oxford: Clarendon Press, 1972.

Reist, Thomas. *Saint Bonaventure as a Biblical Commentator: A Translation and Analysis of his Commentary on Luke 18, 34–19, 42.* New York: Lanham, 1985.

Rusconi, Roberto. "Alla ricerca delle autentiche tracce di Gioacchino da Fiore nella Francia meridionale," *Florensia* 6 (1992): 57–71.

————, ed. *Gioacchino da Fiore tra Bernardo di Clairvaux e Innocenzo III.* Atti del quinto congresso internazionale di studi gioachimiti, San Giovanni in Fiore, 16–21 settembre 1999. Rome, Viella, 2001.

Schlageter, Johannes. "Die Auseinandersetzung zwischen griechischem und biblischem Menschenbild im franziskanischen Freiheitsverständnis des Petrus Johannis Olivi O.F.M." *Wissenschaft und Weisheit* 60 (1997): 65–86.

————. "Die Bedeutung des Hoheliedskommentars des Franziskanertheologen Petrus Johannis Olivi. Argumente für eine neue Edition." *Wissenschaft und Weisheit* 58 (1995): 137–51.

————. "Von göttlicher in menschlicher Liebe. Petrus Johannis Olivi: Expositio in Canticum Canticorum." *AFH* 91 (1998): 519–34.

————. "Von göttlicher in menschlicher Liebe. Überlegungen zum Canticum Kommentar des Fr. Petrus Johannis Olivi O. Min. (+ 1298)." In *Pierre de Jean Olivi (1248–1298): Pensée scolastique, dissidence spirituelle et société,* edited by Alain Boureau and Sylvain Piron. 121–34. Paris: Librairie Philosophique J. Vrin, 1999.

Selge, Kurt-Victor. "Trinität, Millennium, Apokalypse im Denken Joachims von Fiore." In *Gioacchino da Fiore tra Bernardo di Clairvaux e Innocenzo III,* edited by R. Rusconi. Atti del quinto congresso internazionale di studi gioachimiti, San Giovanni in Fiore, 16–21 settembre 1999. Rome, Viella, 1995.

Simoni, F. "Il *Super Hieremiam* et il gioachimismo francescano." In *Bullettino dell'Istituto Storico Italiano per il Medio Evo* 82 (1970): 13–46.

Smalley, Beryl. "Glossa Ordinaria." *Theologische Realenzyklopädie* 13 (1984): 452–57.

————. *The Gospels in the Schools c. 1100–1280.* London: Hambledon Press, 1985.

————. *The Study of the Bible in the Middle Ages.* 3rd ed. Oxford: Basil Blackwell, 1983.

Southern, R. W. "Aspects of the European Tradition of Historical Writing: 3. History as Prophecy." *Transactions of the Royal Historical Society* 21 (1972): 159–80.

Steiner, M. *La tentation de Jésus dans l'interprétation patristique de Saint Justin à Origène.* Paris, 1962.

Thomas, Antoine. "Le vrai nom du frère mineur Petrus Johannis Olivi." *Annales du Midi* 25 (1913): 68–69.

Thussen, J. M. M. *Censure and Heresy at the University of Paris 1200–1400*. Philadelphia: University of Pennsylvania Press, 1998.

Töpfer, Bernhard. *Das kommende Reich des Friedens*. Berlin: Akademie Verlag, 1964.

Torjesen, Karen Jo. *Hermeneutical Procedure and Theological Method in Origen's Exegesis*. Patristische Texte und Studien Bd. 28. Berlin and New York: De Gruyter, 1986.

Vian, Paolo. "Appunti sulla tradizione manoscritta della 'Lectura Super Apocalipsim' di Pietro di Giovanni Olivi." In *Editori di quaracchi, 100 anni dopo. Bilancio e prospettive. Atti del colloquio internazionale. Roma 29–30 maggio 1995*. Scuola superiore di studi medievali e Francescani. Pontificio Ateneo Antonianum. A cura di Alvaro Cacciotti Barbara Faes de Mottoni (Medioevo 3). 373–409. Roma: Edizioni Antonianum, 1997.

———. "I codici fiorentini e romani della Lectura super Apocalipsim di Pietro di Giovanni Olivi (con un codice di Tedaldo della Casa ritrovato)." *AFH* 83 (1990): 463–89.

———. "L'opera esegetica di Pietro di Giovanni Olivi: Uno status quaestionis," *AFH* 91 (1998): 397–456.

———. "Pietro di Giovanni Olivi." In *Mistici Francescani. Secolo XIV.* 559–87. Milano: Edizioni Biblioteca Francescana, 1997.

Weisheipl, James A. *Friar Thomas d'Aquino*. Garden City: Doubleday, 1974.

Wessley, Stephen. *Joachim of Fiore and Monastic Reform*. New York: P. Lang, 1990.

West, Delno C., ed. *Joachim of Fiore in Christian Thought: Essays on the Influence of the Calabrian Abbot*. 2 vols. New York: Burt Franklin, 1975.

West, Delno C., and Sandra Zimdars-Swartz. *Joachim of Fiore: A Study of Spiritual Perception and History*. Bloomington: Indiana University Press, 1983.

Williams, Ann, ed. *Prophecy and Millenarianism: Essays in Honour of Marjorie Reeves*. Essex, Longman, 1980.

Index

KEVIN MADIGAN is assistant professor of the history of Christianity
at Harvard Divinity School.